Economics of
College Sports

Economics of College Sports

EDITED BY JOHN FIZEL AND RODNEY FORT

Studies in Sports Economics

Westport, Connecticut
London

Library of Congress Cataloging-in-Publication Data

Economics of college sports / edited by John Fizel and Rodney Fort.
    p. cm. — (Studies in sports economics)
    Includes bibliographical references and index.
    ISBN 0–275–98033–2 (alk. paper)
    1. College sports—Economic aspects—United States. 2. College athletes—United
States—Economic conditions. 3. National Collegiate Athletic Association. I. Fizel, John.
II. Fort, Rodney D. III. Series.
    GV350.E36   2004
    796.04'3'0973—dc22   2003060427

British Library Cataloguing in Publication Data is available.

Library of Congress Catalog Card Number: 2003060427
ISBN: 0–275–98033–2

First published in 2004

Praeger Publishers, 88 Post Road West, Westport, CT 06881
An imprint of Greenwood Publishing Group, Inc.
www.praeger.com

Printed in the United States of America

The paper used in this book complies with the
Permanent Paper Standard issued by the National
Information Standards Organization (Z39.48–1984).

10 9 8 7 6 5 4 3 2 1

Copyright Acknowledgments

The editors and publisher gratefully acknowledge permission for use of the following material:

Chapter 5 is reprinted, by permission, from B. Goff, 2000, "Effects of University Athletics on
the University: A Review and Extension of Empirical Assessment," *Journal of Sport Management*,
14 (2): 85–104.

Chapter 10 is reprinted from John Fizel and Timothy Smaby, 1999, "Participation in Collegiate
Athletics and Academic Performance" in *Sports Economics: Current Research* (Westport, CT:
Greenwood).

Chapter 11 is reprinted from John L. Fizel and Michael P. D'Itri, 1997, "Managerial Efficiency,
Managerial Succession, and Organizational Performance," *Managerial and Decision Economics*,
18: 295–308. © John Wiley & Sons Limited. Reproduced with permission.

Contents

Part I
Introduction

1

Economics of College Sports: An Overview

John Fizel and Rodney Fort

INTRODUCTION

College sports are big business. Major college coaches, such as basketball coach Mike Krzyzewski at Duke University or football coach Phillip Fulmer at the University of Tennessee, make headlines when their compensation packages exceed $1–2 million annually, making them the highest paid university and state employees. Coaches often earn additional income through sports camps, media shows, and athletic apparel endorsement contracts. Washington State University, a modestly funded major collegiate sports program, reported athletic revenue of $16.8 million for 1997–1998.[1] College athletic events are held in state-of-the-art facilities, like the University of Maryland basketball program's new $107 million dollar arena. The NCAA reports 2001–02 revenues of approximately $346 million from Division I sports, $14.6 million from Division II, and $11 million from Division III. Television contracts for Atlantic Coast, Big East, Big 10, Pac 10, and SEC conference football are valued at approximately $350 million, not including shares of the $140 million paid out from 1998 post-season Bowl games, while CBS just negotiated an 11-year, $6 billion contract to broadcast the NCAA Division I basketball tournament.

Where do, or should, these lucrative athletic ventures fit in the mission of higher education? To what extent is the central mission of creating an environment for learning and extending the frontiers of knowledge enhanced or limited by college sports? Are declarations by the NCAA to promote amateurism and competitive balance supportive of the university mission? Does the NCAA even follow its purported objectives?

Economics of College Sports contains both empirical and theoretical research to address these and related issues. The book opens with three chapters that provide unique perspectives into the organization of collegiate athletics and the university mission. In the first chapter, Joel Maxcy examines the role and structure of the NCAA in influencing the operations of collegiate athletics and the link between athletics and university educational missions. Specifically, Maxcy addresses how the 1997 restructuring of the NCAA attempted to bring stability to the collegiate athletics and power to university presidents. His analysis suggests that the reorganization has succeeded in appeasing, at least temporarily, the wishes of the least- and greatest-invested universities. The implication of the university presidents' new power to exert control over athletics is less clear.

Paul Staudohar and Barry Zepel critique the findings and recommendations of three major studies that examine athletic programs in the context of the mission of higher education. They conclude that education leaders have the opportunity to greatly reduce the existing conflicts between developing commercialized sports programs and fostering stimulating environments for learning if they adopt the recommendations of these studies. However, there is no centralized authority to mandate support of educational missions, nor do the incentives of the NCAA prompt support of these missions. Implementation requires that university presidents show the fortitude to forego some of the enticements of big-dollar sports and exert their power over athletic activities.

But, what if university presidents believe that institutional academic reputations are based primarily on the quality of graduate school education and the prestigious research activities that emanate from these programs? Athletic revenues may then be an excellent way to fund these programs. And, if undergraduate education is compromised as graduation education is emphasized, then athletic activities may provide entertainment, hence appeasement, for the undergraduate students. This is the "beer and circus" hypothesis that is tested by Evan Osborne in Chapter 4.

Part III includes three chapters on the financial returns to college athletics. "Most college sports lose money" is an assertion commonly made by representatives of college athletic departments and increasingly accepted by the media, despite revenue from monster stadia and arenas that sell out, postseason tournaments, and lucrative private sports contracts.[2] Brian Goff evaluates this premise addressing both the direct and indirect financial impact athletics may have on university costs and revenues. He concludes, with qualifications, that athletic departments do not typically operate in the "red" when the vagaries of accounting convention are replaced with an economic analysis of benefits and costs.

Robert Sandy and Peter Sloane continue to address the direct and indirect impacts of college athletics, but do so in the context of a university contemplating a move in its athletic affiliation from Division II to Division I. Their results clearly indicate a move to Division I is warranted and ask "Why don't all colleges that can possibly beg or borrow the money start Division I-A programs?" The profit incentives achieved by upgrading the affiliation of an institution's athletic programs cause a constant churning within the membership of the NCAA. This churning was the impetus for the restructuring addressed in Chapter 2 by Maxcy.

In Chapter 7, Robert Baade and Victor Matheson investigate the economic returns to a city that hosts the final four for the NCAA post-season basketball tournament. They find that promoters overstate the economic impact of these mega-events because they estimate the increased spending by nonresidents but ignore reduced spending by nonresidents and residents alike. In only two of 48 final four events (men's and women's tournament finals) did the host city experience significant positive income growth.

Part IV includes four chapters that explore the relationships between college athletics and labor issues. Perhaps no issue has caused more controversy for athletic departments than gender equity or Title IX compliance. Recently, athletic departments have attempted to meet Title IX compliance standards by expanding women's sports programs and eliminating non-revenue men's sports, arguing that budget limitations require such trade-offs. Michael Leeds, Yelina Suris, and Jennifer Durkin address this issue by testing the relationship between the success of football programs, the largest of college revenue-producing sports, with the Title IX compliance of the institution. They find little evidence that football funds are used to support Title IX initiatives. Indeed, some of the most successful football programs are actually a drain on funding of women's programs.

The second chapter in this part examines the value or marginal revenue product (MRP) of a college basketball or football player. As college sports are increasingly commercialized, athletes continue to be paid far below what they would earn in a competitive market. "The NCAA operates behind a veil of amateurism as its members generate revenues comparable to professional sports, practice and play in facilities that rival those found in professional sports, and pay their top coaches salaries comparable to those paid to coaches of professional teams. Only the student athletes are bound by amateur status and restricted in their ability to share in the bounty generated by their play."[3] The extent of underpayment is estimated by Robert Brown and R. Todd Jewell, who find that the MRP of a star collegiate football player is approximately $400,000 and the MRP of a star collegiate basketball player is approximately $1.2 million. Each is in stark contrast to the full cost of attending college, the compensation limit imposed by the NCAA.

In Chapter 10, John Fizel and Timothy Smaby compare the academic performance of college athletes relative to all baccalaureate students at Penn

State University. Their analysis is disaggregated for individual sports, and for most sports, participation in intercollegiate athletics has no significant impact on the grade point averages of athletes. However, men's football is the exception. Despite the NCAA's SAT and high school course requirements, the university is able to recruit athletes who have significantly lower SAT scores than their cohorts do. Athletes also appear to opt for less rigorous curricula, and are significantly slower in advancing to an academic degree. The exploitation of the premier, revenue-producing collegiate athlete appears to have been extended to the classroom.

In the last chapter of this part, John Fizel and Michael D'Itri examine the impact of coaching turnover and the rationale for turnover on college basketball performance. Turnover, per se, is found to be disruptive to success. Furthermore, the hiring of a new, less efficient coach can cause a long-term decline in performance. Despite these implications, college coaches are typically dismissed based only on winning percentage rather than efficiency.

Part V contains three chapters that investigate competitive balance in collegiate sports. The NCAA states that fostering competitive balance is one of the organization's key purposes, and historically the NCAA has used competitive balance as a justification for the development and imposition of many of its regulations. Craig Depken and Dennis Wilson use three measures to examine competitive balance in college football from 1888 to 2001. They find that competitive balance has declined over time for all measures. Moreover, structural changes introduced by the NCAA exacerbate the decline in competitive balance when using the measure that best captures intertemporal changes. It appears that special interest groups are able to dictate policy development within the NCAA that runs counter to the purported goal of competitive balance.

In the next chapter of this part, David Berri examines competitive balance in collegiate football, baseball, and basketball and compares the competitive balance in each of these sports to their professional counterparts. Collegiate baseball and basketball have less competitive balance than collegiate football. Berri argues that competitive balance is directly related to the population of the athletes available for employment in a given sport which, in turn, is related to the number of choices athletes have available. If athletes have the option to turn pro early in their collegiate careers, the employable population is diminished and competitive balance compromised.

In the final chapter of the book, Craig Depken and Dennis Wilson estimate the impact of NCAA football probations and investigations on various measures of competitive balance in Division IA football conferences. If an institution pays athletes in an environment where other institutions abide by the NCAA's no-pay rule, the cheating institution can gain a talent advantage which can ultimately generate revenue from post-season play and additional media coverage. If sanctions are effective, cheating should be reduced and competitive balance enhanced. On average, however, Depken and Wilson find that sanctions have reduced competitive balance. They do note that the impact on competitive balance is diminished the larger the conference membership and that some conferences may exhibit an increase in competitive balance.

Economics of College Sports addresses issues in the reemerging and growing area of collegiate athletics. Perhaps the most important contributions focus on the interactions between legal and institutional aspects of the NCAA and their impact on the objectives and goals of university education. However, all of the contributions provide insights that will generate significant discussion about policies necessary to sustain the vitality and integrity of the university education-sports coalition. The major issues include:

- The restructuring of the NCAA
- The university objective function
- Sports corruption and impact on university education
- Implications of Title IX compliance
- Cartel rents for collegiate athletes
- Institutional changes and competitive balance in collegiate sports

We hope you find the research in *Economics of College Sports* to be useful, thought-provoking, and enjoyable.

NOTES

1. See Fort (2003), p. 426.
2. See, for example, *USA Today,* July 15, 1999.
3. See Fizel and Bennett (2001), p. 349.

Part II

Structure of College Sports and the University Mission

The 1997 Restructuring of the NCAA: A Transactions Cost Explanation

Joel G. Maxcy

INTRODUCTION

The National Collegiate Athletic Association (NCAA) underwent a significant change in its organizational structure in 1997. The restructuring transformed the Association's system of governance from a single body to a federated system where each of its three competitive divisions formulates separate policy. More significantly Division I, the most competitive classification, replaced a one-member, one-vote direct democracy with a representative system where the basis of representation is determined by conference membership.[1] A Board of Directors composed entirely of institutional CEOs now approves all Division I legislation. This change is especially significant because representatives from Division I-A conference institutions, although composing only about one-third of the division's total members, are mandated majority representation on the Board.[2] Divisions II and III continue to approve all legislation by a vote of the membership at an annual convention, but the legislative sessions are now separate and specific to each division.

The restructuring received considerable attention from the media and public forums because of the apparent shift in organizational control from athletic directors to university presidents. Although university presidents (and faculty representatives) had been involved in NCAA governance from its inception, a perception existed that athletic departments, whose objectives are often implied to conflict with the university mission, had gained excessive control of the organization. Under the new structure of the composition of the Board of Directors, university CEOs are given full charge of Division I policy. Additionally, Divisions II and III each established Presidents Councils to oversee the policy changes to be voted on by the membership. These changes were recognized as a shift from an emphasis on business interests to academic interests. It will be argued in this paper that presidential control is primarily a superficial revision. The shift to a federated system where the major revenue-producing football conferences are mandated a majority on legislative issues is in point of fact the significant change.

The proposal to formally restructure was concurrent with serious consideration of an NCAA-sanctioned Division I-A football play-off. All sports with the exception of Division I-A football compete for an NCAA-sanctioned (national) championship in their respective divisions. The NCAA collects all championship event revenue and redistributes a significant portion to individual members. Revenues derived from television rights currently account for about 80% of the Association's gross revenue. This can be seen in the 1998–2000 budgets shown in Table 1. The contract between the CBS network and the NCAA for Division I men's basketball tournament makes up by far the bulk of this revenue. The net revenues from the tournament are reallocated to the membership using a formula that rewards conference tournament performance; nonetheless all NCAA members, regardless of division, receive a share.

Table 1
NCAA Budget 1998–99 and 1999–2000

Revenue	Approved 1998-99 Budget	Approved 1999-2000 Budget	Percentage of Total Operating Revenue/Exp.
Television	226,400,000	241,550,000	79.63%
Championships Revenue:			
Division I men's basketball	18,235,000	19,274,000	6.35%
Other Division I championships	8,481,000	9,393,000	3.10%
Division II championships	540,000	540,000	0.18%
Division III championships	303,000	265,000	0.09%
Total Championships Revenue	27,559,000	29,472,000	9.72%
Licensing and Royalties	18,370,000	21,056,000	6.94%
Investments	7,000,000	7,150,000	2.36%
Sales, Fees, and Services	3,661,000	4,107,000	1.35%
Totals NCAA Operating Revenue	282,990,000	303,335,000	100.0%

Source: The NCAA Online Financial Section, http://www.ncaa.org/financial/.

Post-season play in Division I football consists only of bowl games. Bowl organizers and promoters are independent of the NCAA. Bowl revenue is not redistributed across the Association, as payouts stay entirely within Division I and nearly all go directly to participating schools and their conferences. Since an antitrust ruling against the NCAA in 1984, the number of members able to profit from the considerable and fast-growing television revenues from football is limited primarily to the so-called power conferences of Division I-A. It stands to reason the Association was ready to use calls from the public and sports media as leverage to institute a national play-off that would result in significant revenues collected by the NCAA and subject to redistribution. The arrangement between the Division I-A power conferences and the bowl organizers, who also profit substantially from the current system, was (and is) threatened by an NCAA sanctioned play-off.

The NCAA experienced rapid membership growth throughout the first half of the 1990s. The revenues generated by the Division I men's basketball tournament had grown substantially since the early 1980s. The majority of this increased revenue derived from a series of successively larger television contracts with CBS; in fact, rights fees for the tournament increased from $28.3 million in 1985 to $166.2 million in 1995 (Zimbalist, 1999a, 112). The revenue-sharing plan makes the NCAA an attractive alternative in comparison to its only competition, the National Association of Intercollegiate Athletics (NAIA). NAIA members' athletic programs are comparable in size and scope to NCAA Division II and III, and this is where they typically enter if joining the NCAA. The revenue-sharing formula allocates a fixed percentage of the Division I tournament income to Division II and III members (approximately 4% and 3%, respectively). Increased membership therefore reduces the proportion going to an individual institution. It makes economic sense that the lower divisions ask for additional autonomy in determination of their entry rules. Hence a state of affairs is defined by which the bargain for a new organizational structure could be struck.

The NCAA has been the subject of a number of economic studies. Most employ the characterization of the organization as a cartel and focus on monopsony outcomes in input markets, specifically the comparison of the value of college athletes relative to their pay (Becker, 1985; Brown, 1993 and 1994, for example). Zimbalist (1999a) devotes a portion of his analysis to the product market effects of the NCAA cartel. Fleischer et al. (1992) provide a comprehensive analysis of the NCAA organization as a cartel and consider the monopoly effects on output markets as well. The research as to how the NCAA is organized to maintain its economic functions is yet incomplete—and this is amplified by the restructuring. Because of its size, term of existence, and minimal entry barriers, the NCAA is hardly typical of the theoretical economic cartel. Because it functions as a legislative body that both provides public goods and redistributes wealth, it is perhaps most appropriate to evaluate the NCAA under the construct of a political market in reference to the considerable public choice literature stemming from Buchanan and Tullock (1962). This line of analysis is not absent from Fleischer et al.'s economic characterization of the NCAA. But to date, only DeBrock and Hendricks (1996 and 1997) have considered the effect of the Association's voting methods on its organizational structure. The purpose of this paper is to extend the analysis of the NCAA's political markets by focusing on the events and actions leading to the 1997 reorganization. In the analysis of this paradigm shift particular attention will be given to transactions costs (Coase, 1937; Williamson, 1975) and property rights (Coase, 1960; Demsetz, 1967).

The paper proceeds as follows. The following section provides a background on the evolution of the organizational structure of the NCAA and provides the details of the new structure in contrast to the old. The third section discusses the relevant economic theory. Section four integrates economic theory with the forces driving the restructuring. Recent developments, implications, and suggested avenues for additional research conclude the paper.

NCAA ORGANIZATIONAL HISTORY

Fleischer et al. (1992) and others provide an ample history of the NCAA. In brief, the NCAA evolved from a public-good provider (the establishment of rules to reduce violence in football) to a cartel organization that assumed economic control of most college sports markets.[3] Although there is some overlap, the focus here is to trace the organizational changes following a history provided by Mott (1996).

Representatives of universities and colleges founded the organization and held the first convention in 1906. A constitution was drafted and ratified by 38 original members. The organization convened annually, and rule changes and other legislation were determined by vote of the membership. Approval required a simple majority. The members also elected a slate of officers officially called the Executive Committee to preside over the organization. This method of governance remained largely unchanged until 1922.

By the early 1920s the membership of the rapidly growing Association exceeded 100. The NCAA had extended its scope of governance beyond football and included most men's intercollegiate athletic sports offered at the time. In 1922 the first NCAA-sponsored and -sanctioned national championships were held in track and field. With the Association's role in governing intercollegiate athletics increasing in both breadth and depth, a significant organizational change was implemented.

In 1922 the NCAA established the NCAA Council, which essentially came to act as a corporate "board of directors" (Fleischer et al., 1992, 71). The Council replaced the Executive Committee as the NCAA's policy-making body and was granted the authority to act on behalf of the Association between annual conventions. At the time it was established, it was deemed the 14-member Council comprise at least one representative from each of the NCAA's nine geographic districts, with the five other members to include the Association's elected officers. The Council's purpose was to recommend and promote policy in the organization's best interests. The Council's economic mandate grew to include interpretation of the NCAA constitution and bylaws as well as the arbitration of disputes in regard to rule violations. All legislation continued to require approval by a majority vote of the membership. This basic legislative structure remained in place until the 1997 restructuring, although the membership had grown to over 1,000, included women's sports, and had divided into three competitive divisions. An organizational chart of the NCAA before the 1997 restructuring is shown in Figure 1.

From its early days the NCAA has faced internal conflicts primarily based on the institutionally divergent levels of investment in intercollegiate athletics. In 1922 University of Michigan Athletic Director Fielding Yost presented a paper to the convention proposing that the Association be separated into divisions according to the "attitude toward athletics" (Mott, 1996, 10). The

Figure 1
NCAA Organizational Chart Before Restructuring

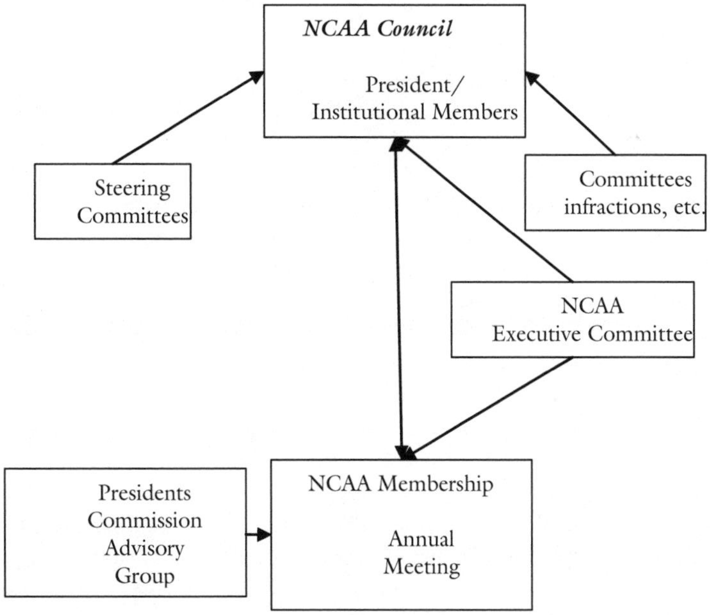

Source: Arthur A. Fleisher, Brian L. Goff, and Robert D. Tollison, *The National Collegiate Athletic Association: A Study in Cartel Behavior* (University of Chicago Press, 1992). © 1992, by the University of Chicago. All rights reserved.

opposing sides in the legislative battles of the 1930s and 1940s were drawn largely—although not completely—along these lines. Despite these conflicts and concerns over "level playing fields" there was no separation of the Association based on level of competition until the 1950s. In 1957 the NCAA sponsored the first lower level or "College Division" men's basketball championship. Throughout the 1960s the NCAA added College Division championships in other sports. By the 1968–69 academic year the membership sponsored College Division championships for nearly all sponsored sports, and individual institutions were asked to choose the level where they wished to compete; 223 opted for the more competitive University Division while 386 chose the College Division.

Although it may have seemed logical to have the divisions separated for the purpose of policy formation as well, this did not occur. The membership continued to vote on legislation as a unified body. There was a fear that divided voting would splinter the membership. The Association instead instituted a policy of "conscience voting" where members were asked to abstain from voting if they had no interest in the legislation. There is speculation that conscience voting was not adhered to and this system encouraged the typical coalition strategy of logrolling (Mott, 1996, 11). The institutions with high athletic investments, which constituted a minority, were not satisfied with their lack of decision-making autonomy within the organization. This gave rise to changes in the 1970s that set the stage for restructure 20 years later.

In 1973 the NCAA voted to create a three-tier system still based on the level of competition. The new divisions were simply numbered I, II, and III. The least competitive, Division III, was reserved for institutions choosing a very low level of investment in athletics, and declined to award athletic grant-in-aid scholarships. At the same time it was agreed to assure a Division I majority on the 14-member Council. Bylaws were changed so that eight slots were reserved for Division I members. The remaining six slots were allocated to Divisions II and III with no stipulation as to the breakdown between the two divisions. The organization expanded to include steering committees for each division.[4] The steering committees' functions included recommending legislation appropriate to the division, but the Council retained ultimate authority and all legislation was still enacted by conference votes of the entire membership.

Institutions were given the freedom to choose their level of competition and 235 initially opted for Division I. The institutions with the greatest investments in football programs quickly showed signs of dissatisfaction with the composition of the highest division. These schools argued that they should vote separately in matters relating to "big-time" football. At issue was NCAA's restrictive television policy. Individual schools were allowed a maximum of two appearances on national television per year. The NCAA controlled all television rights, precluding individual members or conferences from negotiating independent contracts. In 1977 a group of high-investment programs, including all members of the Atlantic Coast, Big 8, Southwest, Southeastern conferences, and Notre Dame, formed an alliance called the College Football Association (CFA). The CFA desired more autonomy for its members and aggressively lobbied for organizational changes, actually threatening secession from the NCAA if concessions were not made. The two other major conferences, the Big 10 and Pac 10, did not join the CFA, limiting their cartel power.[5]

The NCAA divided Division I into two subdivisions in 1978 mainly in response to pressure from the CFA membership. The I-A and I-AA distinction divided schools into two groups based on strict criteria of institutional investment in football programs. This marked the establishment of a formal internal barrier to entry.[6]

The restructuring of Division I granted the football powers some additional autonomy but still did not allow them to vote on legislation independently. More importantly, the NCAA did not change its television policy. The Association had controlled television rights and negotiated a national contract since the early 1950s.[7] The revenues collected from the contract were reallocated to the membership. Those schools appearing in televised contests received greater shares, but the NCAA restricted both the total number of televised games and individual appearances. High investment football programs were left to profit independently of the NCAA only through gate revenue and their conference relationships with post-season bowl games.

Unsatisfied with the restrictive NCAA policy, the CFA negotiated an independent television package with the NBC network in 1980. The NCAA threatened expulsion of the CFA members not only for football, but also for all NCAA sanctioned sports. Rather than follow through on the contract, the CFA responded by filing an antitrust suit against the NCAA. The United States Supreme Court heard the case in 1984 *(NCAA v. Board of Regents of University of Oklahoma & University of Georgia Athletic Association)* and ruled against the NCAA. This opened the door for individual schools and conferences to negotiate their own television contracts. The CFA entered into national-network contracts on behalf of its members. The Big 10 and Pac 10 conferences, which had refused to join the CFA, nonetheless reaped the benefits of the antitrust victory and signed a lucrative joint national television contract (Zimbalist, 1999a, 101). Conferences and individual institutions also sold television rights regionally and to increasingly influential cable networks.

Despite the Association's considerable loss of control over football revenue there was little movement toward substantive organizational alteration at this time. Increased revenues generated from the men's Division I basketball tournament mitigated the NCAA's loss of revenue from the national television contract for football. Noteworthy at this time, however, was the creation of the Presidents Commission in 1984. The Commission's purpose was to facilitate more institutional control over athletic programs, and it was technically established to provide a system of checks and balances to the Council. Fleischer et al. (1992, 71) discount the importance of the role of the Commission, classifying it as simply an advisory group.

Despite the pressure for decision-making autonomy by the high-investment football conferences, the organizational structure remained intact for 10 more years. The Association voted to explore its organizational restructure at the 1994 Convention. A task force for each division was appointed to devise a restructuring plan in early 1995. A proposal outlining specific plans for restructure was presented in December of 1995. The membership approved the restructuring at the 1996 Convention and the new governance structure took effect on August 1, 1997.

Figure 2 shows the organizational chart of the new structure. As previously noted, the major change occurs in Division I. A representative legislative system based on conference membership replaced direct democracy. A 15-member Board of Directors composed entirely of institutional CEOs approves all legislation, and it is required that nine of the fifteen members represent Division 1-A institutions. Division I also replaced committees with four cabinets with specific responsibilities; these are: academic affairs, eligibility and compliance, business and finance, championships and competition, and strategic planning. The cabinets have either 26 or 34 members and each is required to have a majority of members from IA institutions, 14 and 18, respectively. All cabinets report to the 34-member Division I Management Council, which in turn reports to the Board. The Management Council contains athletics administrators and faculty athletics representatives and is empowered to make recommendations to the Board and handle responsibilities delegated to it. It is also structured so that the Division I-A Conferences always have a majority. No legislation is created in Division I by a vote of the membership. Division-wide voting may be done only through an override vote process that requires a written request from at least 30 Division I members. In 1999 an expansion of the Board of Directors to 18 with 11 members representing 1A was approved. An increase in Management Council membership to 49 was also improved. In each case Division I-A conference members will retain their majorities; however, the proportion of members representing the six so-called power conferences is slightly reduced and Divisions I-A and I-AAA gain.[8]

Divisions II and III have nearly identical structures under the new system. Each has a Management Council and presidential board that are similar to the ones in Division I; however, the presidential body is known as the Presidents Council rather than the Board of Directors. Legislation in both divisions is considered through the traditional one-school, one-vote process at the annual Convention.

The entire Association remains under one umbrella. The Executive Committee, composed of institutional chief executive officers, oversees

Figure 2
Current NCAA Governance Structure

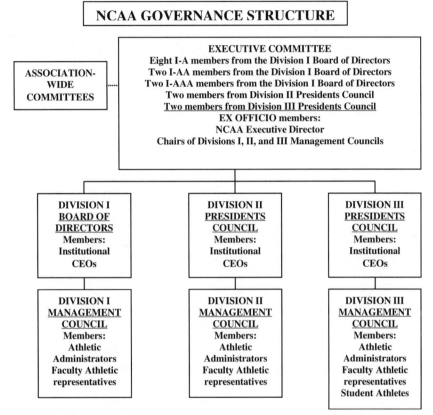

NCAA GOVERNANCE STRUCTURE

EXECUTIVE COMMITTEE
Eight I-A members from the Division I Board of Directors
Two I-AA members from the Division I Board of Directors
Two I-AAA members from the Division I Board of Directors
Two members from Division II Presidents Council
Two members from Division III Presidents Council
EX OFFICIO members:
NCAA Executive Director
Chairs of Divisions I, II, and III Management Councils

ASSOCIATION-WIDE COMMITTEES

DIVISION I BOARD OF DIRECTORS
Members:
Institutional CEOs

DIVISION II PRESIDENTS COUNCIL
Members:
Institutional CEOs

DIVISION III PRESIDENTS COUNCIL
Members:
Institutional CEOs

DIVISION I MANAGEMENT COUNCIL
Members:
Athletic Administrators
Faculty Athletic representatives

DIVISION II MANAGEMENT COUNCIL
Members:
Athletic Administrators
Faculty Athletic representatives

DIVISION III MANAGEMENT COUNCIL
Members:
Athletic Administrators
Faculty Athletic representatives
Student Athletes

Source: The NCAA Online, Governance Structure http://www.ncaa.org/databases/ governancestructure/.

Association-wide issues and is charged with ensuring that each division operates consistently with the basic purposes, fundamental policies, and general principles of the Association.[9] The new role of the Executive Committee is not discernable from the old, as it still does not play an active role in policy formation.

POLITICAL MARKETS, TRANSACTIONS COSTS, PROPERTY RIGHTS, AND RESTRUCTURING

The NCAA is a voluntary organization formed for the purpose of providing common rules and organizing athletic contests among its members.

The organization exists because the collective action benefits its individual members. Given this, it is entirely appropriate to consider the restructured governance under the theoretical construct of the political market. Buchanan and Tullock (1962) assert that collective decisions are determined by an evaluation of the relative weights of two types of costs. The first are the decision-making costs, which include the cost of organizing the group, bargaining, implementing decision-making rules, etc. The second group represents the external costs (net of external benefits) of collective action, which include the costs of inefficient reallocations. This type of externality arises because a majority rule system tends to reward effective coalitions with differentially larger shares of the benefits. Coalitions that form for the specific purpose of obtaining differentially larger shares are described as engaging in what economists call "rent seeking." Buchanan and Tullock claim that decision-making costs are higher under a system of direct democracy but the external costs imposed by effective rent seeking are higher in a representative legislative system, and increasingly so as the degree of representation is diminished. For example, a dictator has minimal decision-making costs but theoretically will impose the highest external cost on other group members. The choice of a representative system versus direct democracy is simply an evaluation of the respective costs. Buchanan and Tullock imply that the representative governance greatly reduces the decision-making costs of direct democracy, and these costs are prohibitive unless the group is small or there are very few issues that must be considered. They do not, however, specifically model the dynamic by which a group that employs direct democracy moves to representative democracy.

Though not directly parallel, the theory of collective action has a number of similarities to the theory of the firm developed by Coase (1937) extended with the transactions-cost economics introduced by Williamson (1975). No claim is made that this observation is unique; there exists an extensive body of public choice literature that invokes transactions costs and principal-agent analysis. It is simply conjectured that it is applicable to this situation.

The two types of categories of costs that determine organizational structure in each theory are directly analogous. Coase's theory provides a more distinct description of the circumstances that motivate a change in decision–making structure. The choice is really nothing more than basic benefit-cost analysis. The optimal firm structure occurs where the marginal cost of learning and haggling over the terms of trade (Buchanan and Tullock's decision-making costs) are equated with the cost of errors associated with concentrating decision-making authority (Buchanan and Tullock's external costs). Changes in the cost structure may tip the balance and motivate an organization to alter organizational structure. Williamson (1975) proposes that informational limitations and asymmetries are also determinants of these "transactions costs" and influence organizational structure.

The role of the legislative process in the determination and assignment of property rights allows us to take the analysis of the NCAA restructuring one step further. Central to the restructure was the battle over the property rights to the television market (and its returns) for Division I football. Jung et al. (1995) suggest that agents may rent-seek over the method that determines property rights distributions. It can be concluded that by the mid-1990s the Association had reached the point where the rents generated by college sports had grown to the point where coalitions that could force an organizational structure in their favor stood to greatly benefit. The next section identifies the development and recognition of the evolving cost structure and analyzes the restructure in this context.

EVOLVING EXTERNAL COSTS AND RESTRUCTURE

Buchanan and Tullock (1962) point out that collective action always results in a reallocation of property. The investment in athletic programs is highly variable across NCAA members even within Divisions; and it can be assumed investment is made on the basis of expected return. A direct democracy with each member's preferences given equal weight will be expected to impose greater external costs on those members that make the greatest investments in athletics (and therefore have highest expected returns). Conversely, if the relative level of investment determined the basis of representation, an outcome that imposes significantly lower external costs in proportion to investment would be expected.

With over 1,000 members and a significant diversity in athletic investment, it would seem by the 1990s that the NCAA had long since surpassed the benefit-cost ratios necessary to maintain direct democracy. The restructuring could thus be characterized as simply a long overdue action. Fleischer et al. (1992) imply that reorganization as a representative democracy was effectively established with the inception of the Council in 1922. In their characterization the elected Council made policy, and the legislative vote served as little more than a rubber stamp. The authors also suggest that the institutions that invested most heavily in athletic programs dominated the Council. There is no argument that this was true given the incentives by such institutions to form coalitions that promote their election. However, there was no decision-making rule in place that assured that Council representation would be based on financial investment in athletics or that Council policies would be approved by a vote of the membership. Certainly the conflict over Division I football policy illustrates the inability of the schools most heavily invested in athletics to force the Association to consent to their wishes. With increasingly lucrative returns from the power conference's television contracts, the disparity of investment within Division I had grown. The Council majority was only required for Division I. Additionally, despite higher organizational costs, there were plenty of incentives for the low-investment majority to form coalitions and seek allocations in their favor. So regardless of their ability to manipulate the system, heavily invested institutions had increasing incentives to make a change.

As previously mentioned, the impetus for restructuring was set with the increasing conflict over football revenue allocations between the powerful football conferences and the weaker Division I members in the 1970s (see Zimbalist, 1999a, and Byers and Hammer, 1995 for specific battle accounts). The formation of the CFA in 1977 represents the zenith of the first stage of this conflict; and the CFA's move to sell football television rights independently set the wheels of restructure in motion. This led to the lawsuit and subsequent Supreme Court decision in the 1984 antitrust case *(NCAA v. Board of Regents)* that enabled CFA members (and other institutions as they wished) to break free of the NCAA for the purpose of controlling television revenues for football.

The decision was crucial to the restructuring 12 years later for two primary reasons. First, institutions making large investments in football realized the benefits of being able to sell their product independently of the NCAA. Second, these schools could compare their revenue shares and revenue growth in football to the NCAA-controlled Division I basketball tournament that was also growing in popularity and profitability. Although institutions investing the greatest amounts in basketball programs do receive a majority of the spoils, Division I basketball tournament revenues are redistributed so that all members receive a share.

The breakup of the NCAA football cartel initially generated a lower level of total revenue. Weiler and Roberts (1998, 765) report that there were three times as many college football games televised in 1983 as in 1984, but the average price-per-game paid by the networks dropped from $1 million to $250,000. Greater quantities at lower prices are the expected result of moving from a monopoly to a competitive market, but lower total revenue is an extreme case. Zimbalist (1999a, 101) also attributes disorganization and a lack of negotiating experience and skills on the part of the CFA and Pac 10/Big 10 coalitions as playing a substantial role in the diminished prices.

By 1990 the revenue generated from the sale of television rights had grown to well in excess of the 1983 levels (Weiler and Roberts, 1998, 765), and the revenue was retained by the conferences that participated in the televised games. The power conferences were not necessarily a unified group. Notre Dame left the CFA in 1990 and entered into an exclusive television contract for televising its home games with NBC. The Pac 10 and Big 10 conferences remained independent of the CFA.

A major side effect of this lack of organization was the inability of Division I-A football to determine a champion on the field. Post-season play in Division I-A football, in contrast to all other divisions, does not include an NCAA-sanctioned tournament as a means of determining a champion. The championship instead is based on two polls, one of sportswriters and the other of coaches. If the two polls do not agree, both winners are declared national champions. College football fans and media have expressed considerable dissatisfaction with the subjective determination of the championship and the possibility that a distinct champion may not be determined. In both the 1990 and 1991 seasons each poll chose different winners, resulting in co-national champions being declared each year. This increased the external and internal pressure to institute a play-off and objectively determine the champion.

The relationship between the power football conferences and the bowl organizers provides the main obstruction to an NCAA play-off. An independent NCAA play-off would compete economically with the bowls, and with history as judge, have a considerable advantage.[10] The bowls responded to this threat by forming a coalition with the CFA following the 1991 season. The Bowl Coalition, as it was known, was in place for three years (1992–94). The Coalition provided a structure which enabled the champions of the Big East and Atlantic Coast Conferences and Notre Dame to meet the champion of the Big 8, Southeastern, and Southwest Conferences in the Orange, Sugar, and Cotton Bowls, respectively. But a championship game between the two highest ranked was guaranteed only in the event that the champions of the Big East and ACC or Notre Dame were ranked number one and two, in which case they would have met in the Fiesta Bowl for the national championship (SEC, 1999).

The Bowl Coalition was hampered by its inability to include the Rose Bowl, by far the most lucrative bowl. Additionally, the Big 10 and Pac 10 conferences held an exclusive contact with the Rose Bowl, committing their respective champions to the game. The Coalition therefore had no hope of staging a championship game if either conference had the first or second ranked team. Frustration over the failure of the bowl system to determine a champion and concerns over the opportunity cost of lost revenues because of this breakdown appeared to reach a head in 1994. The year began with two major news stories emerging from the Association's annual convention. First, Division I-A conference commissioners proposed the overhaul of NCAA structure that led to the restructuring of 1997. Concurrently the Association's leadership announced that it would research the possibilities for an NCAA-sanctioned Division I-A football play-off. A complete record of the arguments, negotiations, discussions, and agreements between all the parties involved is not available. However, implications can be drawn based on accounts of events as reported in the NCAA publications and media outlets over this period.

The declared reasons for restructuring clearly illustrate the motivation. The I-A commissioners claimed their proposal overhaul was as necessary for three reasons (NCAA News, January 12, 1994):

1. The size and complexity of the current structure had become problematic.

2. The current NCAA membership classifications had become cumbersome, inflexible, and overly expensive.
3. The institutions with the greatest investment were not adequately empowered to effectuate policy.

A Board of Directors with a majority chosen on the basis of conference "equity" was a key to the proposal, making it apparent the above list was in reverse order of concern. The equity (investment) needed to gain a majority position was strictly defined along the lines of the conference membership of I-A members at the time. The Big West, Western Athletic, and Mid-American were the only I-A conferences that did not meet the proposed criteria.

NCAA president Joseph Crowley was quoted as saying he believed I-A members had a greater interest in autonomy than in the past based largely out of concern as to how the Association's resources were being deployed. In response to a question of whether a secession of I-A powers could occur, Crowley acknowledged that although ill advised, the possibility existed (NCAA News, January 12, 1994).[11]

The NCAA News reported in January 1994 on a proposal for a six-team play-off including the champions of the five most invested conferences (Big 10, ACC, Pac 10, Big 8, SEC) and Notre Dame. It was suggested the rights could be sold to the highest bidding bowls. At the same time Crowley stated that income generated by a play-off would be distributed throughout the membership and resistance would come from the Division I-A schools that produced this revenue. The strategy employed by I-A members can be inferred from the comments of newly appointed executive director Cedric Dempsey, who stated that a "play-off system must prove it won't lose money" and "the bowls are proven to be profitable" (NCAA News, January 19, 1994).

The demise of the CFA, which elected to disband in 1996, also began in early 1994. Although Notre Dame broke away in 1990 and signed its own television deal with NBC, the organization retained its function as the collective voice and economic agent of the strongest I-A conferences, with the two notable exceptions. In February the Southeastern Conference (SEC) broke ranks and signed a five-year $95 million contract to begin in 1996 with CBS. In March the Big 8 conference and four members of the Southwest Conference (SWC) signed a five-year $100 million contract with ABC for television football rights also to begin in 1996. The deal motivated a merger resulting in the formation of the Big 12 conference. Later that spring the left-out SWC members, with the exception of the University of Houston, merged with the Western Athletic Conference (WAC) in hopes of creating a seventh I-A power conference.

In addition to nearly eliminating the CFA's economic function, these contracts were noteworthy because they demonstrated the tremendous increase in the commercial value of televised college football. The five-year CFA package set to expire in 1995 totaled $300 million (Zimbalist, 1999a, 102). The new deals also made apparent that a one-twelfth share of $100 million is far preferable to one-eightieth of $300 million. This likely furthered the determination to resist any plan resulting in a situation where football revenues would be shared across the NCAA membership. In February the College Football Coaches Association revealed that 70% of its Division I members opposed a play-off system. Questions as to the split of the revenues were cited as a primary concern.

Formal discussions of football play-off proposals continued in May. At this time a play-off review panel indicated that serious consideration should be given to a play-off in light of the revenue potential. The panel revealed the revenue generated by the men's basketball tournament increased by 120% over the previous six years. During the same period football bowl revenue increased by 33% (NCAA News, May 11, 1994).

In June of 1994 the CFA announced that it would seek a new Division (to be called somewhat inaptly Division IV) that would be limited to the I-A power conferences. Again a desire for more autonomy on football matters and control over revenues are cited as reasons for the change. Interestingly, the CFA faculty representatives and coaches were reported as being the most outspoken on this matter (NCAA News, June 8, 1994). Two inferences may be drawn, the first being that faculty motivations in regard to allocative mechanisms between institutions are consistent with their athletic departments. And second, perhaps CEOs and athletic directors had better information on an alternative plan that would play to the same result.

In June the panel studying Division I-A play-off alternatives asked for an extension. Later that month the President's Commission voted to drop the matter entirely and proscribed the extension. NCAA President Crowley commented that there was not enough interest in the matter among the membership to warrant further investigation.[12]

Also of note in 1994 was the Association's accelerated growth. The 39 new members joining that year accounted for the largest single-year jump in the Association's history. The new members were entirely absorbed by Divisions II and III, with 24 and 15 entrants, respectively. As has been noted, each of the Divisions as a whole receives a fixed allocation of the Division I men's basketball tournament revenue. The increasing value of the CBS contract doubtless encouraged entry at these levels. This in turn increased the incentives of existing members to strengthen entry barriers. Evidence of the desire to limit expansion is found in the approval of a provisional membership category at the 1994 convention, which lengthened the application process to three years, and a moratorium placed on entry during the restructuring period (NCAA News, August 31, 1994).

Comparing the revenue growth rates of the men's basketball tournament and the bowls indicates that an NCAA sanctioned Division I-A football play-off had the potential to generate more revenue than the bowl system. However, the money generated by NCAA-sponsored events is collected by the Association and redistributed across the entire membership.

The bowl system, though very popular, lacks the commercial appeal of a play-off. Nonetheless Division I-A members collect all the revenue and it is not subject to NCAA-wide redistribution. Tables 2 and 3 show the compiled revenue allocations by conference. Table 2 shows total Division I allocations from NCAA redistribution each year from 1992–99. As previously disclosed, 80% of the revenue available for redistribution is generated by television rights to the men's Division I basketball tournament. Table 3 shows the portion of the total allocation made up by the basketball fund allocation, which is directly determined by men's basketball tournament performance. Table 4 shows the conference allocations for football bowl games in 1996 and 1999.

Some conclusions can be drawn from the comparisons. The NCAA as a whole may have gained from a Division I-A football play-off, but if implemented with the 1994 organizational structure in place, a revenue sharing plan similar to that in basketball would have been expected. Comparison of the revenues allocated to the I-A power conferences shows that they keep well over 90% of total football bowl revenue but on average less than half of the total basketball revenue. From Table 3 it is apparent that the power conferences perform the best (of course they get the most slots) in the basketball tournament and are rewarded relatively well. They appear to earn on average about 60% of the total basketball fund allocation, but the overall allocation of revenue is by far less lucrative from their standpoint, than it is for football.

The alternatives facing members of the I-A football power conferences were taking a considerably smaller share of a possibly bigger pie versus retaining their current shares of the existing pie. Even if the former were expected to be greater, the I-A conferences would effectively cede control over a major portion of football revenues to the Association for the indefinite future, and if revenues continued to grow, so do their external costs. The preferences of the leadership of the Division I-A institutions were clear from their actions. The goal was to prevent the NCAA from instituting a football play-off, or at least stall action and attempt to alter the organizational structure so that a better allocation results for Division I-A members.

A final category of external costs must be considered in this analysis. A number of writers, including Weiler and Roberts (1998), have noted the courts and law-making institutions have been very sympathetic toward the NCAA. In any other context much of what the NCAA does to control both input and output markets would be subject to legal challenges. The courts have generally taken the viewpoint that college athletics are not a commercial enterprise but are part of the institutions' educational mission. That characterization of the NCAA is not necessarily disingenuous. The vast

Table 2
NCAA Division I Revenue Distribution 1992–99

	1992-93	1993-94	1994-95	1995-96	1996-97	1997-98	1998-99
TOTAL	$81,976,839	$86,130,481	$123,373,226	$137,749,277	$145,046,244	$147,348,995	$140,770,248
I-A Total	48,860,809	50,982,836	74,099,677	87,018,647	92,064,380	94,231,123	88,353,472
I-A Share	59.60%	59.19%	60.06%	63.17%	63.47%	63.95%	62.76%
Power Total	39,297,664	41,462,156	60,487,705	64,707,986	67,481,572	68,316,778	63,858,410
Power Share of I-A	80.43%	81.33%	81.63%	74.36%	73.30%	72.50%	72.28%
I-AA Total	33,116,030	35,147,645	49,273,549	50,730,630	52,981,864	53,117,872	52,416,776
I-AA Share	40.40%	40.81%	39.94%	36.83%	36.53%	36.05%	37.24%

Source: Data is derived from the NCAA Online Financial Section, http://www.ncaa.org/financial/.

Table 3
NCAA Division I Basketball Fund 1992–99

	1992-93	1993-94	1994-95	1995-96	1996-97	1997-98	1998-99
TOTAL	$31,500,001	$31,500,000	$39,999,990	$44,999,997	$49,999,998	$54,999,997	$54,999,998
I-A Total	21,755,088	21,498,642	27,311,825	33,644,293	36,994,607	40,806,450	40,141,128
I-A Share	69.06%	68.25%	68.28%	74.77%	73.99%	74.19%	72.98%
Power Total	18,848,711	18,720,487	24,086,018	26,999,998	29,380,052	32,379,031	32,157,257
I-A Power Share of I-A	86.64%	87.08%	88.19%	80.25%	79.42%	79.35%	80.11%
I-AA Total	9,744,913	10,001,358	12,688,165	11,355,704	13,005,391	14,193,547	14,858,870
I-AA Share	30.94%	31.75%	31.72%	25.23%	26.01%	25.81%	27.02%

Source: Data is derived from the NCAA Online Financial Section, http://www.ncaa.org/financial/.

Table 4
NCAA Division I Bowl Revenue Distribution by Conference 1996 and 1999

Conference	1996		1999	
Division I-A	Major Bowl Revenue	Total Bowl Revenue	Major Bowl Revenue	Total Bowl Revenue
Power Group				
Big 10	16,736,000	23,986,000	18,052,579	25,990,639
Atlantic Coast	8,736,000	1,286,000	13,473,750	18,289,074
Southeastern	8,736,000	15,336,000	16,982,500	28,311,134
Big East	8,484,000	11,534,000	13,473,750	15,776,345
Pac-10	8,250,000	11,400,000	16,543,829	20,844,797
Big 12	16,972,000	21,372,000	13,473,750	21,346,099
Second Tier				
Western	-	2,750,000	1,600,000	4,353,095
Mid-American	-	150,000	600,000	1,350,000
Conference USA	-	800,000	800,000	3,503,095
Big West	-	150,000	300,000	1,050,000
Mountain West	-	-	-	-
I-A Total	67,914,000	88,764,000	95,300,158	140,814,278
PowerTotal	67,914,000	84,914,000	92,000,158	130,558,088
I-A Power Share	100.00%	95.66%	96.54%	92.72%
I-AA Total	0	0	1200000	1200000
I-AA Share	0	0	1.24%	0.84%

Sources: Zimbalist 1999a, p. 107; 1999, NCAA Online Financial Section http://www.ncaa.org/financial/.

majority of schools spend more on athletics programs than these programs generate in direct revenue. Significant profits are shown only at the elite levels of Division I-A (Zimbalist, 1999a, 150). But it was exactly these elite level schools that motivated the restructure, and their purpose seems quite clearly increased control of the commercial benefits.

Roberts (1994) observed that the common thread uniting Division I-A institution was in no sense a common educational mission, but rather the high degree of commercialization. Given this commercialization, Roberts warned that the new organization would face serious antitrust risks. The restructuring also opened the door to a reevaluation of tax law. Nonprofit organizations are typically subject to a 34% tax on revenue produced from activities that are unrelated to the main purpose for which the organization exists (Roberts 1994). The IRS attempted to collect this tax on revenues generated by corporate sponsorship in 1991. Their attempts were thwarted and federal legislation was passed that allowed such revenue to remain exempt from taxes with certain qualifications (Zimbalist, 1999a, 128). Intercollegiate athletics are part of the educational mission of most colleges, but when looking at the behavior of only the I-A institutions it is much harder to draw that connection. It is apparent that a change in mind-set by either the court system or lawmaking bodies could be very costly to NCAA members. Mitigation of such costs must have been considered in the reorganization process.

This helps explain the emphasis and publicity generated by the new structures empowerment of institutional CEOs. By the 1980s there were repeated accusations that "big-time" athletics had grown out of control. A common perception was that athletic departments, whose profit-seeking actions are seen in conflict with university's educational objectives, were beyond reproach. The establishment of the Presidential Council in 1984 is an early attempt at treating this quandary. In response to the deteriorating public image of college sports, the independent Knight Foundation was appointed to examine and make recommendations for improving college athletics. Central to their 1990 report was that athletic programs should be subject to increased institutional control.

Fleisher et al. (1992) discount both the independence of the Foundation and the claim that presidents' incentives are different from the athletic directors'. They point to evidence that the supposed lack of control was more a perception than reality. To further that point, consider this statement by retired NCAA executive director Walter Byers in 1994: "The presidents were put in control of collegiate athletic policy and this reform movement, which has been publicized at every NCAA convention and written about at every NCAA Presidents commission meeting, clearly has become an exercise in meeting more with form and very little substance."[13]

A conflict does develop only over the allocation of revenues within the institution. Athletic directors of course have the incentive to keep the revenue in their departments. Presidents conversely would prefer to have the option to allocate the revenues to their best advantage, which may be elsewhere in the university. This explains why the most significant actions attributed to increased presidential influence are cost controls. Examples include scholarship limits and the restrictions on the size and compensation of coaching staffs. These cost controls may release more funds for university-wide distribution. They also allow for greater profits by increasing the degree of monopsonistic exploitation of input markets and serve to advance the position of the wealthier established programs. Both are outcomes that doubtless also please the athletic department.

The NCAA's emphasis on the complete presidential authority over the restructuring appears to be largely an exercise in propaganda. The reorganization sets the stage for the members with the highest levels of commercial investment in athletics to gain a greater degree of control over the allocation of revenues. This may in turn cause legal institutions to be more likely to consider college athletic programs commercial rather than educational enterprises. The emphasis on presidential control reduces this prospect. The illusion of an organization under the auspices of university presidents creates the impression that education remains the top priority of the NCAA. The Knight Foundation, which had reconvened for the purpose of evaluating academic eligibility standards in the spring of 1995, fully endorsed the restructuring on this basis.

The NCAA also increased its lobbying presence establishing of the Office of Federal Relations in Washington, DC, in April of 1995. A 1996 NCAA News story states that a key decision was to locate the office at One Dupont Circle alongside other higher education associations, including the American Council on Education. The director of the office, Doris Dixon, is quoted: "Because of our office location, we are perceived as and treated as one of the higher education associations."[14] Case closed!

The restructuring proposals for each division were approved by the 1995 convention by an overwhelming majority of 777-91-1. From this it can be surmised that an effective coalition formed of Division I-A schools and Division II and III members who also stood to gain from greater autonomy (or at least were convinced of this). The NCAA News reported that the only objections came from I-AA and I-AAA members who voiced concern over access. The new structure took effect on August 1, 1997. The only change since indicates that the original objections of the I-AA an I-AAA members remained a point of contention as the 1999 expansions of the Division I Board of Directors and Management Council accommodated these interests.

IMPLICATIONS AND SUGGESTIONS FOR FUTURE RESEARCH

The NCAA appears to have settled on a structure that is able to allocate revenues to appease its greatest and least invested institutions. A lack of satisfaction with the new form by those with mid-range investments (Second tier Division I-A and Division I-AA institutions) seems to have become apparent. The expansion of the Division I Board of Directors and Management Councils to include more representation for these members provides substantiation. Whether this sates the schools remains to be seen. However, as of 1999 I-AA schools do receive a share of I-A bowl money (see Table 4).

A national play-off in Division I football also appears very unlikely. The power conferences can be expected to be unwilling to implement such a system unless their current share of revenues (more than 90%) remains with certainty. Even with the current organization, ceding control of football to the Association is a considerable risk. Increasing revenue will only serve to increase the incentives of those currently cut out of the mix. Attempts have been made to appease public demands for an on-field determined national champion. The I-A power conferences have unified and joined with the major bowls to create a system that allows the two top-ranked teams to meet in an unofficial championship game. The unified body replaced the Bowl Coalition, first as the Bowl Alliance and with the Rose Bowl signing on in 1999, the Bowl Championship Series (BCS) (SEC, 1999). It appears well posed to fend off any NCAA threats to establish a play-off system.

The majority of analysis of the NCAA discloses monopoly effects in relevant input and output markets affected. Though the results clearly demonstrate a powerful cartel, the organization itself is an anomaly. To date, analysis of the evolution of NCAA's internal structure that effectively maintains this odd but very effective monopoly is limited. This investigation provides some additional perspective. The inference is drawn that in many respects the organization looks like a government monopoly (the former Soviet Bloc's communist party for example). From its beginnings with its only purpose to provide public goods to its assumption of economic functions and power, the parallels with government institutions are evident. The structural change reveals aspects of coalition building, opportunism, and rent seeking, which characterize public choice and the analysis of institutions.

This research unearths several additional questions. The governance structure emphasizes conference affiliation. Since the restructure there have been numerous conference shake-ups, including expansions, mergers, and new alliances. It may be useful to identify the altered incentives of the new structure on this dynamic. Also interesting is the conference structure given the differences in control and allocation of the football and basketball revenues. Conferences appear less likely to retain the same composition for both sports, especially at the Division I-A level. Does the different reward system have an effect? There are a myriad of public choice questions in regard to principal-agent problems, including relationships between the membership and their elected representatives on the Board of Directors and the Management Council and the Board. The principal-agent relationship between the Association and the Central Office (the agency) is also of interest. The votes of the membership and minutes of Board and Council are part of the public record, making the research plausible.

NOTES

1. Most NCAA institutions have grouped themselves into conferences, some of which predate the NCAA. The primary purpose of conferences is the organization of league play, but conferences also act as economic agents for their membership. Traditional conferences maintain the same members across all NCAA sports. Single sport conferences are now fairly common, however. NCAA governance is essentially based on football conference membership.

2. Division I is divided into three sub-classifications for football only. Division I-A membership is limited to institutions whose football programs meet minimum standards of revenue generation, including minimum stadium size and average home attendance.

3. It is well documented that the organization formed under pressure from President Roosevelt for the purpose of creating a common set of rules aimed at reducing violence in the sport of football. The rule-making function was soon applied to other sports. The common rule-making function and the general organization of competition is a public good. As Fleischer et al. point out, once an organization is intact, cost of assuming economic functions is relatively low.

4. By this time there were numerous other committees representing specific interests and individual sports within the organization. These committees could recommend legislative proposals but all reported to the Council.

5. The Big East, which did not exist as a football conference until the late 1980s, joined the CFA but the Big 10 and Pac 10 remained permanent holdouts.

6. Later a third category, I-AAA, was established to include schools that compete in Division I in basketball but place less (often no) emphasis on football than I-AA.

7. The television rights contract created a monopoly for the network winning the bid as well. The NCAA sold the rights exclusively to one network, most often ABC until 1981. (See Zimbalist, 1999a for a thorough discussion of the NCAA's television history.)

8. The power conferences are the ACC, Big East, Big 10, Big 12, SEC, and Pac 10.

9. All information including the organizational chart is reported in the *NCAA News*, August 4, 1997, in a supplement titled "The NCAA Restructuring Guide."

10. When initially instituted, the NCAA men's basketball tournament had to compete with the well-established National Invitational Tournament (NIT). The NCAA effectively drove the NIT to greatly diminished status. Effective ploys included not allowing NIT participants to compete in the NCAA tournament, and later expanding the NCAA tournament to include multiple conference representatives.

11. Byers and Hammer (1995) claim that a number of CFA threats of secession in the past were much closer to becoming reality than was actually reported.

12. Ironically, Pennsylvania State University of the Big 10 Conference and the Big 8's University of Nebraska both completed undefeated regular seasons that fall. Penn State filled its conference obligation and defeated the University of Oregon in

the Rose Bowl, while Nebraska competed in the Bowl Coalition's Orange Bowl and defeated the University of Miami. Both final polls declared Nebraska the champion, but critics had a field day with the failure of the system.

13. From an editorial comment by Walter Byers, *NCAA News*, June 14, 1994, p. 4.

14. "A capital idea—NCAA's D.C. office has served Association well in its first year" by Sally Huggins, *NCAA News*, June 16, 1996.

3

The Impact on Higher Education of Corruption in Big-Time College Sports

Paul D. Staudohar and Barry Zepel

INTRODUCTION

The purpose of this paper is to examine the principal findings and recommendations of three major studies. The first is a series of three reports produced from 1991–1993 by the Knight Commission on Intercollegiate Athletics.[1] The second is a book published in 2001 called *The Game of Life: College Sports and Educational Values*.[2] The third study is by the Knight Commission in 2001.[3]

These studies lend themselves to analysis and comparison because they examine athletic programs in the context of the mission of higher education. *The Game of Life* covers a longer time span and views college sports comprehensively and at all levels of competition. The Knight Commission reports focus on the sports of football and basketball at Division I-A schools. The studies are particularly worthy of attention because of the objective approach and high quality of the research. Both of the major Knight Commission studies (hereinafter called Knight I—the 1991–1993 studies—and Knight II—the 2001 study) were chaired by William C. Friday, president emeritus of the University of North Carolina, and Rev. Theodore M. Hesburgh, president emeritus of the University of Notre Dame. *The Game of Life* is based on a study by the Andrew W. Mellon Foundation. Author James L. Shulman is the financial and administrative officer, and author William G. Bowen is the president of the Mellon Foundation. Bowen is also a former professor of economics and president of Princeton University.

Prior to examination of these three studies, it is appropriate to review some historical aspects of sports corruption and the institutions that are parties to it.

AMATEURS AND PROFESSIONALS

The first definition of an amateur in the United States was adopted by the National Association of Amateur Athletes of America in 1879. It said that:

> An amateur is any person who has never competed in an open contest, or for a stake, or for public money, or for gate money, or under a false name; or with a professional for a prize, or where gate money is charged; nor has ever at any period of his life taught or pursued athletic exercises as a means of livelihood.[4]

This definition focuses on negative aspects which if committed would disqualify one from amateur status. The main distinction between amateur and professional is receipt of money from athleticism. Later definitions have emphasized the pleasure, leisure, and avocation of amateurism, but receipt of pay has always been the distinguishing feature of the professional.

In early America there were few professional participants in sports. Beginning with baseball in the 1850s, professional teams and leagues were formed. By the late 1880s, college football games between traditional rivals in the Ivy League had become the most popular single spectator event in America, with crowds of up to 40,000 fans. This prompted Harvard president Charles Eliot to lament that "Colleges are presenting themselves to the public, educated and uneducated alike, as places of mere physical sport and not as educational training institutions."[5]

As collegiate athletics began to flourish commercially, covert professionalism crept into certain sports such as rowing, football, and baseball. Monetary aid was provided to athletes in the form of tuition and incidental fees, and clandestine payments to top players were common. In 1906, historian Frederick Jackson Turner said, at an alumni gathering at the University of Wisconsin, that intercollegiate athletics "has become a business, carried on too often by professionals, supported by levies on the public, bringing in vast gate receipts, demoralizing student ethics, and confusing the ideals of sport, manliness, and decency."[6] Despite elements of professionalism in a few sports at a handful of schools, amateurism reigned supreme on college campuses. Nearly all athletes were authentic students and true amateurs.

Americans' fascination with sports continued to grow, however, and by the 1920s we entered what became known as the Golden Age of Sport. Professional athletes like Babe Ruth in baseball, Jack Dempsey in boxing, Red Grange in football, and Bill Tilden in tennis became national heroes. In 1929, the first comprehensive study of collegiate sports in America was undertaken by the Carnegie Foundation for the Advancement of Teaching. A total of 112 colleges and universities were visited, including seven schools in Canada.

The study reported that while many institutions operated on a straightforward basis, there were ". . . acute problems of recruiting and subsidizing, especially with respect to intercollegiate football."[7] Athletes were taken to task in the report for ". . . disreputable and shameful practices for the sake of material returns . . ."[8] and university presidents were faulted for not taking sufficient responsibility for the "shaping of athletic policies."[9]

The last stand on unsullied amateurism was made by Avery Brundage, an American who headed the International Olympic Committee. Brundage championed a notion of amateurism that emphasized high educational and humanistic aims.[10] He fought hard against pay for play and during his tenure many athletes were denied their amateur status by accepting money for performance. In the late 1970s and under the leadership of IOC president Juan Antonio Samaranch (1980–2001), Brundage's ideals were jettisoned and payment of athletes became common. Today, top professionals compete in Olympic sports such as basketball, baseball, and hockey, and even so-called amateurs are paid openly for training and for winning medals.

Are football and basketball players at Division I-A schools amateurs or professionals? The answer is complicated since categorical notions have changed over time, making for an ideological rather than historical assertion. We know that top college athletes have a full-time commitment to their sport; they function in an organization with emphasis on economic goals; they "work" for bosses (coaches, tutors); and they are contracted to play for a particular team. Athletes receive compensation for tuition and books, housing in collegiate facilities, and sometimes financial assistance from boosters. Their main goal is to participate in sports, not to receive an education. There is currently a movement to unionize college athletes, by the United Steelworkers of America, which if successful would be another indication of professionalism. On the other hand, there is no direct payment to athletes in the form of a wage, and an athlete's outside earnings are limited to $2,000 per year.

The purpose of big-time college sports has little if anything to do with the educational mission of the schools. The purpose is to provide entertainment for students, alumni, boosters, and the public-at-large through live game and televised viewing. Elite athletes in top-level programs are ostensibly students, but they are not recruited for academic reasons. Their "scholarships" are based on their playing skills and entertainment value, not on academic capability.

THE BASIC PROBLEM

There is no doubt that sports are a valuable part of students' campus life, whether playing intramural games or attending sports events for entertainment. However, overemphasis on the big-time sports of football and basketball, especially at the 115 Division I-A schools, has created a monster that conflicts with the essential mission of higher education. The dilemma is nicely put by former Harvard president Derek Bok:

> [T]he very success of intercollegiate athletics and the passionate enthusiasms they arouse create constant tendency toward excess, pushing the search for winning teams to extremes that threaten to harm the lives of student-athletes and compromise the integrity of universities as serious educational institutions. And so it is that university presidents find themselves in the strange position of having to regard athletics as a serious ethical challenge.[11]

The mission of a university is to provide an intellectually stimulating environment for teaching, learning, and pushing forward the frontiers of knowledge. How do big-time sports conflict with this mission? One source of conflict is illegal recruiting, which involves bending or breaking university rules in order to attract elite athletes, including transgressions such as altering high school transcripts, deceptions on admissions tests, payment of money as inducement to attend, and providing gifts to athletes and their families.

A second source of conflict is admission of athletes who are unqualified academically. Many schools do not have minimum acceptance requirements and athletes are brought in whose academic grades and test scores do not meet normal admission standards.

A third conflict is that athletes are kept eligible by various proper and improper means. Many schools have programs specially designed for athletes, often in the physical education department, that provide a curriculum of academically inferior courses. Athletes are kept eligible by tutoring arrangements not available to other students and sometimes by having term papers and assignments completed on their behalf by academic advisors.

A fourth source of conflict with the educational mission of the university is that athletes, even though they may be qualified to compete in a rigorous academic curriculum, are typically unable to do so effectively because of the heavy time demands that conditioning, practice, travel, and games involve. It is not uncommon for players to spend 20 to 30 hours per week on these activities, draining time and energy from academic pursuits.

The reason these academic conflicts have arisen lies within the universities themselves. Presidents, boards of trustees, faculty, conferences, athletic departments, and coaches have all played a role in subverting the educational mission. In the final analysis, it is these groups who must come to grips with the conflict in order to regain the integrity of the academy. But there are other institutional actors that are contributing to the schism between academics and athletes. Among the more important of these intertwined actors are television, the National Collegiate Athletic Association (NCAA), the Bowl Championship Series (BCS), and boosters.

Television

Underpinning the commercial development of collegiate sports is network and cable television. The amounts of money paid by television to broadcast games are enormous. From 1994 to 2001, for example, CBS paid the NCAA $1.75 billion for rights to the Division I postseason men's basketball tournament. Starting in 2002, CBS will pay the NCAA $6.2 billion over 11 years to continue broadcasting these games. Football, hockey, and baseball games also provide bountiful revenues from television. Telecasts of college games occur year-round on almost a daily basis.

NCAA

The NCAA was formed in 1906 to establish rules that would minimize injuries to football players, 18 of whom had been killed the year before. Today, 977 colleges and universities are members of the NCAA. Article 2 of the NCAA Constitution states that its basic purpose is to "maintain intercollegiate athletics as an integral part of the educational program and the athlete as an integral part of the student body." Yet the organization sets only minimal standards and uniform playing rules. The NCAA is akin to a professional league. Eighty percent of its revenue comes from television; it has lucrative corporate sponsorships, and resides in a lavish headquarters in Indianapolis. In addition, the NCAA has two major advantages that professional leagues lack: (1) college athletes do not receive salaries, and (2) the NCAA and its member schools do not pay income taxes.[12]

BCS

Ironically, the big-money nature of college sports was ratcheted upward by a 1984 decision of the U.S. Supreme Court, which invalidated the NCAA's monopoly over televising football games. This created a bonanza for already wealthy Division I-A conferences and teams by enabling them to cut their own television deals without having to share revenues with NCAA-member schools. It also led to corporate sponsorship of bowl games and creation of the BCS, which generates substantial revenues for schools with powerhouse football programs. The BCS includes the Atlantic Coast Conference, Big East, Big 10, Pac-10, and Southeastern Conference. The NCAA has no role in the BCS. As a cartel, the BCS seeks to arrange a national championship game and other bowl games among leading contenders. Controversy has swirled around its choices, however, and traditional bowl rivalries have been compromised.

Boosters

Boosters and their clubs provide support to various types of athletic programs, sometimes involving improper payments to players and coaches. In exchange for their legitimate contributions, boosters receive priority seating at games and other perks. Unlike alumni, whose donations have little if any correlation to won-lost records of schools, boosters' support is strongly related to success of the football and basketball teams.[13] Boosters also provide for college athletics prospectively in their wills and insurance policies. Athletic administrators are reluctant to crack down on boosters because of a fear of biting the hand that feeds them. Meanwhile, corruption in college sports is related to boosters who may have little idea of the educational mission of a school or the ethical conduct it is supposed to promote.

KNIGHT COMMISSION I

This section refers to the combined version of three Knight Commission reports: "Keeping Faith with the Student-Athlete" (1991), "A Solid Start" (1992), and "A New Beginning for a New Century" (1993). Shortly before Knight I began, *Time* magazine published a cover story (April 3, 1989) on how the national obsession with winning and moneymaking was turning big-time college sports into an educational scandal that perverted the noblest ideals of both sports and the academy. Time interviewed scores of young men who played college basketball, and concluded that for many, the promise of education was a sham. One of the article's conclusions was that "Equally victimized are the colleges and universities that participate in an educational travesty—a farce that devalues every degree and denigrates the mission of higher education."[14]

Knight I found that during the 1980s, 109 colleges and universities were censured, sanctioned, or put on probation by the NCAA, and that more than half of these schools were at the Division I-A level. Nearly a third of present and former professional football players interviewed said that they had accepted illicit payments in college. Another finding was that among 100 big-time schools, 35 had graduation rates under 20% for basketball players, and 14 had the same low rate for football players. This is not surprising in light of another finding that at half of Division I-A schools, 20% or more of football and basketball players were "special admits," a rate 10 times as high as for the total student body.

At the heart of the problem is the separate nature of football and basketball programs, which are not held to the same standards as the rest of the university. As Knight I put it:

> Athletics programs are given special, often unique status within the university; the best coaches receive an income many times that of most full professors; some coaches succumb to the pressure to win with recruiting violations and even the abuse of players; boosters respond to athletic performance with gifts and under-the-table payments; faculty members, presidents, and other administrators, unable to control the enterprise, stand by it as it undermines the institution's goals in the name of values alien to the best the university represents.[15]

Knight I was convinced that for constructive change to occur, it was absolutely essential that university presidents take the bull by the horns and institute reform. The centerpiece of this reform was what it called the "one-plus-three" model, in which the "one"—presidential control—is directed toward the "three"—academic integrity, financial integrity, and independent certification.

An essential aspect of presidential control, according to Knight I, was that boards of trustees delegate administrative authority to the president to govern the athletics program. Also, alumni and boosters would defer to presidential control.

Sound as this policy might be, it is much easier said than done. Boards of trustees (sometimes called boards of regents) are the ultimate power in American colleges and universities.[16] These boards have the authority to hire and fire presidents and rule on broad matters of academic policy. Many trustees are successful, strong-willed persons who are protective of their power and influence. Thus, it is by no means assured that trustees will cede complete power to presidents over governance of athletic programs, even though it makes good sense to do so.

Regarding academic integrity, Knight I recommended that compromising academic standards in order to admit athletes cannot be tolerated. A "no pass, no play" rule was viewed as essential, with athletic eligibility predicated on continuous progress toward graduation within five years of enrollment, with athlete graduation rates expected to be comparable to those of other full-time students.

On financial integrity, Knight I urged that athletic departments not operate as independent subsidiaries of the university. All funds raised and spent for athletics would be subject to the same oversight and scrutiny as other departments of the university. Boosters and their clubs would not be allowed to support athletic programs outside of the direct control of the university administration. The difficulty here is that although presidents might retake operational control of athletic departments that have run amok, reining in the activities of boosters is harder because they are typically local businesspersons and alumni over whom presidential control is limited.

Independent certification, according to Knight I, means that universities undergo an annual independent audit of all academic and financial matters related to athletics. This would provide verification that athletic departments are following overall university objectives on admissions, academic progress, and graduation rates. It further recommended that the principles of the one-plus-three model be incorporated into the NCAA's certification process, and that schools that refused to correct deficiencies would be isolated. In order to enhance the applicability of these principles, Knight I said that presidents should have ultimate authority over the NCAA, and that presidents should control their institution's involvement with commercial television.

Although several aspects of the one-plus-three model have been adopted by the NCAA, presidents currently do not have complete control of the NCAA. Presidents have some authority over arrangements with television, which is the primary source of revenue to big-time collegiate athletics, but the lure of television monies has compromised constructive use of this control.

Knight I seemed to have a positive effect in a variety of areas. Influential in this regard was the greater role for the Presidents Commission of the NCAA, which had been established in 1984. Among the changes to NCAA rules were that satisfactory progress toward completion of program course requirements and grade point average were established, coaches were required to get prior approval for outside income (including that from shoe and apparel companies), official visits by high school students were limited, and initial eligibility rules were put into effect. But, as seen in the next sections, these reforms, though laudable, have done little to arrest the nature and extent of corruption in collegiate sports and its deleterious effects on the integrity of higher education.

THE GAME OF LIFE

This book, published in 2001, provides the most comprehensive study to date on college sports and the mission of higher education. Its authors, James L. Shulman and William G. Bowen, played sports in college and have had distinguished academic careers.

The research methodology in the book is first-rate. Five categories of selected schools are analyzed: Division I-A private universities (e.g., Duke, Rice, Stanford), Division I-A public universities (e.g., Michigan, North Carolina, Penn State), Division I-AA Ivy League universities (e.g., Columbia, Princeton, Yale), Division III coed liberal arts colleges (e.g., Denison, Kenyon, Swarthmore), and Division III universities (e.g., Emory, Tufts). Selected data also is presented on certain women's colleges such as Smith and Wellesley. Altogether, thirty schools were surveyed longitudinally by the Mellon Foundation, with detailed information from about 90,000 undergraduates who entered college at three points in time: 1951, 1976, and 1989.

Classification of schools allows comparisons on key aspects of athletic programs. The distinct time frames reveal contrasts on features such as educational achievement, attitudes, family circumstances, and career choices. With response rates of about 75%, there is a high degree of reliability in the sample. Also, there are significant findings on women athletes and comparisons of "high profile" sports of football and basketball with "low profile" sports like crew, fencing, tennis, and wrestling.

The study confirms certain preconceptions about the collegiate sports scene, but there are numerous surprises too. Among the key empirical findings that one might expect are that athletes are being recruited far more intensively and offered more scholarships than in the past. The "walk-on" athletes at Division I-A schools in 1951 or 1976 had largely disappeared by 1989. Also, whereas few women athletes were recruited in 1976 (their numbers were negligible in 1951), this practice was common in 1989 at Division I-A and Ivy League schools. Nor is it surprising to learn that athletes are given preferential treatment in admissions. An "athlete culture" has developed on campus, in contrast to earlier times when jocks more closely resembled other college students. Women athletes are following in the footsteps of their male counterparts in this regard, especially in schools that award athletic scholarships.

Despite lower SAT scores, athletes overall were found to graduate at higher rates. However, for both men and women, academic rank is significantly lower than it is for their classmates, and has deteriorated markedly in recent years. As is generally known, male athletes are highly concentrated in certain fields of study, particularly in the social sciences, and women athletes are following this pattern. Among popular fields are business, communication, psychology, economics (when there is no business program), and political science.

Male athletes are apt to pursue post-collegiate careers in business and finance, and less often in medicine, law, science, or engineering. Former athletes in the 1951, 1976, and 1989 cohorts consistently made about 10% more money on average than their classmates.

One might expect that former athletes would be inclined to donate more money to their schools, and they generally do. But high-profile athletes at Division I-A schools are an exception, giving less. This is partly explained by the anecdotal quote from a former athlete who said, "I gave my knee to Stanford—that's all you're getting from me." The data also contradicts a widely accepted myth—that winning teams, especially in football, have a positive impact on giving rates. The authors determined that, except for coed liberal arts schools, winning football teams do not inspire increased alumni donations.

Although one might imagine large profits generated by high-profile sports at Division I-A schools, this is another myth. The authors quote top sports economist Roger Noll as saying, "No university generates a large enough surplus to justify the capital expenditures necessary to field a football team."[17] Reference is further made to the University of Michigan's sports teams in 1998–99, which had excellent records in football, ice hockey, women's basketball, and men's gymnastics, and overall were ranked sixth among colleges nationally. Yet, the athletic department had a deficit of $2.3 million (or $3.8 million when capital expenditures and transfers were added in).

In their proposed direction for change, Shulman and Bowen offer sage advice, generally on closing the growing gap between college athletics and educational values. They think it is important to address the blatant abuses of standards of good conduct, especially in the high-profile sports of football and basketball, and to consider de-emphasizing these sports. The authors note evidence of the rapid growth in the number of coaches and their corresponding emphasis on recruiting, which they perceive as far out of balance with the educational mission.

The Game of Life views Title IX, the law requiring gender equity in athletics for women, as providing an opportunity to rethink the organization of sports on campus. Until now, the approach has been to increase women's sports, which is admirable, but greater equality could be reached by cutting back on men's programs. One idea is to return to single-platoon football; another is to reduce the number of football scholarships.

Whatever the idea for retrenchment, it is difficult to overcome the vested interests in favor of increased commercialization of big-time college sports. The media, booster groups, and former athletes are strong advocates of continued growth, so the academy is held hostage to outside forces. Shulman and Bowen urge college presidents and boards of trustees to face up to problems before they worsen. *The Game of Life* concludes:

> The objective, in our view, should be to strengthen the links between athletics and the educational missions of colleges and universities—to reinvigorate an aspect of college life that deserves to be celebrated for its positive contributions, not condemned for its excesses or criticized for its conflicts with educational values.[18]

The most serious problems identified in *The Game of Life* were with the highly commercialized sports of football and basketball at the Division I-A level. Graduation rates among players in these sports were significantly lower than for other sports, and there is far less compatibility with the objectives of higher education. The book reinforces the findings of Knight I, as well as providing a comprehensive view of how football and basketball fit into the larger picture of sports on campus. We next examine Knight II, which came out shortly after *The Game of Life*, and ten years after Knight I.

KNIGHT II

This report is based on several hearings and interviews conducted in 2000 to 2001. The principal finding of Knight II is that despite rule changes by the NCAA and greater control by presidents, the problems associated with Division I-A football and basketball have worsened. Referring to the model established in Knight I, the new report proposes a revised one-plus-three model emphasizing that a Coalition of Presidents directs an agenda for academic reform that de-escalates the athletics arms race and the commercialization of collegiate sports.

Knight II notes that in the 1990s, 58 out of 114 Division I-A colleges and universities were censured, sanctioned, or put on probation for major violations of NCAA rules, at about the same rate as found in Knight I. These problems continued notwithstanding that two-thirds of the recommendations of Knight I were adopted by the NCAA. Although amateurism was clearly on the way out by the early 1990s, there is no doubt that today it is no longer a cherished ideal. As a result of the relentless shift towards commercial development by forces such as television, marketing, and new stadiums with luxury boxes, the ethos of big-time college sports is now viewed as clearly professional.

Evidencing the corruption in college sports is a spate of ugly incidents that come to light on what seems like a daily basis. These revelations of theft, gambling, violence, drugs, and academic fraud are demeaning to the reputation of the schools. Players who commit violations are identified by the media with their colleges and universities. James Duderstadt, president emeritus of the University of Michigan, testified for Knight II that major college sports "do far more damage to the university, to its students and faculty, its leadership, its reputation and credibility than most realize—or at least are willing to admit."[19]

Three areas of special interest in Knight II are: (1) academics, (2) the arms race, and (3) commercialization. The university's mission of teaching, learning, and generating new knowledge is said to be mocked by, and in some instances, deliberately undermined by big-time college sports. Apart from the issue of player eligibility, athletic departments are said to have little interest in academic affairs.

Graduation rates in Division I-A schools were found to be only 48% for football players and 34% for men's basketball players, and the rates have fallen in recent years. The graduation rate for white football players was 55%, the lowest rate in several years, and it was only 42% for black football players. This compared to an overall graduation rate of 75% for all students who enroll full-time immediately after high school graduation and continue at the same college for up to five and one-half years. A faculty member at a Division I-A school was quoted in the study as saying that there were students on the football team who would graduate without being able to read or write.

The arms race. An NCAA study is cited in Knight II showing that only about 15% of big-time programs are operating in the black, and that deficits at the majority of schools that are losing money are growing annually. Overall, numbers in 2001 for NCAA member schools show revenues of just over $3 billion and expenses of $4.1 billion. These figures do not take into account capital expenditures, debt service, and many indirect program costs.

Despite deficit spending, schools are in a race to build new and ever more luxurious stadiums and arenas. In the past seven years up to 2001, capital expenditures at Division I-A institutions were found to have increased by 250%. If one school in a conference spends enormous amounts of money on rebuilding facilities, other schools feel that they must compete, driving expenditures ever higher. Annual costs per athlete at Division I-A schools were found to be about $100,000, significantly more than the average salary of fully tenured professors at these schools (about $84,000). Even more disturbing is that, according to the latest count, 30 "star" coaches in football and men's basketball were paid $1 million or more annually.

Commercialization

Knight II found that over the past decade, television and shoe deals have burgeoned, and more space in stadiums and arenas was sold to advertisers. It was estimated that each win in the Division I men's postseason basketball tournament brings $780,000 to a school. Cable television presents football and basketball games on weekday evenings and in the early morning and late night hours on Sunday. The appetite for televised sports seems to be insatiable, and even the hallowed Friday nights, previously reserved for high school games, and are being intruded on by the colleges. Ironically, television ratings are down in many cases because of over-saturation of sports programming.

Sports are all business today ("Show me the money," as the saying goes). Relatively new players in the money game are shoe companies. For instance, Knight II refers to a new seven-year deal between the University of Michigan and Nike that is expected to be worth $25–28 million. Schools, coaches, and players have bowed to the influence of sneaker companies. Knight II states that "In allowing commercial interests to prevail over academic concerns and traditions, presidents have abdicated their responsibilities."[20] Even though the NCAA has come under greater presidential control, it cannot do what is necessary to come to grips with the money-sports behemoth that is destroying academic integrity and reputations.

Because presidents have failed to achieve reform individually or within the NCAA, Knight II recommends a revised approach of each president working together with their university's board of trustees to achieve reform. Also, national higher education institutions such as the American Council on Education and the Association of Governing Boards of Colleges and Universities are urged to do more to address corruption in college sports. A Coalition of Presidents should be formed to work with these organizations and the NCAA. This recommendation recognizes that individual presidents appear to be unable to accomplish much toward achieving reform, but may be more effective by acting together. This also was a recommendation made in *The Game of Life*.

Other recommendations from Knight II have considerable merit and deserve immediate action. One is to require athletes to face the same admission standards as other students. Teams would be banned from conference championships and postseason play if they do not graduate at least half of their players. The length of practices and post-seasons should be reduced, and the NBA and NFL are urged to develop minor leagues so that athletes not interested in academic study would have an alternative route to professional careers.

Regarding the arms race, it is recommended that Division I-A scholarships in football and basketball be reduced along with total expenditures on these sports. Compensation for coaches should be brought into line with overall salaries in their institutions. The CBS television contract for the NCAA tournament should be revised to stop basing revenue on winning games.

On the problem of commercialization, Knight II recommends that teams remove corporate logos such as the Nike "swoosh" from their uniforms. Universities alone would determine when games are played and how they are broadcast. Also advocated is federal legislation to ban gambling on college sports in the state of Nevada. Presidents are urged to address illegal gambling on their campuses.

CONCLUDING THOUGHTS

The recommendations contained in the three reports have ample justification, and if fully implemented, would go a long way toward reducing corruption in college sports and returning to the high level of probity for which universities should stand. Given the big-money interests and lack of centralized authority for change, however, one might be skeptical that the current situation will be reversed. We seem to know what to do, but lack the determination to do it.

The top priority is to reduce recruiting and to tighten standards for admission and continued academic progress. Because it is nearly impossible to operate at a high level of sports competition with an honest program these days, schools that commit to reform may have to operate in a lower division or conference. Presidents, in conjunction with boards of trustees, should consider abolishing corrupt programs altogether.

The large amounts of money paid to the NCAA and universities for big-time basketball and football result mainly from the entertainment value of watching these sports on television. While the athletes participating in these shows receive various forms of compensation, they do not receive a wage. Limited as to how much outside income they can earn, it is not surprising that some of these athletes feel that they are being exploited because they bring in far greater revenues to their schools than the cost of the benefits they receive. The Collegiate Athletes Coalition (the organization supported by the Steelworkers Union) is trying to improve conditions for athletes in Division I men's football and basketball. This group, founded by former UCLA football player Ramogi Huma, has already signed up dozens of players and was featured in a televised program on *60 Minutes*.[21]

The organization of players may be a good idea if it provides a more equitable distribution of money to athletes. Although supported by the Steelworkers, the players' group is not a union as such. According to the National

Labor Relations Act, rights to unionize exist only for "employees," and under their current status, college athletes would not be considered employees because they do not receive a wage.

But perhaps it is time to change the nature of big-time athletic programs in a radical restructuring. Athletes could have a real union and be paid a wage for their services. This would get rid of the hypocrisy of the "student athlete" at schools with corrupt programs and provide honest for-pay entertainment. If such a change were enacted, programs would become self-supporting and not subsidized by public funds. Big-time college sports programs would function as a minor league feeder system to the NFL, NBA, and other major leagues. They would continue to provide entertainment, but as professionals not operating under the guise of amateurism.

If athletes playing for universities under these revised programs want to pursue academic studies, they could do so. But they would have to compete in admissions fairly, pursue authentic curricula with real scholarly content, and be treated and judged just like other students. For most athletes, successful educational pursuit would have to wait until their playing days were over.

NOTES

1. Knight Foundation Commission on Intercollegiate Athletics, *Reports of the Knight Foundation Commission on Intercollegiate Athletics*, March 1991–March 1993 (Charlotte, NC: Knight Foundation, 1993).

2. James L. Shulman and William G. Bowen, *The Game of Life: College Sports and Educational Values* (Princeton, NJ: Princeton University Press, 2001).

3. Knight Foundation Commission on Intercollegiate Athletics, *Ten Years Later* (Miami: Knight Foundation, 2001).

4. Quoted in Howard J. Savage, *American College Athletics* (New York: The Carnegie Foundation for the Advancement of Teaching, 1929), p. 37.

5. Quoted in Andrew Zimbalist, *Unpaid Professionals: Commercialism and Conflict in Big-Time College Sports* (Princeton, NJ: Princeton University Press, 1999), p. 7.

6. Quoted in Ronald A. Smith, *Sports and Freedom: The Rise of Big-Time Athletics* (New York: Oxford University Press, 1988), p. 214.

7. Savage, *American College Athletics*, p. 225.

8. Ibid., p. 297.

9. Ibid., p. 80.

10. John J. MacAloon, "Are Olympic Athletes Professional?" in *The Business of Professional Sports*, ed. by Paul D. Staudohar and James A. Mangan (Urbana, IL: University of Illinois Press, 1991), p. 287.

11. Derek Bok, "Intercollegiate Athletics," in Contemporary Issues in Higher Education: Self-Regulation and the Ethical Roles of the Academy, ed. by John B. Bennett and J.W. Peltason (New York: Macmillan Publishing Company and American Council on Education, 1985), p. 124.

12. Zimbalist, *Unpaid Professionals*, pp. 4–5.

13. Murray Sperber, *College Sports Inc.: The Athletic Department vs. The University* (New York: Henry Holt and Company, Inc., 1990), pp. 72–73.

14. "Foul!" *Time* cover story, April 3, 1989.

15. Knight Foundation Commission, *Reports*, p. 21.

16. Numerous good examples of the relationships between these boards and presidents can be found in Clark Kerr, *The Gold and the Blue: A Personal Memoir of the University of California, 1949–1967*, Volume 1, *Academic Triumphs* (Berkeley: University of California Press, 2001), pp. 154–156, 162–163, 174–175.

17. Shulman and Bowen, *The Game of Life*, p. 250.

18. Ibid., p. 309.

19. Knight Foundation Commission, *Ten Years Later*, p. 13.

20. Ibid., p. 20.

21. Carolyn Said, "Power Play for Pay," *San Francisco Chronicle*, February 15, 2002, p. B1.

4

Motivating College Athletics

Evan Osborne

INTRODUCTION

Intercollegiate athletics is a substantial enterprise. The National Collegiate Athletic Association's 2001–2002 budget lists revenues of $345,815,000 and expenses of $228,337,000 in Division I, $14,653,000 in Division II and $10,663,900 in Division III. The NCAA itself notes that its television contract is more lucrative than that of every professional sports league in North America except for the National Football League, and even the merchandising associated with NCAA sports is itself an extensive commercial activity. Much of this revenue surely comes from enthusiasm for college athletics by people who have little or no association with the teams that happen to be playing on any given day.

A moment's reflection reveals that the prominence of intercollegiate athletics in higher education is a puzzle. Universities exist the world over, as does rabid enthusiasm for professional sports, and yet only in the United States do universities send out athletic teams to gladiate on behalf of students, faculty, alumni, and fans generally.[1] Noll (1999, 25) asserts that foreigners view big-time intercollegiate athletics in the United States as a "pagan ritual." In a famous remark, the one-time president of the University of Chicago, Robert Hutchins, is said to have sarcastically dismissed the illogic of college sports: "A college racing stable makes as much sense as college football. The jockey could carry the college colors; the students could cheer; the alumni could bet; and the horse wouldn't have to pass a history test."

The attachment to college sports is all the more remarkable because of the periodic embarrassment it brings to many universities. The recent accusations of academic misconduct at the University of Minnesota and the University of Tennessee, point-shaving scandals at Arizona State and Northwestern, as well as other sorts of embarrassing behavior by prominent athletes, are hardly novel, despite the damage they presumably do to the schools' public images. At the same time, the NCAA has had to labor mightily to promote relatively modest minimum academic standards for its student-athletes in the last two decades.

Why, in light of these reputation costs, do schools go out of their way to promote college athletics? The answer, presumably, is because sports contribute to their objective functions. Higher education in the United States is in fact substantially different from that of other countries in several ways, especially the widespread use of large land-grant universities and the major commitment to research. Thus, it is not surprising that colleges and universities in the United States might be outliers in other respects. But what objective is served by college sports? This chapter seeks to shed light on this question. It does so first by laying out some of the basic empirical contours of college athletics, then proposing several hypotheses for their popularity, and empirically testing the contrary predictions of two of the most prominent hypotheses.

SOME BASIC FACTS ABOUT COLLEGIATE ATHLETICS

Data on college athletics have historically been somewhat hard to come by. The NCAA does keep track of spending by member institutions on athletics but, asserting confidentiality, does not release data by particular schools. However, it does release figures for each division. Figure 1 shows the growth in average revenue and expenses in Division I-A from 1985 to 1999. While the NCAA's numbers should be taken with a grain of salt, owing to a relative lack of transparency, they indicate that many schools lose money on athletics. In fiscal year 1999, 29% percent of Division I-A programs had expenses in excess of revenues when institutional support (e.g., concession revenue that can be attributed to food services or the athletic program) was included in athletics, while 54% had expenses exceeding revenue when institutional support was not. In Division II, 63% of programs reported expenses exceeding revenue when institutional support was included, and 94% when it was not. If these numbers are at all accurate, they demand an explanation. Standard economic theory would predict that activities that generate losses cannot maintain their claims to the scarce resources needed to engage in them, and hence should shut down. The "explanation of the many" (e.g., Zimbalist, 1999a) may provide a rationale for the persistence of loss-driven activities. Many if not most divisions of a university lose money in isolation, but are

Figure 1
Average Revenues and Expenses at a Division I-A Program

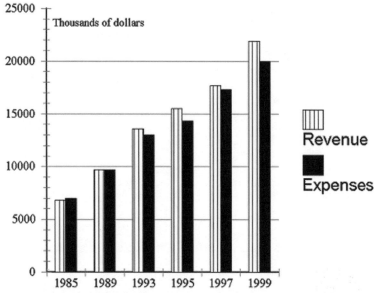

Source: NCAA 2001–02 Average Revenue and Expenses for a Div. I-A Program,
http://www.ncaa.org/financial/2001-02_budget.pdf.

seen as part of a comprehensive educational package. It is possible to think of the basketball team, the philosophy department, and the glee club as indissoluble parts of a single composite commodity. It might then be rational for some characteristics of that commodity to earn losses in isolation. Certainly, if all academic departments were required to have revenue in excess of expenses, modern universities would be lean indeed.[2]

Nonetheless, a presumption of a puzzle to be explained can surely be established. Administrators sometimes explain the substantial athletic empires on campus, as well as the relaxed admissions standards that support them, as part of the thorough environment that any comprehensive college or university should have. Athletes enhance the variety of the academic environment in the same way that students possessing any other unusual skill might. But this is an argument that is hard to take at face value. The idea is that athletes, whose practice schedules and separate dining and training facilities leave them substantially sequestered from the rest of the campus, are contributing to a diverse campus menu in the same way that a flute player or an art history major does. The major athletics programs, and the stretching of the traditional university mission they bring with them, need a better explanation than this.

Table 1
Spending on College Athletics per Enrolled Undergraduate

Top 20 Schools		Bottom 20 Schools	
1. Temple	$6127	283. South Alabama	$184.60
2. Hampton	$5913	284. Illinois-Chicago	$184.00
3. Vanderbilt	$4111	285. Cal St.-Long Beach	$170.90
4. Stanford	$3226	286. UC-Irvine	$170.60
5. Syracuse	$3213	287. Cal St.-Sacramento	$168.00
6. Lafayette	$2988	288. Florida-Internat'l	$167.00
7. Tulsa	$2854	289. Florida Atlantic	$164.00
8. Colgate	$2721	290. SW Texas St.	$162.00
9. Wofford	$2688	291. Central Michigan	$157.00
10. VMI	$2589	292. Penn	$153.00
11. Wake Forest	$2501	293. Wisc-Milwaukee	$150.00
12. Holy Cross	$2453	294. Chicago St.	$145.00
13. Furman	$2428	295. UT-Arlington	$140.00
14. Richmond	$2143	296. IUPUI	$138.00
15. Southern Methodist	$2106	297. Cal St.-Fullerton	$134.00
16. Tennessee	$2078	298. Cornell	$118.00
17. Oregon St.	$2074	299. Cal-Santa Barbara	$116.00
18. Army	$2032	300. Texas-San Antonio	$113.00
19. Northwestern	$2027	301. SE Louisiana	$87.00
20. Clemson	$1995	302. St. Bonaventure	$78.00

Some hints of an explanation are offered by a brief examination of who does and does not spend great amounts of money on intercollegiate athletics. The Equity in Athletics Disclosure Act of 1994 requires all schools that participate in student financial-aid programs to release data on spending on men's and women's athletics. Table 1 contains the top 20 and bottom 20 colleges and universities in spending per enrolled student in the 1997–1998 academic year. The mix of high-spending schools contains public and private universities, including one private and one public historically black university, and major research as well as more teaching-oriented schools. Some are stereotypical big-time athletics schools, and some are not.

But there is significant consistency in the bottom 20 schools. Most of the schools are secondary state universities, and have at least one corresponding major land-grant university in their state that participates in major-league Division I athletics. Some are themselves Division I members, others are not. However, in contrast to most of the top schools, few have Division I-A football teams, with their huge entry costs (DeBrock and Hendricks, 1997). This clustering of branch public universities in the lower end of the funding distribution is a stylized fact to note.

WHY DO COLLEGIATE ATHLETICS EXIST?

The money-losing aspect of the sports programs at many universities is at first puzzling, but only if athletics are seen as something that contributes no revenue other than the obvious ones of ticket sales, revenues distributed by the NCAA, and so on. Several possibilities suggest themselves. There is of course a huge incongruity between the amount of attention and resources lavished upon college athletics compared to what is given to other non-classroom aspects of the making of the broader college graduate (music, community service, and the like). For that reason, I do not take seriously the aforementioned assertion that the primary motivation for universities cultivating an environment in which 100,000 fans travel substantial distances to eat and drink (occasionally to excess) much of the day before removing their shirts and cheering a team whose players often mingle little if at all with average students is simply a workday broadening of the educational mission.

RAISING THE ADMISSIONS HARVEST

Another common assertion claims that college athletics yields increased admissions. There are two existing versions of this argument. One is that mere participation in big-time athletics is a way to increase the exposure of the university, causing it to draw new applicants and thus to be more selective in admitting students (McCormick and Tinsley, 1987). The main mechanism posited here is advertising, i.e., a comparatively low-cost way for universities to make their offerings known to students facing relatively high search costs, who would otherwise be unaware of the school. An implication of this view, presumably, is that as search costs fall (e.g., because of improvements in communications technology), the need to engage in athletics would decline.

Another version of this enrollment-drive view is that athletic success brings with it increased admissions from would-be students who seek the consumption benefits of attending games, rooting for successful teams, and so on. Murphy and Trandel (1994) do find a positive association between a university's football winning percentage and the number of applicants it gets. But Sperber (2000) is deeply skeptical of claims of bottom-line admissions benefits. He argues that most increased applications effects from unexpected athletic success, such as Doug Flutie's famous touchdown pass to Gerard Phalen for Boston College on national television on Thanksgiving weekend or the performance of the men's basketball team at the University of Massachusetts while Marcus Camby was a student there, are ephemeral at best. It is certainly true that by the very nature of athletic competition, success in football and basketball cannot simultaneously accrue to all or most schools. Thus, one could infer that the pursuit of athletic success by many schools simultaneously will create many losers for every winner, damaging the vast majority of schools that spend liberally in an attempt to achieve athletic success.[3] This argument is reminiscent of Frank (1999), who describes the damage that can occur from competitions in which a small number of people at the top of the competition receive substantial rewards, while most receive little if any. For every school that makes the successful leap to significant athletic success, there will be many universities who fritter away their resources and reputations in a futile chase for prizes that can by construction only be obtained by a few competitors. To be fair, the weakness of this argument is the absence of a rigorous way of distinguishing between excessive "winner-take-all" contests and ordinary competition. If there are 300 Division I universities chasing a few places available for consistently successful basketball programs, or 100 Division I-A schools chasing a single national championship, why is that intrinsically different from seven restaurants competing vigorously in a town that only has the demand to support two, or several hundred car companies in the United States in the 1920s competing to be whittled down to a handful by the 1950s?

But another possibility is a hybrid: students like the participation in athletics, and success, if it matters, is a bonus. In this case, universities pursue major sports programs because it increases students' willingness to pay, but athletic success is not required in and of itself. This hypothesis has the advantage of explaining why schools would continue to support programs despite long-term lack of success. It seems reasonable that, all things being equal, students prefer their schools to win rather than lose, and yet it may be that the "consumption capital" provided by attendance at games and creation of lifetime memories is the biggest attraction of major athletics for students. Many students may see athletics as an essential part of the college experience.

DISTRACTING STUDENTS, DEVOTING RESOURCES TO RESEARCH

One of the most provocative hypotheses is that of Sperber (2000), who argues that athletics is a way for schools to fund more prestigious research activities and graduate education. Since research and graduate education are often the cornerstones of perceived university quality, university decision-makers value these activities, but face budget constraints governing how much they able to spend on each. Those budget constraints in turn depend on the willingness of undergraduate students to pay tuition. If undergraduates value athletics and quality education, but some students are willing to substitute some athletics (entertainment) for educational quality, then universities are apt to divert resources from their undergraduate educational budgets to graduate education, research, and athletics budgets.

ALUMNI CONTRIBUTION AND POLITICAL SUPPORT

It is also possible that athletic success spurs greater donations by graduates to the university. McCormick and Tinsley (1990) find evidence that athletic success is correlated with alumni giving to both athletic and academic programs. Unfortunately, their paper is confined to only one school, Clemson University. Grimes and Chressanthis (1994) find a positive relation between athletic success and alumni giving to non-athletic missions, but again at only one school (Mississippi State). Shulman and Bowen (2001) do not find such an association, except for a positive relation between success and contributions by former athletes in particular at Division III schools. In general, the empirical literature does not demonstrate that athletics yields rewards in the form of alumni donations to nonathletic programs.

EXTERNALITIES FOR THE COMMUNITY

It could be true that the same thing motivates college athletics as motivates cities, counties, and states to spend large amounts of public funds on professional sports—enhanced economic activity in the local area. While possible, this should presumably be true only for public universities, some of whose spending decisions might plausibly be determined at the level of state legislatures. One would imagine that private universities would be motivated little if at all by returns to surrounding restaurants, taverns, and so on, as well as higher local employment that might be generated from local expenditures on athletics.

TESTING THE DETERMINANTS OF ATHLETIC SPENDING

In each of the hypotheses sketched above there is an implicit belief about university objectives—e.g., maximizing profits or maximizing the utility of research activity—as well as a belief that universities compete for students. Data are available for discriminating in particular between the demand-driven and distraction hypotheses. To do this it is necessary to establish what it is that students value when they attend a given school. One way to accomplish this is to test which activity costs can be successfully incorporated into tuition. Unfortunately, tuition rate (i.e., price) data in isolation can be somewhat deceptive. While all universities have posted tuition rates, schools can and do engage in extensive price discrimination by offering different financial-aid packages to students judged to have different willingness to pay.

In an attempt to solve this problem, data on total tuition revenue available from the National Science Foundation is used. They maintain a Web site (http://caspar.nsf.gov) at which they archive a wide variety of data on colleges and universities. Among those data are annual figures for revenue from tuition. To obtain a proxy for what is actually paid by undergraduate students, I take this figure and first divide it by the number of students who are undergraduates. These figures come from the College Board (2000).

Using these data I estimate the following equation:

$$\text{TUITION} = a_0 + a_1 \text{ STUDENTS} + a_2 \text{ ATHLETIC} + a_3 \text{ TEACHPC} \quad (1)$$
$$+ a_4 \text{ OWNRESPC} + a_5 \text{ SAT} + a_6 \text{ PUBLIC STUDENTS}$$

where STUDENTS is the number of undergraduate students, and is meant to test for possible economies of scale (or crowding costs) in the provision of education. ATHLETIC is total university spending on intercollegiate athletics. Athletic spending per student could be used as the independent variable, but athletic consumption has substantial public-goods components to it. Activities such as attending the big game generate utility that is substantially noncompetitive. Throughout the paper, using total rather than per capita spending yields a better model fit. The data on athletic spending are for the 1997–1998 year, and are filed by universities in compliance with the Equity in Athletics Disclosure Act. The Chronicle of Higher Education on its Web site, at http://www.chronicle.com/stats/genderequity, makes them available.

TEACHPC is per-undergraduate student spending, and here there are substantial rivalrous aspects to consumption. While lectures may be simultaneously delivered to many students, individual faculty attention, grading of assignments, and many other components of instruction can only be done using resources unavailable for at least some other students. INSTRPC is research spending by the institution itself (as opposed to spending funded by grants or government expenditures). These two variables also come from the NSF. Finally, PUBLIC is a dummy variable taking the value of one if the university is a public one.

The results in Table 2 show that both athletic spending and instructional spending can be passed on, so that (presumably) students value more instructional quality and athletic spending, all things being equal and up to a point, enough to pay more for them. ATHLETIC and TEACHPC both have positive signs at high levels of statistical significance. INSTRPC, the per-student school expenditure on research by the institution (as opposed to that which is funded by external sources), is not associated with higher tuition. Universities seem to have no power to pass on their own research costs to students. The negative result for STUDENTS indicates that there are some crowding costs in higher education. Interestingly, after standardizing for characteristics, research spending, and the number of undergraduates, public universities do not appear to charge less than private ones at a statistically significant level.

Table 2
Tuition Regression

Variable	*Coefficient*
INTERCEPT	6.2209**
	(6.36)
STUDENTS	-0.0005**
	(-6.59)
ATHLETIC	2.8352E-07*
	(3.04)
TEACHPC	0.8240**
	(20.21)
OWNRESPC	0.0024
	(0.59)
PUBLIC	-0.0001
	(-0.61)
$R^2 = 0.7841$	$F = 24.20**$

*Denotes statistical significance at one-percent level.
**Denotes statistical significance at 0.1-percent level.

Figures in parentheses are t statistics.

STUDENT QUALITY AND ATHLETIC SPENDING

To further discriminate between the distraction and admissions hypotheses, in this part I carry out a more sophisticated version of the McCormick and Tinsley (1987) experiment on the relation between student quality and school athletic participation. The tactic is to measure the relation between the SAT scores of incoming freshmen and the variables emphasized in that piece, augmented by some data that are now available and relevant to the two hypotheses. Of particular interest is the contrast between the student-distraction and admissions-harvest hypotheses with respect to the predicted relation between SAT scores and athletic spending. Sperber's (2000) claim implies that students with better SAT scores would tend to get less athletic spending, because they must be attracted purely on the basis of educational competence. He argues (p. 109) that of the schools classified by the *Princeton Review*, a widely used guide to higher education for high school seniors, as excellent in teaching, only one (Rice) is a Division I school. He also asserts that research universities and extensive athletics programs would lose students if not for their highly selective honors programs, which draw high-caliber students who would otherwise flee the prevailing anti-educational environment in pursuit of better instruction elsewhere. Higher SAT scores should be negatively associated with athletic spending and positively associated with educational spending. Under the hypothesis that athletics responds to student demands, however, athletics and instruction ought to be tools that schools use jointly to compete for more-desirable students. Higher SAT scores ought to be positively associated with both more educational and more athletic spending. To test these contrary predictions, the following equation is estimated:

$$\text{SAT} = b_0 + b_1 \text{ TEACHPC} + b_2 \text{ ATHLETIC} + b_3 \text{ REPERCAP} \qquad (2)$$
$$+ \ b_4 \text{ LIBRARY} + b_5 \text{ PUBLIC} + b_6 \text{ TEACHRES}$$

REPERCAP is the university's total research spending per terminal-degree faculty member. It is used rather than INSTRPC because if research affects the student mix it will surely be total spending, including external funding, rather than the institution's own spending. LIBRARY is the number of books in the university's library. McCormick and Tinsley (1987) also used this variable. Here the figure comes from the American Council on Education (1997). TEACHRES is an interaction term between UGTEACH and REPERCAP. The Sperber argument hinges on research (except perhaps pedagogical research) being negatively related to student achievement, and there is some evidence to support this claim (Terenzini and Pascarella, 1991, in Sperber). However, many university administrators (not to mention department hiring committees) are convinced that those professors who conduct the most research are those most familiar with state-of-the-art knowledge, and hence likely to be the best teachers. In addition, it is possible that student participation in research improves the productivity of a given amount of instructional resources, which would imply a positive coefficient for TEACHRES.

The results in Table 3 are in line with the hypothesis that universities offer athletics, and even research, because students demand it.[4] The sign of ATHLETIC is positive and highly significant, as are those of TEACHPC and RESEARCH. The coefficient of TEACHRES is highly significant and negatively signed, while that for PUBLIC is highly significant and negatively signed. Overall, the results are in accord with McCormick and Tinsley (1987), albeit (because of more data available) more compelling. While they were only able to use a dummy variable for membership in what they argued to be the six major Division I athletic conferences, here the continuous variable of spending on intercollegiate athletics is much more refined. Despite that, the relation between athletic spending and student quality is strong and positive. The more schools spend on intercollegiate athletics, the better the students they draw. However, more total spending on research does seem to lower the ability of more teaching resources to attract students.

Table 3
SAT Regression

Variable	Coefficient
INTERCEPT	*1027.1360** (56.75)*
TEACHPC	*9.53384** (56.75)*
ATHLETIC	*0.00000491* (3.29)*
REPERCAP	*0.00437* (5.58)*
LIBRARY	*0.00000885 (1.39)*
PUBLIC	*-78.54681** (-5.08)*
TEACHRES	*-0.00049460** (-5.06)*
$R^2 = 0.5056$	$F = 24.20**$

*Denotes statistical significance at
one-percent level.
**Denotes statistical significance at
0.1-percent level.

Figures in parentheses are *t* statistics.

There are only two interpretations of student preferences and school constraints that are consistent with the findings. One is that better students actually have a higher preference for athletics, and schools that cater to such students provide them with it. Otherwise, universities with more resources at their disposal spend more on athletics, and get better students as a result. The positive sign and significance of all the outlets for university spending (athletics, research, and instruction) suggest the latter interpretation. Schools spend resources on athletics because it, along with better education, is what students by and large want.[5]

CONCLUSION

It would be surprising if it were otherwise. Schools compete vigorously for students, and students attend them to a substantial degree to improve their earnings prospects. If the quality of undergraduate education is analogous to its rate of return in the job market, the idea that schools could get away for any extended period with allowing this return to deteriorate is somewhat difficult to believe. It does seem to be true that colleges and universities are in the end behaving like any other profit-maximizing firm in a highly competitive market, providing product features that the market seems to be demanding. Having said that, given the data on colleges and universities that now exist, much more study of the motivation of intercollegiate athletics can be justified.

Note finally that the findings here are complementary to some of the existing literature. Previous work on the benefits for schools of college athletics has concentrated on the ability to increase the university's exposure. Here the findings also suggest that universities can have their cake and eat it too by investing in college athletics, because students seem to desire it. In light of this, the widespread popularity of college athletics is not so surprising.

NOTES

1. The historian Paul Kennedy ("The Eagle Has Landed," *The Financial Times,* Feb. 2, 2002) estimates that the world's top 12 to 15 research universities are all in the United States.

2. Another is the claim that athletic departments, as members of a cartel, cannot possibly lose money.

3. For an interesting account of the difficulty in creating a successful Division I athletics program, see Grant Wahl and George Dohrmann, "Welcome to the Big Time," *Sports Illustrated*, Sept. 19, 2001.

4. In saying this I assume that any school would desire a student body with higher SAT scores, other things equal.

5. It is possible that certain subsets of students do not have a taste for athletics. For a useful discussion of different student subcultures, see Clark and Trow (1966).

Part III

Financial Returns to College Sports

5

Effects of University Athletics on the University: A Review and Extension of Empirical Assessment

Brian Goff

INTRODUCTION

Many factors may influence strategic decisions concerning athletic programs. Certainly university executives responsible for these decisions ought to take into consideration a wider spectrum of information than can be obtained solely from analyzing the impact of athletics on financial and other quantitative variables. For example, other relevant benefits are the positive influence of intercollegiate athletics on issues such as institutional unity and loyalty (Beyer and Hannah, in press) and on an institution's reputation (Shanley and Langfred, 1997). Nonetheless, carefully scrutinized empirical data about quantitative impacts of intercollegiate athletics are very important decision-making considerations.

This paper assesses extant research concerning several quantifiable effects of intercollegiate athletics. It is hoped that this effort will contribute to our state of knowledge and provide more accurate information for university executives and faculty responsible for directing athletics policy. Existing evidence is surveyed, evaluated, and extended. Although in some cases the data can be analyzed from a purely statistical standpoint without reference to economics, in other areas insights from economic analysis are important for properly evaluating existing data and for pointing empirical work in potentially fruitful directions.

The next section examines the evidence concerning the direct impact of revenues and expenses of intercollegiate athletics on university finances.

Various indirect financial and nonfinancial impacts are then considered, followed by some concluding remarks.

DIRECT FINANCIAL IMPACTS

The importance of accurately assessing the direct financial impact of university athletics hardly requires justification. The "profitability issue" has attracted considerable attention in the popular media in books such as *College Sports, Inc.* (Sperber, 1990) and *Keeping Score* (Sheehan, 1996) and in newspapers and magazines such as *USA Today,* the *Chicago Tribune, U.S. News and World Report, Academe,* and the *Chronicle of Higher Education.*[1] The studies reported in these outlets challenge the "myth," allegedly held by many, that college athletics is a significant net contributor to university treasuries; instead, these reports have estimated that even some of the giants of college sports operate in the red. For instance, the University of Michigan, Auburn University, and even Notre Dame University have been estimated to be losing up to $3 million per year on their athletics programs. As discussed below, such claims are muddled by the not-for-profit setting of universities and related accounting practices.

The denial that big-time college athletics is a net revenue generator runs counter to intuition and to evidence based on simple economic insights. Athletic programs such as those of Michigan and Notre Dame generate revenues exceeding $20 million per year (approaching professional team revenues) while avoiding the $30 million dollar payrolls that professional teams must meet. The NCAA earns hundreds of millions of dollars every year from its contract with CBS to televise its basketball tournament. Brown (1993) has estimated that better college football players could earn $600,000 or more per year if paid market-based salaries, while basketball players could earn even more. The kinds of revenues available to major NCAA programs, restrictions on payments to players, and avoidance of antitrust regulation, seemingly signal a very profitable enterprise. From this viewpoint, reported losses for programs are more likely due to misleading accounting methods and university budgetary practices than to a lack of economic viability.

A basic issue that we address is whether intuition based on principles of economics or published reports alleging college sports' losses are correct. Only two detailed, peer-reviewed studies of college sport finances, which fully utilize appropriate economic/managerial accounting methods, have been published.[2] These are studies of athletics at Utah State University (Skousen and Condie, 1988) and Western Kentucky University (Borland, Goff, and Pulsinelli, 1992). Rather than relying on institutional figures reported at high levels of aggregation, these studies use detailed information from university accounts to determine the flow of dollars into and out of universities because of athletics programs. The widely circulated reports of losses among college sports programs utilize much less detailed data usually drawn from aggregate university budget figures.

Key questions that were asked in these two studies are important for an assessment of an athletic program's financial situation. What revenues would be lost if a sport is dropped, and what expenses would be saved if a sport is dropped? Although these questions are simple, arriving at accurate answers is not. Because of complex organizational arrangements, accompanying interunit transfers, noneconomic valuation methods, and university-specific accounting conventions, merely taking data about revenues and expenses reported by institutions at a high level of aggregation leads to the errors and to wide variances in reported estimates. Attention here is centered on football and basketball because, for most universities, these are the sports that raise significant revenues and that often subsidize the other "non-revenue" sports.

Adjustments are necessary to arrive at accurate assessments:

1. Valuing grant-in-aid expenses at their true incremental expense to the university. Most universities value athletic grant-in-aid expenses at their "list price" (full tuition price, full housing price, full book price). This can account for $1 million to $5 million of athletic expenses, depending on tuition at a specific university. However, the amount of money that a university actually spends to instruct and house one hundred additional football and basketball players is only a fraction of the "list price." The incremental instructional expense is nearly zero because at universities, where even small amounts of excess capacity exist, few, if any, additional faculty or staff must be employed to accommodate the additional student-athletes.

2. Attributing athletics-produced revenues to non-athletic accounts. At most universities, all, or some of, merchandise sales, concession revenues, parking receipts, and related revenues, are attributed to the general fund or to a nonathletic unit of the university. Such revenues can be substantial. In many cases, even the revenues paid by athletic foundations for athlete tuition are credited directly to the general fund so that grants-in-aid deliver a "double blow" to athletics—overvaluation on the expense side and undervaluation on the revenue side.

3. Attributing athletics-produced expenses to nonathletic accounts. Items such as the custodial care and maintenance of sporting venues may be charged as an expense to units other than the athletic department. While occurring, the evidence in the studies cited above indicates that this is a relatively minor adjustment.

For Utah State and Western Kentucky, estimates of operating profits/losses differed widely from publicly reported estimates that were based on university figures. Table 1 presents the comparison. Utah State's program, publicly reported to be experiencing a loss of almost $700,000, actually turned a $366,000 profit. Western Kentucky's program, publicly reported to be experiencing a $1.2 million loss, was losing money, but just over

Table 1
Summary of Detailed Studies of Intercollegiate Cash Flows Publicly Reported

Source	Institution	Cash Flow*	Adjusted Figure/Main Adjustments
Skousen and Condie (1988)	Utah State University	-$680,000	+$360,000/grant-in-aid expenses lowered, tuition revenue included
Borland et al. (1992)	Western Kentucky University	-$1.2m	-$330,000/grant-in-aid expenses lowered; food services revenue included; maintenance expenses included; athletic credit hour revenues included

Note: The Sheehan figures are from Sheehan (1996, 266). The tuition adjusted figures add $800,000 for public universities and $1.5m for private universities. The basis for this adjustment is explained in the text.

$300,000 per year. Neither of these studies incorporates athletics-induced merchandise sales that would increase adjusted revenue figures.

Because the data required to make the appropriate adjustments exists only in very detailed university accounts, and gathering it requires intimate knowledge of a university's accounting conventions, arriving at such detailed estimates for a few, or even for one, athletic department is a daunting challenge. However, if we take the two studies described above as indications of the average amount of adjustment necessary at public universities and adjust more recent estimates based on aggregate level data by this amount, we can gain a more realistic assessment than currently exists. In fact, the Skousen and Condie (1988) and the Borland et al. (1992) studies provide minimum adjustments because neither of the programs examined are near the top of college revenue producers. As a result, omitting revenues such as merchandise would not have as big an effect as it would for a program such as Michigan's, where merchandise sales attributable to athletics would run into the millions.

Sheehan (1996) has written the most recent study of college football and basketball (i.e., not the entire athletic program) finances. He has gone to greater lengths than most studies' authors in attempting to collect accurate figures. Yet, by his own admission, his figures do not adjust for accounting conventions at universities or take into account merchandise sales due to athletics. The first column of Table 2 reports relative frequency distributions for profits/losses at 109 NCAA Division I universities using Sheehan's figures. According to his figures, 16% of the schools lose money and 29% earn less than a $1 million profit (a profit large enough, by his estimation, to compensate for state subsidies). Even though these results show that most

Table 2

Frequency Distributions of Operating Profits for Top 109 Programs

Programs with Profits ($m)	Sheehan-Based		Tuition-Adjusted Estimates	
	Relative	Cumulative	Relative	Cumulative
< (- 1.0)	7%	7%	0%	0%
(-0.1) – (-1.0)	9%	16%	10%	10%
0.0 – 0.9	13%	29%	11%	21%
1.0 – 1.9	13%	42%	7%	28%
2.0 – 3.9	20%	62%	24%	52%
4.1 – 6.9	17%	79%	22%	74%
7.1 – 9.9	7%	86%	11%	85%
> 9.9	14%	100%	15%	100%
Median	$2.5m		$3.9m	

Note: The Sheehan figures are from Sheehan (1996, 266). The tuition adjusted figures add $800,000 for public universities and $1.5m for private universities. The basis for this adjustment is explained in the text.

programs contribute net revenues to the university, the results have been used to indicate the lack of financial health of college athletics.[3]

In order to obtain more realistic estimates of the financial health of athletic programs, Sheehan's results are adjusted for the accounting problems discussed above. Without detailed accounting information from each school, a complete revision is not possible. However, revisions based on estimates of undervaluation of revenues and overvaluation of expenses are possible given the results of the Skousen and Condie (1988) and Borland et al. (1992) studies. Based on these studies, which suggest adjustments of $1,040,000 and $870,000 respectively, we add a conservative amount, $800,000, to the profits of the athletic programs of public universities in Sheehan's study. No detailed study of necessary valuation adjustments for private universities exists; we add $1.5 million, which assumes that tuition for athletes at the private schools is slightly less than double the tuition for athletes at public schools. The third and fourth columns in Table 2 report relative frequency distributions for profits/losses for the 109 universities after making these adjustments. The results indicate that only 10% of the schools lost money. All but three of these are in the Mid-American Conference—universities whose football programs would rate at the lowest level of Division I-A schools and whose basketball programs would rate below the top seven or eight conferences. After the tuition adjustment, 79% of schools exceed $1 million in annual profits, with 72% exceeding $2 million. Although used as evidence of faltering financial performance in college athletics, Sheehan's data show just the opposite, even without including further adjustments such as revenues for sales of merchandise.

In addition to the issues related to accurate accounting for university athletics discussed above, three others are worth noting. First, at universities where enrollments are relatively fixed (mainly selective private schools), admitting one hundred athletes may or may not reduce admission of paying students so that tuition revenue may or may not be foregone due to athletics. Whether, and the extent to which, revenue is actually lost depends upon the admission and tuition practices of a specific school. If a school were to admit one hundred students paying full tuition (say $20,000 per student) in place of student athletes, the revenue foregone would be substantial. If the school were to admit one hundred students paying the average tuition among students (always less than full tuition), revenue foregone would be reduced. If the school were to admit one hundred students with full tuition grants themselves, or if the school did not increase admissions of nonathletes after dropping athletics, then revenue foregone would be zero.

Second, the assessment of financial viability depends on whose perspective is taken. If it were the perspective of a university president, then any revenue from state treasuries that is received because of athletics would be included in financial calculations. If the perspective is that of the state legislature—the ultimate policy-making body for public universities—such revenues would be excluded.

Finally, the difference between for-profit environments and the not-for-profit setting of universities must be taken into account when interpreting profit-loss data. As in other not-for-profit settings, unit directors in universities (e.g., department chairs, deans, athletic directors) do not typically have an incentive to maximize profits (budget surpluses). If surpluses are experienced or anticipated, most unit directors increase expenditures in order to fully utilize their budgets. As a result, expenses rise to match, and often exceed, budgets regardless of revenue. So it should come as no surprise that expenses for even the largest revenue producers in college sports are frequently reported as equal to, or greater than, revenues, especially when relying on self-reported figures.[4]

INDIRECT IMPACT OF ATHLETICS

While much more could be said concerning inaccurate analyses of the direct revenues and expenses of major college athletics, other issues relevant to making strategic decisions concerning university athletics could also be quantitatively addressed. There are many anecdotal, or isolated, reports of indirect impacts (e.g., increased visibility, applications, donations) of newfound athletic success. A recent example is Northwestern University's turnaround football seasons in 1995–1996. There exists, however, minimal work concerning the extent of indirect impacts of such turnarounds across different campuses using rudimentary descriptive statistics, much less using sophisticated statistical analyses. Below, the empirical literature relating to these issues is summarized and then extended.

The most valid means of assessing indirect impacts would be to accumulate data related to athletic success (e.g., win-loss records, bowl games and tournaments attended, conference championships, etc.), data for the variables potentially influenced by athletics (e.g., student applications, student retention, alumni giving, etc.), and data on other factors related to these latter variables (e.g., general trends in student applications and alumni giving, economic conditions, etc.). Such data would be collected either for a wide cross-section of schools and/or for a time series of 30 or more years for one school. With this kind of database, regression analysis or similar methods could isolate the effects of athletics while controlling for other systematic influences.

As with many multidimensional statistical inquiries, data is either not forthcoming or very costly and time-consuming to obtain. In the absence of sizable cross-sectional, or time-series data, one can still proceed beyond mere anecdotes or reports of individual cases by making use of descriptive statistics that provide some comparisons across schools or over time.

UNIVERSITY EXPOSURES:
THE MECHANISM FOR INDIRECT IMPACTS

The most common skepticism related to measurements of the indirect impacts of athletics pertains not to the statistical methods utilized, but to the credibility of sizable effects.[5] The skepticism usually grows out of a misunderstanding of the mechanisms by which athletics influence seemingly unrelated behavior. A question arises in the minds of many, especially university faculty: Outside of hardcore fans, are there enough people who care so strongly about athletics to alter enrollments, giving, and other oft-touted outcomes?

This question presumes that the primary mechanism of athletics' influence is via sports fans and boosters. When 100,000 people attend a football game, as they do at places such as the Universities of Michigan and Tennessee, six or seven times per year, turning people into university boosters would appear to be a viable means by which athletics could influence indirect outcomes. The means to influence outcomes extends considerably more broadly, however. Athletics is an integral source of name exposure for almost every university, and is often the only frequent source of exposure for schools possessing little in the way of academic reputation. Even for institutions with highly regarded academic reputations, many potential donors and potential students are more likely to become aware of, and interested in, the institution due to its participating in a major owl game of the NCAA "Sweet Sixteen" than they are due to the work of a Nobel prize–winning chemist. Also,

Figure 1
Newspaper References for Northwestern University and Western Kentucky
University, 1990–96

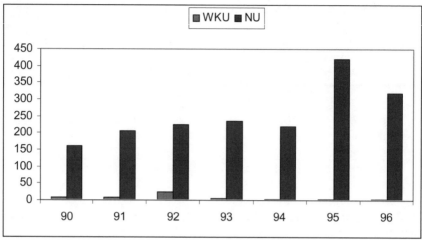

athletic events provide opportunities for large numbers of prospective students and their parents—some of whom may have only a passing interest in the athletic event—to visit campuses they might not otherwise visit.

Figure 1 presents evidence related to university exposure due to athletics at two very different academic institutions. The evidence is the number of articles in which Northwestern University—a very selective private institution with a heavy orientation toward research and graduate education—and Western Kentucky University—a midsized, regional public institution with an undergraduate orientation—appear in eight leading newspapers over the period 1991–1996.[6]

A review of this data leads to two noteworthy conclusions. First, athletic success translated into substantially increased exposure for both institutions. Articles about Northwestern jumped by 185% during 1995, the season leading to Northwestern's Rose Bowl visit, in comparison with the prior three-year average. Articles about Western Kentucky University jumped from about 2 or 3 in typical years to 13 and 30 in 1992 and 1993 when the men's and women's basketball programs enjoyed atypical successes, a final 16 appearance for the men, and a final 4 appearance for the women. Second, even in years without special success, athletic articles were an important source of exposure. In 1992, for instance, Northwestern athletics accounted for almost 70% of the coverage of the university. In contrast, research related stories accounted for less than 5%. For Western Kentucky, nonathletic stories were either zero or one in each year.

Many factors contribute to the decisions of boosters and students. The evidence presented here about the exposure from athletics is not intended to suggest that athletics is the only determinant of these decisions. However, the influence of such exposure may be very important.

GENERAL CONTRIBUTIONS TO UNIVERSITIES

One of the most contentious debates surrounding the indirect effects of athletics concerns its impact upon nonathletic gifts to universities. The major improvements of programs at Northwestern in 1995 and Georgia Tech in 1991 prompted speculation and some anecdotal evidence supporting the argument that athletic success contributes to additional general giving.[7] However, this evidence, and the proposition behind it, has often met strong rebuttal.

The reasons behind the challenges are easy to understand; the likely impacts of athletics on general giving are much harder to unambiguously assess than are the types of effects we have discussed to date (athletic department revenues and expenses, media coverage). Moreover, the cause-effect relationships can be quite ambiguous. Some benefactors are interested in both athletics and general university welfare but have a fixed amount of money they are willing to donate. In such cases, increased athletic success may help steer these donors toward athletic giving and away from general gifts. On the other hand, greater exposure for a university, whatever its source, may help spur giving across many fronts. The effect that is expected to dominate (athletic vs. general giving) cannot be theoretically determined.

Comparisons across empirical studies are complicated by the use of different dependent variables, use of different variables to account for athletic success, different control variables, and a lack of investigation of lag relationships. For example, Baade and Sundberg (1996) try to explain gifts per alumnus for 167 schools over an 18-year period, Grimes and Chressanthis (1994) consider annual gifts for one school over a 30-year time frame, and McCormick and Tinsley (1990) use individual-level contributor data for one school over 14 years. While Baade and Sundberg (1996) consider the effects of winning percentages in football and basketball along with postseason play, McCormick and Tinsley (1990) estimate the relationship between athletic gifts and general giving. Even if effects are determined using comparable methods for different institutions, the answer as to whether athletic success and athletic giving reduce or increase general giving may depend on the specific university in question as well as the specific circumstances surrounding its athletics success (e.g., how "big" and how novel the success was).

Existing Studies

Table 3 is presented in an effort to condense available, useful information on this issue. It summarizes the most important features of three of the

Table 3
Summary of Regression Studies of Athletics-Contributions Relationship

Study	Data	Main Results
Baade & Sundberg (1996)	Gifts per alumni for 167 institutions over 1973-90; controls for 2 student attributes, 4 institution attributes, fund raising intensity	40% to 54% increase for bowl game appearances; 35% increase for basketball appearances; very small increases for increased winning at liberal arts colleges
Grimes & Chressanthis (1994)	Alumni contribution over 1962-91 for Mississippi State; controls for alumni base, enrollment, government appropriations, income	$200,000 increase for each 10% increase in winning percentage; $200,000 to $300,000 increase for TV appearances.
McCormick &Tinsley (1990)	Cross-sectional data on gifts per alumni over 1979-93 for Clemson University; controls for tuition, regional characteristics of alumni/students – income, enrollment, agricultural employment, school expenditures, distance to Clemson	10% increase in athletic booster donations associated with 5% increase in general contributions – no "crowding out"

more recent empirical studies of the athletics–general giving relationship.[8] Each of these studies has appeared in peer-reviewed outlets; each uses regression methods to control for a number of factors influencing giving.

In what is likely the most comprehensive study, Baade and Sundberg (1996) use data from over three hundred institutions of various types over the years 1973–1990. They find that general giving depends very little on overall winning record. However, bowl appearances and basketball tournament appearances were found to raise general giving by 35% to 55%. Using data from Mississippi State covering 1962–1991, Grimes and Chressanthis (1994) find a positive effect of basketball winning percentage (an extra $200,000 to $1 million depending on the size of the increase in winning) as well as a $200,000 to $300,000 increase for television appearances, most directly related to College World Series appearances. Using data at the level of individual contributors over a five-year period at Clemson University, McCormick and Tinsley (1990) find that general giving and athletic giving complement, rather than take away from, each other.

New Assessments

As an additional source of information on the relationship between athletics and contributions, we collected market value endowment data for Northwestern and Georgia Tech Universities to test whether the years of major football success translated into additional giving. These two schools were selected because of the rapid and significant degree of athletic success they recently enjoyed after many years of poor to moderate performance.

Because the time frames over which the data were available are limited to 1979–1996, not all useful time series statistical methods can be utilized. Still, basic regression analysis is possible. To adjust for correlated residuals, changes in the market value of endowments are used as the dependent variable rather than the level of the endowments. The explanatory variables included in the equation, control for market conditions that influence the return on the endowment funds by including changes in the S&P 500 Index.[9] To control for general trends in giving to higher education, a time trend variable is included. Differences between Northwestern and Georgia Tech are controlled by including a dummy variable for Northwestern. Finally, the vastly improved football success for Northwestern in 1995 is estimated by including a dummy variable equal to one for 1996 and zero otherwise. The success for Georgia Tech is measured by including a dummy variable equal to one for 1991 and 1992, the two years after the university won a share of the national championship in football (1990).

Overall the equation explains 76% of the endowment changes. The variable for Georgia Tech's athletic success is not statistically different from zero. Alternative formulations of this variable (to include more years) also did not show any effects.[10] The variable for Northwestern's football success, however, indicates an increase of almost $200 million. In commenting on these results, however, Henry Bienen, President of Northwestern, indicated that a large part of this increase was due to his having moved a substantial amount from cash into long-term equity during the period we studied. Our assessment of the relationship between athletics and contributions, therefore, is more suggestive of the difficulty of conducting such research purely with secondary data than it is of the relationship of interest.

While the data used to generate this estimate are accurate with respect to publicly reported figures, consistent with arguments made elsewhere in this paper, assessing the indirect effects of intercollegiate athletics is fraught with methodological challenges. Among these that are relevant here are the necessity of considering complex organizational arrangements, including interunit transfers and university-specific accounting conventions, and the development of sound knowledge of a university's accounting conventions. In short, great care is necessary in conducting and reporting such research.

STUDENT INTEREST

Athletic success may also have an effect on student interest measured by the number of students desiring to attend a university and/or the quality of those students. For public universities with relatively open enrollment policies and with funding being dependent on enrollment figures, enrollment might be the best gauge of the effect of athletics upon student interest. For universities with more selective admission policies where enrollments stay relatively fixed over time, application data and/or data on academic aptitude of incoming students (e.g., SAT scores), are more relevant measures for assessing the athletics–student interest link.

Existing Studies

Using time series methods on data covering 30 years, Borland et al. (1992) find substantial effects for basketball and smaller effects for football on enrollments at Western Kentucky University. A movement from a winning percentage of 0.50 to one of 0.75 in the prior two seasons resulted in estimated enrollment increases of about 430 students. Post-season play in football was estimated to increase enrollment by about 340 students, but the statistical significance of this result was marginal (0.10). Mixon and Hsing (1994) also find effects of athletic success on enrollments. In a statistical model explaining the percentage of out-of-state students across universities, they estimated that membership in the NCAA's highest division increased the percentage by 2 to 4 points after controlling for a number of other university characteristics.

If, in fact, enrollments increase due to athletic success, a closely related question follows: What kinds of students are being attracted? One might assume that students who focus excessively on sports and, therefore, are of questionable academic quality, are responsible for enrollment increases. Interest on the part of better students may also increase, however, as a result of the increased exposure due to athletic success. Theory does not provide an unambiguous answer.

Table 4 summarizes the empirical evidence on this issue. Controlling for a number of factors associated with student quality, McCormick and Tinsley (1987) use data from 150 schools to assess both relationships within a single year (1971) and changes across years (from 1981 to 1984). These researchers find a positive relationship between major athletic success and student quality for the single year, but only marginally positive or no relationship for the changes across years. Using essentially the same control data used by McCormick and Tinsley for bowl game and basketball tournament appearances in the years 1989 and 1981–1989, Bremmer and Kesserling (1993) cannot find any SAT effects of athletic success. In an imitation of McCormick and Tinsley, Tucker and Amato (1993) find effects of football success and

Table 4
Summary of Regression Studies of Athletics–SAT Relationship

Study	Data	Main Results
McCormick & Tinsley (1987)	SAT scores for approx. 50 schools for 1971 and changes for 1981-84; controls for tuition, library volumes, salaries, ages, private/public, student-faculty ratio, enrollment, endowment, PhDs awarded, gender	SAT levels approx. 30 points higher at schools in 7 major conferences and major independents, marginally positive or no effect of winning on SAT changes over time
Bremmer & Kesserling (1993)	Model imitates McCormick & Tinsley but with 1989 data and changes for 1981-89	No effects for football bowl games or basketball tournament appearances
Tucker & Amato (1993)	Model imitates McCormick & Tinsley but only for the 63 "big time" schools for 1989 and changes from 1980-89	Index of football success (based on AP rankings) exhibits small effect on SAT in cross section but not over time; no basketball effects
Mixon (1995)	A comment on Bremmer and Kesserling; uses full sample and restricted samples for Division I-A and tournament participants only	Number of basketball tournament games rather than appearances over 1978-92 indicates positive impact on SAT scores; 20 more games increases SATs by 30+ points

no effects of the basketball success. At the average level of football success, SAT scores increased by about 3% relative to a school with very poor football performance. Using the number of games played in NCAA basketball tournaments over 1978 to 1992, Mixon (1995) finds a positive impact of basketball success. His results indicate SAT scores increase by 30 points for a difference of 20 games played in the tournament.

New Assessments

We supplement existing evidence on the effects of athletic success on enrollment with data from three universities: Wichita State University (WSU) and The University of Texas-Arlington (UTA), both of which dropped football, and Georgia State University (GSU), which added football at the I-AA level. The value of examining the effects at these three schools is that the changes involved more than just incremental changes in athletic performance, which may or may not be the result of strategic decisions by university executives. Instead, the changes involved major strategic moves with respect to athletics.

Regression methodology is used to examine the relationships. The dependent variable is changes in enrollment for these schools from 1960 to 1993. Enrollment changes are used rather than levels to control for autocorrelation. We also include a control for general enrollment trends in higher education as measured by changes in U.S. higher education enrollment.[11] School-specific differences in enrollment trends are controlled by including a dummy variable equal to one for Wichita State and zero for the other schools as well as another variable equal to one for UT, Arlington. This makes Georgia Southern the reference group. Finally, the effect of adding or dropping athletics is controlled by the inclusion of a dummy variable football/no football (no football = 1).

The results appear in Table 5. Overall, the independent variables explain only a small part of the total variation in enrollments (about 14%). The low explanatory power is due to using changes in enrollments. Although enrollment trends for these schools are highly correlated with U.S. enrollment trends, the annual changes that make up these trends are highly individualistic. The football/no football variable, however, is significant below the 1% level. The coefficient of this variable indicates that, on average, "no-football" years were associated with about a 550-student decline relative to years with football across the three universities. If the equation is reestimated, including only the two schools that dropped football in the mid-1980s (Wichita State and UT, Arlington), the estimated impact is slightly larger—a decline of just over six hundred students. Estimates for Georgia Southern alone indicate a 500–student increase from adding football with a big increase in overall explanatory power of the equation to 36%.[12]

As mentioned earlier, for a university with more selective admission policies, the number of applicants is a more appropriate measure of student interest than is enrollment. Using freshman applications from Georgia Tech, which enjoyed a share of the national football championship in 1990, a very simple estimate of the relationship between the dramatic athletic success and applications filed is generated based on applications to Georgia Tech from 1982 to 1996.[13] These estimates appear below with p values in parentheses:

Number of = 812.4 + 610.7 Change in U.S.   + 1526.7 Post
Freshman   (0.84)   (0.25) Higher Education   (0.01) Championship
Applicants   Enrollment   Years

$R^2 = 0.80$ F-Statistic = 18.5   Mean of Dependent Variable = 6354.8

A 28% (1,686 applicants) increase in applications occurred for 1991–93 in comparison with 1988–90. The average increase from 1991–94 was 34% higher than the average from 1983–90.[14] Both of these reflect statistically

Table 5
Athletics–Enrollment Relationships: Adding/Dropping Football at Wichita State, Texas-Arlington, and Georgia Southern

Variable	Coefficient	p-value
Constant	571.4	<0.01
Change in U.S. higher education enrollment	870.8	0.04
Wichita State (all years)	-325.5	0.09
Texas-Arlington (all years)	-92.4	0.62
Years with no football	-547.2	0.01
R^2	0.14	
F-Statistic	3.82	
Mean of dependent variable	391.91	
S.D. of dependent variable	755.25	

Note: Dependent variable is annual change in fall enrollment.

significant increases when tested by simple r tests. These results are intended as being suggestive of fruitful lines of research rather than as stringent tests of hypotheses.

ATHLETICS AS AN ALBATROSS

In this section we address whether athletics can have negative effects on the types of outcomes addressed above. This question is similar to one academics ask about their own work: Does a citation that criticizes a work negatively affect a scholar's reputation or, on the other hand, does it enhance it, though to a lesser extent than a positive mention? The evidence presented so far indicates that athletics has either positive or no indirect effect on a number of university outcomes. In several of the empirical studies, teams performing at high levels generated improved outcomes compared with teams performing at low levels; but this is a relative effect. The research does not indicate that poor performance leads to absolute declines in any of the outcomes studied.

However, the design of most of the studies reported above severely restricts the opportunity to find any negative effects because they estimate linear coefficients, which permit only the relative effects of different degrees of success to be estimated. As a result, they are not well suited to address the question of declines in areas such as giving and student applications due to negative athletics outcomes. The data that is available is discussed below and summarized in Table 6.

Table 6
Evidence on Effects of NCAA Sanctions

Variable	Estimate	Basis of Estimate
Alumni Giving	$1.6 million reduction in general giving to Mississippi State due to football probation	Grimes & Chressanthis (1994) regression model
Alumni Giving	$31 million per year reduction in giving to SMU due to death penalty for football program	Inclusion of SMU giving and death penalty into regression applied to Northwestern and Georgia Tech data described earlier
Applications	7% decline in 3-year average of applications after vs. before imposition of death penalty	Author's calculation

Existing Study

An important exception to the research limitations described just above is the study of Grimes and Chressanthis (1994). These authors include a variable for NCAA sanctions in their equation estimating contributions to Mississippi State. While sanctions made no difference in their general equation, their equation, which included only football-related variables and sanctions, did find an effect. In particular, they found that football sanctions reduced contributions to the university by $1.6 million per year, a sizable reduction given average contribution levels.

New Assessments

The case of Southern Methodist University permits an estimation of negative publicity in an extreme case. SMU's athletic program had improved substantially in the late 1970s and early 1980s, earning a second place finish in football polls at the end of the 1982 season. Because of repeated violations of NCAA rules, however, the NCAA imposed a "death penalty" on SMU's football program for 1987 and 1988, banning their participation in these years and severely restricting football scholarships in following years. The severity of the penalty brought substantial publicity to the university. Using data from newspaper citations, one can observe the jump in (negative) publicity surrounding this event. The same eight leading newspapers that are referred to above devoted 133 stories to SMU between 1987 and 1988 compared with a range of five to eight stories per year for 1991 to 1995.

Due to limitations on data availability, only limited assessment of effects of the sanctions on SMU endowments and applications are possible. Changes in the market value of SMU's endowment were available for 1980–1996.[15] Examination of the data without controls for other factors highlights two points. First, SMU enjoyed large increases in its endowment from 1982 to 1986, following its highly successful 1982 campaign and its emergence as a national football power. Market value grew over 156% from 1982 to 1986. Second, although SMU's endowment did not fall in the post-penalty years, the increases fell back into line with those prior to its 1982 success.

These same effects result from regression analysis with changes in the market value of the endowment as the dependent variable, and dummy variables for the successful years (1983–1986) and the post-penalty years (1987–1990). The results appear below with p values in parentheses:

$$\text{Endowment Changes} = 16 + 26.7 \ \text{Success Dummy} + 2.8 \ \text{Penalty Dummy}$$
$$(< 0.01) \qquad\qquad (0.60)$$

$$R^2 = 0.64 \qquad \text{F-Statistic} = 12.9 \qquad \text{Mean of Dependent Variable} = 23.5$$

Altering the penalty dummy variable to include more or fewer years and including controls for the S&P 500 index and a time trend do not alter these results. The years of marked improvement in football appear to have benefited SMU. However, it does not appear that the sanctions decreased SMU's ability to attract funds other than those funds that were attracted due to its becoming a national football power. Thus, while the "death penalty" did not result in endowment decreases, it did result in increases falling back to what they were prior to the 1982 and subsequent football successes.

Data on applications to SMU from 1985 to 1996 were also analyzed. As with the endowment data, because data in years prior to the sanctions are limited, conclusions must be tentative.[16] The number of applications fell by 12% from 1985–1986 to 1987–1988. However, by 1989–1990 applications jumped 30% over this low point. These data may indicate a decline due to the negative publicity followed by a boost due to positive exposure associated with reestablishing the program on a more reputable footing. On the other hand, these data may merely indicate variations due to other factors. Without additional data, the two conclusions cannot be distinguished.

CONCLUSIONS

The purpose of the evidence presented here is to provide a review and extension of empirical assessments of university-wide effects of intercollegiate athletics and to provide university personnel with improved information with which to formulate strategies with respect to intercollegiate athletics. The results presented above permit several conclusions to be drawn.

- For nearly all universities in major conferences (most Division I-A football and top tier Division I basketball), direct revenues from football and basketball are greater than direct expenses; for at least 70% of the schools, the difference is greater than $1 million.

- For universities below the major conferences (Division I-AA football and second tier Division I basketball), the difference between direct revenues and expenses may be negative but is likely less than $1 million.
- Athletic success, particularly significant improvement, can substantially increase national exposure for universities regardless of their academic reputation.
- Achievements in athletics (e.g., bowl trips, basketball tournament wins, college world series appearances) appear to substantially increase general giving to universities; these effects are present for both average and major improvements in athletics.
- Major achievements in athletics appear to spark additional interest from prospective students, even at schools with highly rated academic programs.
- Major achievements in athletics may lead to an improved pool of entering students (in terms of aptitude tests) at selective universities.
- Dropping football can have measurable, negative impacts on enrollments and possibly other indirect variables (e.g., giving), even for universities that do not have top tier programs.
- Negative exposure due to NCAA sanctions may offset the gains made by past athletic success, but the evidence to date does not show that such negative exposure does more than negate the positive influence of past success.

As with any empirical study, or review of empirical studies, qualifications are in order. For one, not all of the influences of athletics on outcomes reported here have been discussed. For example, issues such as the academic standards and performance of athletes, compensation of athletes, and organization and governance of athletics within and between universities, though relevant, have not been addressed here.[17]

Second, the evidence reported here is based on either observable data or responses to surveys about observable data. This has substantial benefits in that the analysis is based on how people behave rather than on their evaluation of that behavior. Coupled with this, it reduces, although does not completely eliminate, the problem of non-sampling error that plagues surveys addressing unobservable data. The weakness of this kind of evidence, however, is that it limits investigation to the most readily observed variables. More comprehensive future studies should likely include the more readily measured impacts of athletics addressed here as well as other factors for which subjective evaluations are necessary (e.g., donor and student applicant motivation). Assessing such motivations must await future research.

Finally, in a similar vein, most, though not all, of the regression evidence on the impacts of athletics uses school-level rather than individual-level data. This also has benefits. Most importantly, school-level outcomes related to enrollments, applications, giving, and so on are what seemingly matters most to university administrators regardless of what the individual-level motivations may be. Also, some of the influences that tend to be important when examining behavior across individuals, such as distance from school in enrollment regressions or income of givers in contributions equations, are not large sources of variability across schools. On the downside, school-level studies may omit details regarding individual behavior, the consideration of which may more fully explain the mechanisms behind the outcomes observed at the school level. Also, more highly aggregated data are usually more susceptible to spurious correlation problems. It should be noted, however, that research using individual-level data, such as McCormick and Tinsley (1990), confirms results found with school-level data.

Investigations of the role of athletics on the type of university outcomes addressed here would be aided considerably by more careful attention to database management. Data that is often necessary is not typically collected or is not collected in a sufficiently detailed fashion. Heading the list of such variables would be sales of team-related merchandise with attention given to game-day sales, off-campus sales, sales through booster organizations, and so on. More attention should also be given to developing time series data. Personnel collecting data on university outcomes in university research offices are frequently acquainted with purely descriptive statistical analysis. Data collection typically reflects this in that piecing together time series (30 years and longer) to be accessed through electronic means is apparently not a high priority. Even when such data is available, university personnel may be reluctant to share the information with external researchers. As addressed earlier, idiosyncratic accounting conventions obscure accurate assessment of the financial status of programs and comparisons across programs. Such practices are not easily overcome even by extensive, detailed examination and review of university accounting procedures and records. The study of appropriate interunit (transfer) pricing mechanisms is another important, underdeveloped, and underappreciated area. Many of the opaque accounting conventions exist because university executives want to keep certain information confidential and to diminish scrutiny.

ACKNOWLEDGMENTS

The author acknowledges helpful comments from Richard Wolfe; the Academy of Management Symposium discussant, Henry Bienen; three anonymous reviewers; and the assistance of institutional research offices at Georgia Tech, Northwestern, and Southern Methodist Universities.

NOTES

1. See, for instance, Shannon Brownlee, "The Myth of the Student Athlete," *U.S. News and World Report*, 8, 1990, pp. 50–52; Barbara Bergman, "Do Sports Really Make Money for Universities?," *Academe* (January/February 1991), pp. 28–30; Andrew Bergnato, "Against The (Cash) Flow," *Chicago Tribune*, February 23, 1997; Welch Suggs, "A Look at the Future Bottom Line of Big-Time Sports," *The Chronicle of Higher Education*, Nov. 12, 1999; and Erik Lords, "Move to Big Time

Yields Losses and Second Guessing," *The Chronicle of Higher Education,* Dec. 10, 1999.

2. The NCAA-sponsored study of its members' revenues and expenses, most recently by Fulks (1998), is excluded from this list because it is an "in-house" project and is based on self-reported data.

3. See, for example, Bergnato, *Chicago Tribune,* February 23, 1997.

4. Newspaper reporters are not the only ones who pass over this seemingly simple point. The distinguished professor of economics who wrote the Academe article cited in note 1 missed it as well.

5. Examples of this kind of skepticism are seen in "Do Winning Teams Spur Contribution?" *The Chronicle of Higher Education,* January 13, 1988, pp. 32–34.

6. These papers are *The New York Times, The Wall Street Journal, The Washington Post, The Boston Globe, The Atlanta Constitution, The Los Angeles Times, The Chicago Tribune,* and *The Christian Science Monitor.* This information was obtained using the Pro-Quest CD-ROM Retrieval system.

7. For instance, two articles in the December 15, 1995, *USA Today* deal with benefits to Northwestern from its Rose Bowl march. More recently, *USA Today,* July 11, 1997, updated these figures.

8. Not many systematic statistical studies of the athletics—contributions relationship exist. Two of the earliest are Sigelman and Carter (1979) and Brooker and Klastrom (1981). Sigelman and Carter estimated the effects of athletics on three different giving variables for each year from 1961 to 1976. They found virtually no athletic effects; however, they did not control for any other giving factors. Brooker and Klastrom used 1961–1971 data from Division I programs dividing them into various groupings such as private and public and controlled for GNR. They found positive and significant effects of athletics for most regression estimates.

9. Endowment data for Georgia Tech were obtained from its Office of Institutional Research and Planning. For Northwestern, these data were obtained from *The Digest of Education Statistics.* The S&P 500 data were obtained from the Economic Report of the President. The reported endowment data covers the entire time frame but skips every other year. The missing data were interpolated along the linear trend between the existing data.

10. These alternatives included estimating longer and shorter post-success effects as well as estimating the Georgia Tech and Northwestern data separately. Using the Chow Test to compare the residual sum of squares from the separate and pooled regressions, we determined that the fit was not significantly improved by estimating separate equations. See Hall et al. (1995) for details of the test.

11. U.S. higher education enrollment is the number of students at four-year institutions based on data from *Fact Book on Higher Education.* Enrollment data for each school were obtained from the *World Almanac and Book of Facts.* Market value endowment data were obtained from U.S. Department of Education, *Digest of Education Statistics.*

12. Using the same type of Chow Test as with the endowment data (note 11), the squared residuals are not significantly diminished by estimating separate regressions. Therefore, the pooled estimates are retained. The restricted sample estimates are not reported in the table but are available from the author.

13. The Georgia Tech applications data are taken from the Georgia Tech Factbook website.

14. Increases in applications at Northwestern University also appeared after their Rose Bowl season of 1995 (Shanley and Langfred, 1997).

15. The SMU endowment data are taken from the *Digest of Education Statistics* with the same adjustments for missing values as with the Northwestern and Georgia Tech data (see note 9).

16. These data were made available by the SMU Office of Institutional Research.

17. Examples of studies concerned with such issues include Long and Caudill (1991), Tucker (1992), Maloney and McCormick (1993), and Shughart et al. (1986).

6

Why Do U.S. Colleges Have Sports Programs?

Robert Sandy and Peter Sloane

INTRODUCTION

When the Faculty Senate at IUPUI was considering a motion to endorse a switch from National Collegiate Athletics Association (hereafter NCAA) Division II to NCAA Division I-AAA, the campus administration argued that switching to the higher-level sports program would increase both student numbers and quality. They claimed that the one hundred extra athletes required for the higher-level program to be recruited through athletic scholarships would directly increase enrollments.[1] In spite of the fee increase charged to all students to support the athletics program, it was argued that the sports program's publicity and favorable image would attract additional students who had no connection to athletics. The higher-profile athletics program would supposedly draw between two and four additional students per athlete to IUPUI. Moreover, the athletes' SAT scores and ranks within their high school graduating classes would be higher than the average of the rest of the IUPUI student body. The administration's sanguine predictions appear to be completely at odds with the claims in many books and reports on the impact of intercollegiate sports aimed at the general public, i.e., almost all sports programs drain university resources and reduce student quality. (Duderstadt, 2000; Knight Commission Report, 1999; and Sperber, 1990 and 2000).

Intercollegiate sports in the United States are comparable to professional team sports in terms of their drawing power, in the case of both live attendances and television audiences. Thus, Leeds and von Allmen (2002) report that the existing TV contract for the NCAA men's basketball tournament is worth more than $1.7 billion over eight years. This was to be replaced in 2002 by a new 11-year contract with CBS worth no less than $6 billion. Zimbalist (1999b) points out that intercollegiate sports have experienced strong revenue growth since 1960. In the 150 top institutions the annual revenue growth was 8% between 1960 and 1981 and 8.9% between 1982 and 1997. Kotlyarenko and Ehrenberg (2000) claim that having a college or university team that wins a conference title in a major sport can have a substantial effect on the institution's revenues, as well as influencing the quality and quantity of high school applicants for places. It is not surprising, therefore, that universities are prepared to accept athletes with lower admission standards and to award them athletic scholarships.

Another way to quantify the size of intercollegiate sports is to look at the attendance figures. Putting it in a European context, the attendance at college football games is greater than that of all of the attendances in English professional soccer. In 1999, U.S. college football attendance was 39.5 million. The teams with the highest average home game attendance figures, Tennessee and Michigan, had 106,500 people per game. Added across its four divisions (premier, 1st, 2nd, and 3rd), English professional soccer had almost the same attendance (38 million).

Table 1 compares attendance for the two revenue sports at the top level of intercollegiate sports, Division I, to attendance in the top levels of the U.S. professional sports, the four major leagues.

An overall revenue comparison among the NCAA Division I revenue sports and the major league professional sports is more difficult than a comparison of attendance figures and ticket revenue. More than 95% of Division I-A programs require a "donation" to the foundation supporting its

Table 1
1999 Attendance and Average Ticket Prices in NCAA Division I Football and Men's Basketball and in the NBA, NFL, NHL, and MLB

Sport	Total Attendance[1]	Average Ticket Prices[2]	Total ticket revenue[3]
MLB	45	14.91	671
NCAA Division I Football and Men's Basketball	59	12.83	757
NBA	20	48.37	967
NFL	16	45.63	730
NHL	16	45.70	731

[1] Millions.
[2] Dollars.
[3] Millions of dollars.

athletics programs either as a condition for being allowed to buy a season ticket or, for the slightly less popular programs, a season ticket in a desirable location.[2] The real ticket revenue for a college is the sum of the donation and the price of the season ticket.

Given the above features, it is difficult to establish the real costs and revenues of college athletics programs. The disagreement over the net costs of intercollegiate sports programs appears in more academically oriented articles and books by economists as well as in more popular publications. Indeed, the most debated question among sports economists with respect to intercollegiate sports is whether colleges make or lose money on these programs. To date, this debate has been largely sterile because with the available data it is impossible to determine the real costs of having an intercollegiate sports program. For example, in NCAA Division I-A programs a major claimed cost is the grants-in-aid covering tuition and room-and-board for 350 to 700 athletes. The true costs of these grants-in-aid depend on the marginal cost to the college of providing room and board and class seats as well as how many of the athletes on grants-in-aid could be replaced by full-fee paying students of similar academic quality if the college either reduced the level of its sports program or dropped intercollegiate sports altogether. Even careful case studies devoted to one university have a difficult time estimating these marginal costs and opportunity costs.

Intercollegiate athletics programs are thought to bring in more students simply because some of the athletes have friends who want to attend the same college they attend. Also, the publicity from athletics programs makes it more likely that students will have at least heard of the college and thus will be more likely to bother to open its advertising mail. With over one thousand baccalaureate degree–granting colleges competing for students in the United States, name recognition is a serious consideration. One study at the University of Alabama at Birmingham concluded that each varsity athlete generated four more students.[3] A window into how the college administrators view athletics programs is the computer program Virtual U, sponsored by the Alfred P. Sloan Foundation. This program simulates managing a university.[4] It is meant to guide the planning of actual university administrators toward raising enrollment, revenue, and prestige. In addition to sections on tuition pricing, capital campaigns, and so on, the simulation allows the virtual college administrator to upgrade intercollegiate sports programs from NCAA Division III to II to I, and to vary the resources devoted to athletics scholarships.

An example of the recruitment effect of intercollegiate athletics is the University of Mary Hardin-Baylor, which was a women's college until 1971. In 1997 it had 2,313 students, of whom 70% were women. Mary Hardin-Baylor wanted to attract more male students, so it started a football team in 1998. It competes at the no-athletics-scholarships NCAA Division III level. The new team attracted 200 additional men who wanted to play football, enrolled in Mary Hardin-Baylor, and tried out for the team. The college started a junior varsity football squad to accommodate the overflow.[5]

There are similarities as well as differences to debate on whether colleges make or lose money on their sports programs and the debate initiated by one of the authors on whether the owners of professional sports teams are profit maximizers (Sloane, 1971). In both professional team sports and collegiate sports, entry is difficult because the incumbents control the sanctioning bodies that admit new competitors. These sanctioning bodies are the leagues or federations in professional sports and primarily the NCAA in collegiate sports. The barriers to entry at least allow the incumbents in both professional and collegiate sports to pursue goals other than profit maximization. The main difference is that since almost all U.S. colleges are not-for-profit institutions, they cannot legally make any profits. They cannot pay dividends to owners. Fort and Quirk argue that the legal restrictions make no practical difference. Instead of a profit, there is a surplus from the collegiate sports program that could be captured by coaches or by the college's administration, or applied to the college's general operating expenses (Fort and Quirk, 1999).

A second similarity between the research on profit maximization in professional sports and surplus maximization in collegiate sports is the difficulty level of these questions. While there are examples in both sectors of non–profit maximizing behavior, it is not clear whether these examples are any more important than the occasional manufacturing firm whose owners eschew profit maximization.[6] One reason for the difficulty in measuring professional team profits and college sports surpluses is problems in interpreting accounting data. Professional sports teams can hide their profits by underpricing their broadcast rights when the same entity owns the team and the media company. Similarly, they can assign revenues to affiliated firms that control stadium parking and concessions, and off-site ticket orders. Most professional teams in the United States are privately owned and their books are not public. Because of Title IX, colleges have to report their sport's revenues and expenditures. However, arbitrary shifts in revenue occur there as well. The colleges can assign parking, concession, and licensing revenues to non-sports entities. Public colleges can list either the out-of-state or the in-state tuition rates as a cost of providing grants-in-aid. Duderstadt (2000) argues that the common practice among Big 10 universities of listing the tuition costs of out-of-state athletes at the in-state rate represents a large understatement of the true costs of the athletics programs. However, the 10 out of the 11 Big 10 universities that are public draw the vast majority of their students from their own state.[7] It is implausible that the athletes could all be replaced with out-of-state students. Another accounting data issue is that colleges do not have to reveal donations to the separate charitable foundations set up to receive gifts to their sports programs.

Economists have addressed the question of profit maximization in professional sports by comparing the marginal revenue products of players with their salaries. (See, for instance, Atkinson, Stanley, and Tschirhart, 1988; MacDonald and Reynolds, 1994; Krautmann, 1999.) This paper also takes an indirect approach to the make-or-lose-money question. Intercollegiate sports programs are organized into tiers of affiliation. In descending order these are NCAA Divisions I-A, I-AA, I-AAA, II, III, and National Association of Intercollegiate Athletics (hereafter NAIA). Each tier has different requirements for the minimum number of sports teams and the number of athletes on grants-in-aid. The lowest NCAA tier, Division III, does not allow grants-in-aid. The NCAA I-A programs have the large football stadiums (60,000 seats are common and 100,000 seats are not uncommon) and require the most grants-in-aid.[8] The NCAA I-AA schools usually have football teams (the most expensive sport) but at a much lower level. The NCAA I-AAA programs are known as "basketball schools."[9] Most NCAA II schools have football, but at a modest level. The NAIA allows grants-in-aid but does not specify school minimums. Colleges have some discretion over their level of affiliation. Clearly, any of them could opt for no participation. The smallest and most resource-constrained colleges would find it impossible to meet the minimum stadium size, average attendance at home football games, and minimum number of grants-in-aid required of NCAA I-A, but colleges as small as 2,807 undergraduates (Rice University) are in Division I-A.

Figure 1 shows box-and-whisker plots for the number of undergraduates for colleges in Divisions I-A, I-AA, I-AAA, II, III, NAIA, and no affiliation. The data are for 1999. The respective counts of the number of colleges in the seven categories are: 114, 122, 85, 293, 420, 254, and 170.[10] The line inside of each box represents the median undergraduate enrollment in that category. The boxes cover the central 50% of each distribution. The circles and asterisks mark respectively outliers and extreme outliers. Even though there is a clear downward trend in the median enrollment going from I-A to the category "no affiliation," Figure 1 also shows that there is a wide overlap in enrollments across the categories.

If colleges surplus maximize, they must adjust the level of their intercollegiate sports program according to whether they are gaining or losing money at a given level. Thus, the level of affiliation should be precisely predicted by factors tied to costs and revenues. Most of the variables we use to proxy costs and revenues in ordered probit models of level of sports affiliation have an obvious connection to costs and revenues, e.g., undergraduate enrollment, tuition rates, room-and-board rates, dormitory capacity, and so forth. We also include variables measuring the college's prestige and selectivity, such as the *U.S. News & World Report* ranking, SAT scores, and acceptance rates. A high-quality student body is effectively a capital asset to a college because these students are more likely to graduate, have higher lifetime earnings, and donate

Figure 1
Box-and-Whisker Plot of Enrollment by Affiliation Level

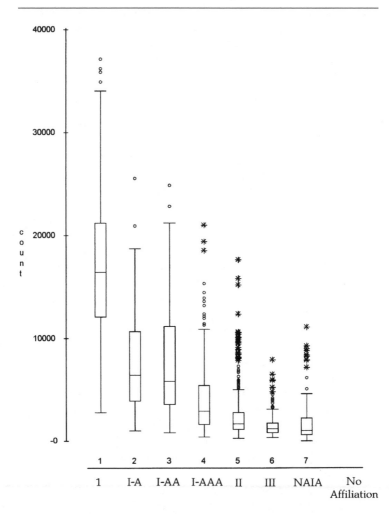

money to their alma mater. Holding tuition and room and board rates constant, colleges that could fill their current physical capacity with high-quality full-fee paying students give up much more money when they offer athletic grants-in-aid than do colleges that draw low-quality students and have unused dorm space and classroom space. The colleges with empty dorm rooms and empty class seats may have a marginal cost for grants-in-aid close to zero. We find a very close fit between our cost/revenue proxies and the level of affiliation over the categories NCAA Divisions I-A, I-AA, I-AAA, II, III, the NAIA, and no affiliation. Further, other things equal, we would expect highly selective/highly ranked colleges to have lower levels of sports programs.

If colleges are surplus maximizers, switches to higher levels of affiliation for a given college must raise either student numbers or student quality or both in order to justify their higher costs. The one clear result from the previous studies is that the gains in donations and ticket revenue are, on average, simply too small to cover the added costs. One hundred and twenty four colleges or roughly 13% of all colleges changed the level of their sports affiliation between 1991 and 1999. Of these 124, 109 raised their level of affiliation. We use a fixed-effects panel framework to estimate the gains in enrollment and student quality in response to changes in affiliation. We find that there are substantial gains in student numbers and in student quality when a given institution raises the level of its sports affiliation.

Having point-in-time distribution of colleges among levels of sports programs closely tied to their cost and revenues and the changes to higher levels of affiliation associated with increases in enrollment and student quality is consistent with colleges operating their sports programs as surplus maximizers. The costs of sports programs at a given school are primarily determined by the level of affiliation because of the NCAA requirements on the number of sports and the minimum number of scholarships. The travel expenses and the recruiting expenses are also tied to the level of affiliation. For example, Division III schools have minimal travel costs because that Division is set up around local or within-state rivalries. At the other end of the spectrum, the Division I-A schools routinely recruit athletes internationally and schedule out-of-conference matches across the United States. While there are a few "powerhouse" programs such as the University of Michigan that fund seven hundred athletes and compete for national championships nearly every year in nearly every sport, most schools have one or two sports with consistent winning records while the rest of their teams hover around 50% wins. Since there is little promotional benefit and perhaps some loss to fielding a full complement of teams with consistent losing records, the choice of the level of affiliation constrains the schools to spend enough to have at least mediocre athletic success at that level. That is why we focus on the level of affiliation. Short of being able to determine the actual marginal revenues and costs of each level of affiliation, our research strategy is the best available method for establishing surplus maximization. We believe this is the first time this method has been used to address this question.

PREVIOUS STUDIES

James L. Shulman and William G. Bowen are the latest authors (Bowen is an economist) to conclude that almost all colleges lose money on sports programs (Shulman and Bowen, 2001). They have proprietary data on 30 colleges that no one else has been able to gather and they attempt to consider every financial aspect of college athletics. Other economists on the "lose money" side of the issue are Roger Noll (1999) and Andrew Zimbalist

(1999a, b). The economists on the "make money" side include Arthur Fleischer, Brian Goff, Robert Tollison (1992), and Kotlyarenko and Ehrenberg (2000) for the Ivy League. Except for Kotlyarenko and Ehrenberg, these studies have a common method. They add up the costs and revenues for a sample of colleges mainly based on NCAA reports or Title IX reports and then adjust these figures with estimates of donations, capital depreciation, etc.[11] The essential difference between the one colleges-make-money-on-intercollegiate-athletics study and the others is that it placed more weight on the ability of an intercollegiate athletics program to draw additional students. Fleischer, Goff, and Tollison rely on two case studies for colleges that appeared to be in deficit but were shown to make money after allowing for the recruiting effect.

Shulman and Bowen's data set concentrates on private colleges near the top of prestige rankings. It was originally collected to study affirmative action programs at elite colleges. There are 114 Division I-A football programs and 318 Division I basketball programs. Obviously, many schools with Division I programs do not even make the *U.S. News and World Report* national rankings, the top group in the prestige rankings that has just 210 universities. Indeed, many of the universities with Division I sports programs are near the bottom of the *U.S. News and World Report* regional rankings.

Although they mention the possibility that the marginal cost of a grant-in-aid might be less than the list prices of tuition, room, and board, Shulman and Bowen treat the grants-in-aid as costing colleges their face value. However, even some of the schools on their list would have a difficult time replacing athletes with students whose families could pay the full tuition and who had academic records near the average of their current students. Moreover, schools at the top of the prestige rankings discount their tuition rates, i.e., they provide scholarships, to more than half of their nonathletes. If Shulman and Bowen's data set consisted of more typical Division I schools, say public colleges such as Boise State University in Iowa, which has a Division I-A football program and is ranked in the third tier of the regional universities, their decision to ignore the true costs of providing grants-in-aid would have been conspicuous. The relevance of their universities being mostly private instead of public is that public universities have much lower tuition rates. A highly ranked private university such as Northwestern or Stanford on the Shulman and Bowen list does give up a real $25,000 in tuition revenue every time it hands out a tuition grant-in-aid because it could easily let in an equally qualified or perhaps a better qualified applicant for the same slot.

DATA

The universe in this study is all accredited by the regional accreditation bodies and ranked by the *U.S. News and World Report* baccalaureate degree–granting colleges in the United States. The data are assembled from four sources. The NCAA and the NAIA provided membership lists. The prestige ranks, acceptance ratios, and SAT scores came from the *U.S. News and World Report*. College characteristics such as enrollments, tuition rates, room rates, and board rates came from the Integrated Postsecondary Educational Data System (IPEDS) federal database. Appendix A has the definitions of every variable used directly in the analysis or as a screen to create the data set. We treated some of the most obscure intercollegiate athletic affiliations as being the same as no affiliation. These included the National Small College Athletics Association, the National Christian Collegiate Athletics Association, and a catch-all indicator for any other athletics association. We also eliminated some professional schools such as schools of pharmacy or seminaries that had NAIA affiliation.

One complication is that some schools compete at different levels of affiliation according to the individual sport. For example, the wrestling team might compete at the I-A level but the rest of the college's teams at Division II. Another example is that every team is at the I-AAA level, except for football, which is at the Division II level. Whenever there were ambiguities about the level of affiliation, we used participation in the I-A and I-AA football as determining the overall level of affiliation or Division I basketball only for belonging to the I-AAA category. A few colleges had both NCAA and NAIA affiliations depending on the sport. These were treated as NCAA schools.

The most recent year available in IPEDS is 1999. The earliest year available in IPEDS is 1991. For the fixed-effects panel regression we used those years and 1995 as an intermediate year. Table 2 shows the number of colleges changing their sports affiliation status between 1991 and 1995 and between 1995 and 1999. There were 109 shifts up in status and 15 shifts down. Approximately half of the movement was out of the NAIA into NCAA I-AAA, II, and III. The NAIA lost a net total of 63 colleges over the period. It is remarkable that no colleges dropped intercollegiate sports. Division I picked up 34 colleges and 5 colleges took the most expensive step of moving to Division I-A.

Some colleges do not report even the most basic data to the federal government such as enrollment. After dropping colleges that did not report data or were not accredited, our sample was reduced to 693 colleges for the panel regressions. With a net increase in status of 94 in a sample of 693 colleges, the clear picture is that colleges overall are moving to higher profile sports programs.

EMPIRICAL ANALYSIS

Our first results are the ordered probit regressions of status. The same specifications were used for the years 1991, 1995, and 1999. Negative coefficients imply a higher-level sports program because the dependent variable

Table 2
Counts of Status Changes

	Shifts Up	
	1991 to 1995	1995 to 1999
NAIA to III	10	24
NAIA to II	19	16
NAIA to I-AAA		2
III to II	2	2
II to I-AAA	1	1
II to I-AA	5	5
I-AAA to I-AA	14	3
I-AA to I-A	1	4
Total	52	57
	Shifts Down	
I-A to I-AAA	1	
III to NAIA	2	
II to NAIA		6
II to III	2	2
I-AA to I-AAA		2
Total	5	10

was coded from 1 for Division I-A to 7 for no affiliation. In Tables 3A and 3B we present the regression output for all three years plus tabulations of the counts of the predicted versus actual affiliations.

The estimating model is

$$Sportingstatus_{it} = a_0 + a_1collegestatus_{it} + a_2women_{it} + a_3black_{it} + a_4public_{it}$$
$$+ a_5count_{it} + a_6sat_{it} + a_7accept_{it} + a_8statusrvl_{it} + a_9roomcap_{it} + a_{10}roomamt_{it}$$
$$+ a_{11}boardamt_{it} + a_{12}h_{it} + \varepsilon_{it}$$

where the independent variables are as defined in Appendix A, with "h" a measure of the highest degree offered, and ε is a random error term.

The results across the three years are similar. First consider the variables that are consistently statistically significant. At a point in time having more undergraduate students, count, is associated with higher-level sports programs. This variable has the highest z-score in all of the regressions. With very high significance levels, other things equal, women's colleges are associated with lower level sports programs, and historically black colleges have higher level sports programs. Presumably this reflects a differential in the recruiting benefits of intercollegiate sports programs for women versus African-Americans. The argument is that the African-American students who might be recruited by a historically black college are more interested in either participating in intercollegiate sports or attending games, or are more drawn by the school spirit/school identification aspects of intercollegiate sports, than the women who might be recruited by women's colleges.

Next consider the variables with mixed results on significance. Being a public college is significantly associated with a higher-level sports program in 1999 and 1995, but is not significant in 1991. Offering students remedial classes, statusrv1, is significantly associated with higher-level programs in 1999 and 1995 but just marginally significant in 1991 ($z = 1.74$). Lower student SAT scores are significantly associated with higher-level programs in 1999 and 1995 but not 1991 (the z-score for 1991 is 1.48). Higher acceptance rates (accept) are significantly associated with higher-level sports programs in 1999 and 1995 but again not 1991 (the z-score for 1991 is -1.24). These results support our thesis that, all things being equal, colleges with better students would be less willing to devote resources to intercollegiate sports. Our thesis that colleges with fewer dorm rooms (roomcap), and higher room and board charges (roomamt and boardamt), would have lower levels of intercollegiate sports had more mixed results. Only the room capacity was significant in all three regressions but the coefficient was negative in 1991 and 1995 and flipped to positive in 1999. The tier variables for the *U.S. News and World Report* ranks were mostly significant. These are dummy variables for prestige rankings ranging over the four quartiles of national universities as identified by the Carnegie classification for research universities, to four quartiles of regional universities that have limited graduate programs, to the four quartiles of nationally ranked liberal arts colleges that have no graduate programs, down to the four quartiles of the regional liberal arts colleges. There were 40 coefficients in the three regressions and of these 27 were significant. However, lower tiers were always associated with lower-profile sports programs compared to the omitted tier of the top quartile of national universities. This result was contrary to our expectations. Given that the SAT variable and the acceptance rate variable and the remedial classes variable had the expected signs and were significant in 1999 and 1995, we are left wondering what the *U.S. News and World Report* rankings measure other than the broad type of college. These rankings receive a great deal of attention among the top 50 national universities, but they may not mean

Table 3A
Ordered Probit Regression Results (1991)

Variable	Coefficient	Std. Error	Pr > |z|
Women	0.813	0.243	0.001
Black	-0.796	0.184	0.000
Tier 2	0.339	0.357	0.343
Tier 3	0.017	0.356	0.961
Tier 4	0.463	0.377	0.219
Tier 5	0.119	0.341	0.726
Tier 6	0.669	0.345	0.053
Tier 7	0.388	0.529	0.464
Tier 8	0.710	0.365	0.052
Tier 9	0.675	0.347	0.052
Tier 10	0.975	0.397	0.014
Tier 11	1.323	0.384	0.001
Tier 12	1.378	0.362	0.000
Tier 13	1.207	0.426	0.005
Public	0.137	0.118	0.247
Count	-0.0001	0.00001	0.000
SAT	0.0007	0.0005	0.139
H2	0.288	0.335	0.390
H3	0.140	0.088	0.111
H4	-0.033	0.145	0.815
H5	-0.263	0.151	0.083
Accept	-0.349	0.282	0.216
Statusrvl	0.182	0.104	0.082
Roomcap	-0.0002	0.00005	0.000
Roomamt	0.0001	0.00007	0.148
Boardamt	0.0001	0.0001	0.383
Wald χ^2 =606.4	**Log likelihood = -1268.3**		**Pseudo R^2 = .25**

much for student decisions below that level. The last variables are a set of dummy variables, H2 through H5, for the highest degree offered. The omitted category is just a baccalaureate degree. The H2 is some post-baccalaureate degree. The H3 is master's degrees. The H4 is some post-masters degree. The H5 is offering a Ph.D. These variables were not consistently significant.

Turning to the Table 3b of predicted versus actual status, a high fraction of the predictions are correct. A college was predicted to be in whichever category was its highest probability. A second observation on these tabulations is that most of the observations are close to the principal diagonal. Thus, when our predictions are off they are not very far off. The weaknesses in the model show up in all three tabulations. We never predict a school to

Table 3A (*Continued*)

Variable	Coefficient	Std. Error	Pr > |z|
Women	0.062	0.214	0.004
Black	-0.729	0.220	0.001
Tier 2	0.631	0.357	0.077
Tier 3	-0.274	0.382	0.473
Tier 4	0.637	0.405	0.116
Tier 5	0.692	0.356	0.052
Tier 6	0.833	0.379	0.028
Tier 7	1.144	0.407	0.005
Tier 8	1.290	0.428	0.003
Tier 9	0.431	0.342	0.208
Tier 10	0.933	0.359	0.009
Tier 11	0.895	0.381	0.019
Tier 12	1.158	0.407	0.004
Tier 13	1.097	0.375	0.004
Tier 14	1.419	0.407	0.000
Tier 15	1.508	0.413	0.000
Tier 16	1.848	0.457	0.000
Tier 17	1.183	0.467	0.011
Public	0.228	0.132	0.085
Count	-0.0001	0.00001	0.000
SAT	0.001	0.0004	0.026
H2	0.516	0.278	0.064
H3	0.046	0.103	0.651
H4	-0.083	0.164	0.611
H5	-0.072	0.172	0.673
Accept	-0.717	0.310	0.021
Statusrvl	0.237	0.104	0.023
Roomcap	-0.0003	0.00005	0.000
Roomamt	0.0001	0.00007	0.037
Boardamt	-0.0001	0.0001	0.105
Wald χ^2 =584.5	**Log likelihood = -1238.2**		**Pseudo R^2 = .24**

be in Division I-AAA. We tried many other specifications, including inter-action terms and any additional variables we could think of such as the age of the university. We were never able to get a single college to fall into the I-AAA category. The other systematic weakness is under-predicting the num-ber of colleges with no affiliation.

To summarize these results, the combination of factors that would cause a college to be most likely to have a Division I-A program would be being a very large, public, historically black college offering remedial classes and

Table 3A (*Continued*)

Variable	Coefficient	Std. Error	Pr >|z|
Women	0.477	0.178	0.007
Black	-0.801	0.212	0.000
Tier 2	0.719	0.377	0.057
Tier 3	0.572	0.413	0.167
Tier 4	1.169	0.414	0.005
Tier 5	1.028	0.372	0.006
Tier 6	1.469	0.402	0.000
Tier 7	1.651	0.424	0.000
Tier 8	1.818	0.444	0.000
Tier 9	0.978	0.365	0.007
Tier 10	1.185	0.377	0.002
Tier 11	1.312	0.392	0.001
Tier 12	1.908	0.437	0.000
Tier 13	1.594	0.389	0.000
Tier 14	1.860	0.418	0.000
Tier 15	1.899	0.439	0.000
Tier 16	2.487	0.488	0.000
Public	-0.447	0.128	0.000
Count	-0.0001	0.00001	0.000
SAT	0.001	0.0006	0.036
H2	0.479	0.430	0.265
H3	-0.156	0.106	0.143
H4	-0.224	0.162	0.169
H5	-0.344	0.147	0.020
Accept	-0.636	0.306	0.038
Statusrvl	0.196	0.102	0.056
Roomcap	0.0001	0.00005	0.019
Roomamt	-0.0001	0.00005	0.030
Boardamt	-0.0002	0.00007	0.000
Wald χ^2 =624.1	**Log likelihood = -1168.15**		**Pseudo R^2 = .25**

having a high acceptance rate and a low SAT average. We think it seems reasonably clear from these cross-section results that opportunity costs and potential revenues are closely tied to a college's choice of level of sports affiliation.

The fixed-effects panel estimates address the question of what happens over time to the enrollment and student quality college that switches its level of sports affiliation. The fixed-effect model holds constant any unobserved variation within a college that is constant over the time period. The actual switches for any college in the data set could be at any time between 1991

Table 3B
Predicted Versus Actual Affiliation (1991 Tabulation of Status by Predicted Status)

Status	Total	Predicted Status						
		1	2	3	4	5	6	7
1	87	**64**	14	0	6	3	0	0
2	77	17	**27**	0	26	7	0	0
3	75	5	16	**0**	24	27	3	0
4	161	0	12	0	**46**	81	22	0
5	232	3	5	0	31	**117**	74	2
6	232	0	0	0	7	71	**150**	4
7	73	1	0	0	0	14	52	7
Total	937	89	74	0	140	320	301	13

(1995 tabulation of status by predicted status)

Status	Total	Predicted Status						
		1	2	3	4	5	6	7
1	73	**51**	15	0	5	2	0	0
2	95	17	**34**	0	20	24	0	0
3	58	5	13	**0**	17	23	0	0
4	166	3	15	0	**34**	105	9	0
5	266	1	10	0	25	**196**	33	1
6	185	0	1	0	1	104	76	3
7	63	0	0	0	1	32	28	2
Total	906	77	88	0	103	486	146	6

(1999 tabulation of status by predicted status)

Status	Total	Predicted Status						
		1	2	3	4	5	6	7
1	86	**65**	16	0	5	0	0	0
2	94	14	**34**	0	29	17	0	0
3	61	8	11	**0**	25	17	0	0
4	188	2	15	0	**50**	119	2	0
5	297	1	9	0	38	**243**	6	0
6	126	0	0	0	0	116	**8**	2
7	39	0	0	0	1	28	8	**2**
Total	891	90	85	0	148	540	24	4

Table 4A
Fixed-Effects Panel Estimates for Number of Students (n = 2079)

Variable	Coefficient	Std. Error	Pr > $|t|$
Status 2	-2159.024	438.822	0.000
Status 3	-2095.166	472.196	0.000
Status 4	-2291.717	485.407	0.000
Status 5	-2266.834	500.087	0.000
Status 6	-2323.432	491.980	0.000
Status 7	-2054.932	502.111	0.000
Rank	-9.356	15.416	0.544
Roomcap	0.203	0.054	0.000
Roomamt	0.183	0.055	0.001
Boardamt	0.002	0.106	0.984
Statusrvl	117.569	141.581	0.406
Y95	-104.628	53.200	0.049
Y99	-88.494	86.984	0.309
Constant	6345.43	521.76	0.000
R^2 within = 0.03 R^2 between = 0.62 R^2 overall = 0.60		σ_U = 5187.56; σ_e = 851.39 ρ = 0.973	

and 1995 or between 1995 and 1999. The observed responses in enrollment are thus fairly short-term, between one and four years after a switch. We do not think it makes sense to look for contemporaneous enrollment responses to rise in status because the gain in name recognition will take some time. Conversely, the loss in name recognition from a decrease in status will take some time. However, the Mary Hardin-Baylor example cited above suggests that a rapid response is sometimes possible.

The model contains similar variables as in the ordered probit, except that sporting status is now an independent variable. We have three models: one to estimate student numbers, one to estimate SAT scores, and one to estimate acceptance rates. Tables 4a, b, and c have the fixed-effects panel results. The same specification is used with three dependent variables: number of undergraduates (count) reported in Table 4a, SAT score in Table 4b, and acceptance rate in Table 4c. The year dummy for 1999 is not significant, implying no differences relative to 1991 in enrollments per college in this sample. The year dummy for 1995 is significant (z = 1.97), indicating a loss of 104 students. There is a numerically small but significant upward trend in SAT scores and in acceptance rates. The other variables, other than level of affiliation, are not consistently significant. An increase in room capacity in a given college is significantly associated with a lower student count, which

Table 4B
Fixed-Effects Panel Estimates for SAT Scores (n = 2032)

Variable	Coefficient	Std. Error	$Pr > |t|$
Status 2	-12.988	23.364	0.578
Status 3	-7.121	25.135	0.777
Status 4	-50.417	25.900	0.052
Status 5	-45.125	26.668	0.091
Status 6	-51.515	26.251	0.050
Status 7	-43.853	26.782	0.102
Rank	-1.203	0.829	0.147
Roomcap	0.091	0.002	0.002
Roomamt	0.008	0.002	0.005
Boardamt	0.003	0.005	0.513
Statusrvl	0.613	7.720	0.937
Y95	17.045	2.895	0.000
Y99	73.604	4.695	0.000
Constant	997.77	27.971	0.000
R^2 within = 0.49 R^2 between = 0.10 R^2 overall = 0.18		$\sigma_U = 99.142$; $\sigma_e = 45.317$ $\rho = 0.827$	

Table 4C
Fixed-Effects Panel Estimates for Acceptance Rates (n = 2079)

Variable	Coefficient	Std. Error	$Pr > |t|$
Status 2	-0.088	0.042	0.038
Status 3	-0.109	0.045	0.017
Status 4	-0.133	0.046	0.005
Status 5	-0.115	0.048	0.017
Status 6	-0.116	0.047	0.015
Status 7	-0.099	0.048	0.041
Rank	0.002	0.001	0.041
Roomcap	5.09e-06	5.26e-06	0.334
Roomamt	1.87e-07	5.35e-06	0.972
Boardamt	-2.68e-06	0.00001	0.795
Statusrvl	0.011	0.013	0.390
Y95	0.019	0.005	0.000
Y99	0.022	0.008	0.008
Constant	0.815	0.050	0.000
R^2 within = 0.04 R^2 between = 0.01 R^2 overall = 0.003		$\sigma_U = 0.141$; $\sigma_e = 0.082$ $\rho = 0.746$	

is contrary to expectations. The main interest in Table 4 is the effect of changes in the level of sports affiliation on enrollments, SAT scores, and acceptance rates. The changes are interpreted as relative to the omitted category of Division I-A. The negative signs on the coefficients are interpreted as the loss resulting from a move from Division I-A to one of the other categories. Sixteen of the 18 coefficients are statistically significant. The signs are always negative, indicating losses in enrollment, SAT scores, and acceptance rates for going to lower levels of affiliation. The differences in SAT scores are from 7 to 51 points, with smallest losses generally for the steps closest to Division I-A. The acceptance rates range from 9% to 13% lower for schools switching to lower levels of sports affiliation, but there is no clear progression across the categories. The losses in enrollment range from 2,054 to 2,323 with a slight tendency to be greater for going down the list of affiliations. These estimated losses in enrollment for going down in affiliation or conversely gains for going up in affiliation are large.

CONCLUSION

The results raise some interesting questions. One is that if they are true, why don't all colleges that can possibly beg or borrow the money start Division I-A programs? One response is that they are doing that. It is difficult if not impossible to jump many steps on the sports affiliation ladder at the same time, but the 109 net increases in affiliation level from 1991 to 1999 suggest that colleges are charging up the ladder at a rapid pace. The NCAA has placed new restrictions on entry into Division I-A, such as increases in average attendance at football games, as a way of slowing down this flow. A second question raised by these results is whether they are too high to be plausible. Sports affiliation status is an endogenous choice for colleges, and there may be other changes aimed at attracting students taking place over the same period at the colleges that switched affiliation. We do not have instruments for why a college would change its affiliation level and we cannot control for advertising or other means of attracting students. A third puzzle is why any college would lower its level of sports affiliation. This decision may be due to severe financial pressures forcing a college to cut anything that is expendable. The number of colleges going down in affiliation is small enough that this question could be addressed by checking the finances of each college.

The most interesting question is why there is such an apparent strong response to level of sports affiliation. We think that there is a high income-elasticity to leisure activities. A generation ago in the United States, children would play pickup games of baseball and basketball or football. Now most parents can afford uniforms for their five-year-olds along with trophies and victory banquets. The increased sensitivity of college students to the availability of intercollegiate sports as a participatory activity is just an extension of increased interest in sports. College-age students would like to continue with the uniforms and camaraderie of youth sports.

Many college administrators talk about the sports "arms race" in victory banquets. College-age students would like to continue with the uniforms and camaraderie of youth sports with bigger stadiums, more elaborate training facilities, and amenities such as chartered jets required to attract outstanding athletes and remain competitive in sports. There is also an arms race in sports affiliation. The colleges that are gaining students are presumably taking them away from other colleges. The net gain across all colleges due to students who would not go to college but for the opportunity to play intercollegiate sports or to attend games must be trivial. What may be individually rational from the point of view of one college administrator may be collectively insane. Many commentators, among whom the most fervent and most frequent is Murray Sperber, have described college presidents as a group as myopic optimists deluded by their athletics administrators into thinking that their teams would draw the golden ring of basketball or football championships. It is hard to believe that so many of them are so consistently making mistakes in terms of their own interests.

Presumably, some collective action reducing spending on sports programs would be Pareto improving. Such action would face legal hurdles. MIT lost its case when it tried to defend a collective setting of academic scholarships. Similarly, assistant coaches sued when the NCAA limited the salaries that colleges could pay them. The NCAA lost that case. The prospects for any collective action seem grim in spite of the efforts of the Knight Commission to de-emphasize collegiate sports and reduce the "arms race." The Knight Commission is made up primarily of college presidents, a group that should have the power to take collective action to reduce spending on collegiate sports.

ACKNOWLEDGMENTS

We thank Feng Liu for excellent work in entering and organizing the data and for programming in STATA. Cay Hamby of the NAIA provided data on that organization's membership for the years 1991 and 1995. We also thank Mary Johnston of the NCAA for substantial help with NCAA data and Vic Borden of IUPUI's Office of Institutional Research for help in accessing the IPEDS database. Any errors are entirely our responsibility.

NOTES

1. These claims are made in a report, "Intercollegiate Athletics at IUPUI: Proposal for Division I Status Prepared for the Meeting of the Trustees of Indiana University on October 30, 1997 at IU Southeast." The report is available from the authors of this paper.

2. See Shulman and Bowen (2001).

3. As stated by the Athletics Director of the University of Alabama at Birmingham during the NCAA Convention in January 1996.

4. http://www.virtual-u.org/

5. Associated Press, "Texas School to Play First Game," August 21, 1988.

6. An example in professional sports would be DeBartolo and the San Francisco 49ers. An example at the collegiate level would be Stanford University, which could easily replace all of its athletes on grants-in-aid with full tuition paying students with better academic records. Ben and Jerry's Ice Cream at least had the reputation of foregoing profits while fostering social causes.

7. The Big 10 originally had 10 universities. It kept that name when Pennsylvania State was added in 1990.

8. The NCAA also requires schools to meet a number of qualifying criteria for I-A status. Thus in football these include a requirement that a college has at least 30,000 permanent seats in its home stadium and averages an attendance of at least 17,000 in any single year and 20,000 over the previous four years.

9. The NCAA website, www.ncaa.org, lists the basic facts on different tiers. In 1999 for Division I-A, I-AA, and I-AAA the average operating budget for intercollegiate athletics is $6,425,827. For Division II schools with football programs the average budget is $1,950,00. For Division III schools the average budget is $663,000. The NAIA does not list the average operating budget on its website. A random sample of 30 NAIA schools from the United States Department of Education website, http://ope.ed.gov/athletics/, yielded an average expenditure on athletics of $385,781.

10. These 1,458 colleges are the universe of accredited baccalaureate degree-granting colleges in the U.S. in 1999. Because of missing data our ordered probit regressions have between 891 and 937 colleges depending the year. Our fixed-effects panel data regressions have 693 colleges.

11. Zimbalist (1999b) shows that the number of schools with surpluses since 1985 in the CFA rose from 43.6% (23 of 53 schools) in 1989 to 63% (34 of 54) in 1995 and the share of Division I-A schools reporting a surplus rose from 41.6% (37 of 89) in 1985, to 55.2% (48 of 87) in 1989 and to 75.3% (67 of 89) in 1995. However, he argues that when institutional support is excluded more than half of these schools operate in deficit. He also argues that the evidence for indirect effects such as increased donations and increased applications is inconclusive. He himself conducted a variety of (unreported) econometric tests on 1980–95 data from 86 Division I-A colleges. While athletic success did tend to increase applications to these schools, he was unable to detect any significant relationship between various measures of athletic success and average SAT scores.

APPENDIX A: VARIABLE DEFINITIONS AND SOURCES

(All data are from the IPEDS database unless indicated otherwise.)

Status: takes the values for NCAA status 1–I-A, 2–I-AA, 3–I-AAA, 4–II, 5–III, 6 for NAIA and 7 for no affiliation.

Women: 1 if women's college, else 0

Black: 1 if black college, else 0

Tier: *U.S. News* rankings

1992

national, top 25 & quartile	1
national, quartile	2
national, quartile	3
national, quartile	4
top regional universities	5
regional universities	6
national liberal arts, top 25 & quartile 1	7
national liberal arts, quartile 2	8
national liberal arts, quartile 3	9
national liberal arts, quartile 4	10
top regional liberal arts	11
regional liberal arts	12

1996 & 2000

National Universities Tier 1	1
National Universities Tier 2	2
National Universities Tier 3	3
National Universities Tier 4	4
Regional Universities Tier 1	5
Regional Universities Tier 2	6
Regional Universities Tier 3	7
Regional Universities Tier 4	8
National Liberal Arts Colleges Tier 1	9
National Liberal Arts Colleges Tier 2	10
National Liberal Arts Colleges Tier 3	11
National Liberal Arts Colleges Tier 4	12
Regional Liberal Arts Colleges tier 1	13
Regional Liberal Arts Colleges tier 2	14
Regional Liberal Arts Colleges tier 3	15
Regional Liberal Arts Colleges tier 4	16
Unranked	17

To reconcile the 1991 coding with the later coding, we changed the 1996 and 2000 codes 7 & 8 to 6, 9 to 7, 10 to 8, 11 to 9, 12 to 10, 13 to 11, and 14, 15 & 16 to 12. The ranks in the years 1992, 1996, and 2000 are based on data for the prior academic year.

Public: from *U.S. News*
1 – public
0 – private

Count: undergraduate students' number, including full time and part time. From *U.S. News* magazine 2000

Sat: midpoint of the SAT 25th-75th percentile, from *U.S. News* magazine 2000

Accept: Acceptance rate, from *U.S. News* magazine 2000

Roomcap: Total dormitory capacity during academic year

Roomamt: Typical room charge for academic year

Boardamt: Typical board charge for academic year

Y95: a dummy variable in the panel regressions indicating year 1995

APPENDIX B: SUMMARY STATISTICS

1991					
Variable	Obs	Mean	Std. Dev	Min	Max
status	937	4.453575	1.726562	1	7
women	937	0.033084	0.178952	0	1
black	937	0.041622	0.199831	0	1
tier	937	7.395945	3.492988	1	13
count	937	4895.499	6086.621	247	41071
sat	937	979.5176	117.4736	600	1375
accept	937	0.742487	0.161539	0.12	1
public	937	0.379936	0.487825	0	2
hloffer	937	7.064034	1.493632	5	9
statusrv1	937	0.827108	0.378356	0	1
roomcap	937	1692.361	1876.609	11	17281
roomamt	937	1855.839	678.8536	0	4560
boardamt	937	1776.716	472.3761	0	3625

1995					
Variable	Obs	Mean	Std. Dev	Min	Max
status	906	4.395143	1.670855	1	7
women	906	0.03532	0.18469	0	1
black	906	0.040839	0.198026	0	1
tier	906	8.657837	4.582205	1	17
count	906	4593.521	5525.169	224	37754
sat	906	1008.389	122.1615	630	1415
accept	906	0.7528808	0.1570747	0.1	1
public	906	1.660044	0.4739555	1	2
hloffer	906	7.116998	1.487182	5	9
statusrv1	906	0.8256071	0.3796566	0	1
roomcap	906	1683.439	1825.112	30	17047
roomamt	906	2177.519	771.2428	0	5500
boardamt	906	2030.424	524.2795	0	3850

1999					
Variable	Obs	Mean	Std. Dev	Min	Max
status	891	4.178451	1.619622	1	7
women	891	0.037037	0.1889586	0	1
black	891	0.043771	0.2047002	0	1
tier	891	8.368126	4.443813	1	16
count	891	4946.366	5928.409	240	37203
sat	891	1071.799	120.6436	665	1610
accept	891	0.7536476	0.1621902	0.13	1
public	891	0.35578	0.4790179	0	1
hloffer	891	7.32211	1.506747	5	9
statusrv1	891	0.7946128	0.4042112	0	1
roomcap	891	2684.584	952.8725	0	7410
roomamt	891	1812.297	1977.009	40	21001
boardamt	891	2384.384	629.1212	0	4670

Total					
Variable	Obs	Mean	Std. Dev	Min	Max
status	2079	4.244348	1.629828	1	7
women	2079	0.031265	0.174075	0	1
black	2079	0.031746	0.1753654	0	1
tier	2079	7.756133	4.075406	1	17
count	2079	5055.942	5931.547	270	37754
sat	2032	1027.148	115.722	600	1610
accept	2079	0.7576597	0.1499063	0.1	1
public	2079	0.7926888	0.7610744	0	2
hloffer	2079	7.205868	1.498136	5	9
statusrv1	2079	0.8162578	0.387367	0	1
roomcap	2079	2207.201	1323.393	0	17281
roomamt	2079	1844.115	1580.709	40	17197
boardamt	2079	2067.037	573.4021	0	4370

7

An Economic Slam Dunk or March Madness? Assessing the Economic Impact of the NCAA Basketball Tournament

Robert A. Baade and Victor A. Matheson

INTRODUCTION: BRIEF HISTORY OF NCAA BASKETBALL TOURNAMENT

The Super Bowl, Olympic Games, all-star games, and league play-offs for the four major professional sports leagues, and the National Collegiate Athletic Association (NCAA) basketball tournament, qualify as sports mega-events in the United States. Convinced that these sports events produce substantial incremental economic activity, cities compete as vigorously to host them as do the athletes who participate in the events. Seduced by the promise of an economic windfall, cities have spent significant amounts of money to host the NCAA basketball tournament. Are the benefits derived from hosting tournament regional games or the NCAA Final Four (FF) as substantial as boosters claim? The primary purpose of this paper is to assess the economic impact of the NCAA FF. In so doing, at least three other questions will be addressed. First, does the size of the host city correlate in some way with the economic impact induced by the event? Second, how does the economic impact of the FF for women (FFW) compare to that of the FF for men (FFM)? Third, does the size of the facility in which the FF games are played influence the economic impact? Before addressing these questions directly, it is useful to consider how the NCAA has evolved in a financial sense, and how the NCAA has been able to parlay the popularity of its basketball tournament into considerable wealth. The evolution of its television contracts provides some particularly meaningful insight.

The NCAA basketball tournament currently commands among the most lucrative broadcast contracts in U.S. sports history. When the tournament began in 1939, few could have anticipated the financial significance the event would achieve. In the financial equivalent of an air ball, the National Association of Basketball Coaches, the event sponsors that first year, lost about $2,500 (Yoder, 2002). Fifty years later the television broadcast rights alone for the tournament exceeded $100 million. To be precise, in 1991 CBS paid $143 million for television rights, an increase of $89 million from the 1990 rights fee of $54 million. In the latest contract iteration announced November 18, 1999, CBS Sports extended its current pact with the NCAA to 2014. The $6-billion, 11-year new contract, one of the largest in U.S. sports history, represents a 220% increase defined in annual terms over the seven-year, $1.725 billion deal which expired in 2002. CBS has had the TV rights to the Division I tournament since 1982, but it should be noted that the latest agreement between CBS and the NCAA includes merchandising rights for tournament related products as well as rights to the games' content on the Internet (*CNN Money*, 1999).

The lucrative television contract reflects successful ratings. The FFM typically rates among the most watched sporting events for any given year. For example, in 2000, only the Super Bowl, the Orange Bowl, and the Olympics opening ceremony achieved higher ratings than the NCAA men's championship game (Isidore, 2001). Despite a ratings slippage from previous years, the number of viewers for the NCAA men's final exceeded the average rating for the World Series and the NBA finals average by almost 10%. Over the past five years the average share for the NCAA men's final exceeded the World Series and NBA finals averages by more than 30% (Isidore, 2001).

Growth in gambling revenues related to the event provides additional evidence on the tournament's significance in the world of sports. The Federal Bureau of Investigation estimates that $2.5 billion is bet illegally on the NCAA basketball tournament each year (Atkins, 1996).

The NCAA has developed a financial dependency on the tournament; it derives 90% of its budget from the event. In all likelihood, Cedric Dempsey, the NCAA president, would be unlikely to command a salary of $525,000 per year in the absence of the tournament.

The popularity and economic success of the NCAA tournament has attracted interest from other quarters to include cities throughout the United States. At a time when cities have attempted to bolster their sagging economies through reinventing themselves as cultural or recreational destinations, the NCAA basketball tournament represents an event that fits that developmental strategy.[1] Hosting an FF employs the tourist infrastructure cities have created in the last two decades. Utilization of this infrastructure is critical to the economic viability of the cultural destination strategy, and cities have competed vigorously for the NCAA tournament as a consequence.

Evidence on the NCAA's success in negotiating with networks for the rights to broadcast their games indicates that the NCAA has learned to use its market power to extract monopoly rents. Cities have to pay at least in kind to host the event, and the sizeable public expenditure required to accommodate the tournament often necessitates convincing a sometimes skeptical public that the event's public benefits exceed the civic costs. Economic impact studies relating to the FF have predictably proliferated. If we assume that cities are rational, then they presumably would not be willing to pay more to host an FF than the benefits derived from the event.[2] Assuming that cities have perfect information relating to the impact of the FF, then the price they pay to host it will not exceed their perceived marginal social product. Using the upper bound for estimating the cost a city incurs in hosting an FF would be the incremental economic activity the event stimulates. Indeed, if the NCAA appropriates all monopoly rents, then in a world of perfect information, the cost to the city equals the estimated economic impact.

CITY PERCEPTIONS ON THE ECONOMIC IMPACT OF THE NCAA BASKETBALL TOURNAMENT

The estimated economic impact for the NCAA Final Four basketball varies widely as do the estimated impacts for all sports mega-events. For example, a series of studies for the NBA All-Star game produced numbers ranging from a $3 million windfall for the 1992 game in Orlando to a $35 million bonanza for the fame three years earlier in Houston (Houck, 2000). In January 2001, *The Sporting News* designated Indianapolis as "the Best Final Four Host." In celebrating the designation, the Indianapolis Convention & Visitors Association (ICVA) indicated that the 2000 FFM, which Indianapolis hosted, brought an estimated 50,000 visitors to Indianapolis and generated $29.5 million in economic impact (ICVA, 2001). This estimate of economic impact equaled slightly more than one-quarter of the $110 million economic impact estimated for an FFM reported in a 2001 article about the impact of the NCAA tournament (Anderson, 2001). The authors found a low booster economic impact estimate for the FFM registered $14 million, or approximately 13% of the high estimate (Associated Press, 1998).

Estimates for the FFW typically run less than that for the men's tournament, and the authors' research indicated a range of $7 million, for the FFW in Cincinnati in 1997 (Goldfisher, 1999) to $32 million for the event hosted by San Jose in 1999 (Knight Ridder News Service, 1999). In deriving his economic impact estimate for Cincinnati, Donald Schumacher opined: "Our feeling is that the dollars that those people were to spend on entertainment and food was going to happen anyway" (Knight Ridder News Service, 1999).

The range of estimates suggests that in addition to correlating with tournament gender, the economic impact may systematically vary with the size

Table 1
Estimated Economic Impact Estimates for the NBA All-Star for Selected Years

Year	City	Arena	Attendance	Days	Estimated Revenue	Revenue Per Visitor Day
1985	Indianapolis	Hoosier Dome	43,146	2	$ 7.5M	$86.91
1989	Houston	Astro Dome	44,735	2	$35.0M	$391.19
1992	Orlando	Orlando Arena	14,727	2	$ 3.0M	$101.85
1997	Cleveland	Gund Arena	20,592	4	$23.5M	$285.30

Source: Jeff Houck, "High-Stakes Courtship: Cities Build New Arenas to Bring in Major Sports Events, Hoping to Make Big Money," FoxSportsBiz.com, January 21, 2000.

of the city and the facility in which the games are played. The nature of the correlation between economic impact and the size of the city and/or the facility is sometimes difficult to discern from booster estimates, however. In Table 1 estimates have been provided for the economic impact of an event similar to the FF, the NBA All-Star game, on host cities for selected years.

The information recorded in Table 1 fails to reveal a pattern with regard to the relationship between the size of the city, facility, or attendance and economic impact.

While booster estimates show a wide variation on the economic impact of the FF, economists offer a more uniform appraisal of the economic impact of sports mega-events. In short, economic scholarship indicates that these events have relatively little impact on metropolitan economies. For example, Stanford economist Roger Noll estimated a "zero" economic impact of the FFW on San Jose's economy. This estimate stands in stark contrast to the $20 to $30 million in economic impact estimated by various civic groups in San Jose (Knight Ridder News Service, 1999). What accounts for the dramatic difference? Economist Philip Porter summarized possible reasons for the inflated estimates provided by civic groups in commenting on the economic impact of the Super Bowl on South Florida's economy. Porter opined:

> Investigator bias, data measurement error, changing production relationships, diminishing returns to both scale and variable inputs, and capacity constraints anywhere along the chain of sales relations lead to lower multipliers. Crowding out and price increases by input suppliers in response to higher levels of demand and the tendency of suppliers to lower prices to stimulate sales when demand is weak lead to overestimates of net new sales due to the event. These

characteristics alone would suggest that the estimated impact of the mega-sporting event will be lower than impact analysis predicts. When there are perfect complements to the event, like hotel rooms for visitors, with capacity constraints or whose suppliers raise prices in the face of increased demand, impacts are reduced to zero. (Porter, 1999)

Economists Robert Baade and Victor Matheson (2000) also challenged an NFL claim that as a result of the 1999 Super Bowl in Miami, taxable sales in South Florida increased by more than $670 million dollars. Their study of taxable sales data in the region concluded that the NFL has exaggerated the impact of the Miami Super Bowl by approximately a factor of 10 even when using assumptions that favored identifying a strong economic impact. Are booster estimates on the economic impact of the NCAA basketball tournament similarly inflated? Given that these estimates often serve as a justification for significant expenses incurred in hosting the FF, the answer to this question should concern public officials. Theoretical issues that have implications for the size of the economic impact estimates are identified and analyzed in the paper's next section.

THEORETICAL ISSUES

The exaggeration of benefits induced by a sports mega-event occurs for several reasons. First, the increase in direct spending attributable to the event may be a "gross" as opposed to a "net" measure. Some subsidy advocates have estimated direct spending by simply summing all receipts associated with the event. The fact that the gross-spending approach fails to account for decreased spending directly attributable to the event represents a major theoretical and practical shortcoming.

Eliminating the spending by residents of the community would at first blush appear to account for a significant source of bias in estimating direct expenditures. Surveys on expenditures by those attending the event, complete with a question on place of residence, would appear to be a straightforward way of estimating direct expenditures in a manner that is statistically acceptable. While such surveys may well provide acceptable spending estimates for those patronizing the competition, such a technique, however, offers no data on changes in spending by residents not attending the event. It is conceivable that some residents may dramatically change their spending during the competition given their desire to avoid the congestion at least in the venue(s) environs. A fundamental shortcoming of economic impact studies, in general, pertains not solely to information on spending for those who are included in a direct expenditure survey, but rather to the lack of information on the spending behavior for those who are not.

Economists have cited that the failure to account for this important distinction between gross and net spending has been a chief reason why sports events or teams do not contribute as much to metropolitan economies as boosters claim they do (Baade, 1996). The national appeal of the NCAA tournament, however, arguably allows for a convergence of the gross and net spending figures given the fact that the attendees come from outside the host city. A national sporting event could be characterized as "zero sum" from a national perspective, while still exercising a strong, positive economic impact on the host city. Stated somewhat differently, spending at the NCAA basketball tournament qualifies as export spending since most of it is thought to be undertaken by people from outside the city.

A second reason economic impact may be exaggerated relates to what economists refer to as the "multiplier," the notion that direct spending increases induce additional rounds of spending due to increased incomes that occur as a result of additional spending. Hotel workers and restaurant workers experience increases in income, for example, as a consequence of greater activity at hotels and restaurants. If errors are made in assessing direct spending, those errors are compounded in calculating indirect spending through standard multiplier analysis. Furthermore, precise multiplier analysis includes all "leakages" from the circular flow of payments and uses multipliers that are appropriate to the event industry. Leakages may be significant depending on the state of the economy. If the host city is at or very near full employment, for example, it may be that the labor essential to conducting the event resides in other communities where unemployment or a labor surplus exists. To the extent that this is true, then the indirect spending that constitutes the multiplier effect must be adjusted to reflect this leakage of income and subsequent spending.

Labor is not the only factor of production that may repatriate income. If hotels experience higher than normal occupancy rates during a mega-event, then the question must be raised about the fraction of increased earnings that remain in the community if the hotel is a nationally owned chain.[3] In short, to assess the impact of mega-events, a balance of payments approach should be utilized. That is to say, to what extent does the event give rise to money inflows and outflows that would not occur in its absence? Since the input-output models used in the most sophisticated *ex ante* analyses are based on fixed relationships between inputs and outputs, such models do not account for the subtleties of full employment and capital ownership noted here. As a consequence, it is not clear if economic impact estimates based on them are biased up or down.

As an alternative to estimating the change in expenditures and associated changes in economic activity, those who provide goods and services directly in accommodating the event could be asked how their activity has been altered by the event. In summarizing the efficacy of this technique Davidson opined:

> The biggest problem with this producer approach is that these business managers must be able to estimate how much "extra" spending was caused by the

sport event. This requires that each proprietor have a model of what would have happened during that time period had the sport event not taken place. This is an extreme requirement, which severely limits this technique. (Davidson, 1999)

An expenditure approach to projecting the economic impact of mega-events is likely to yield the most accurate estimates. Do *ex post* estimates on the economic impact of the NCAA basketball tournament conform to *ex ante* economic impact estimates on host cities provided by boosters of the event? In the next section of the paper, the model that is used to develop after-the-fact estimates is detailed.

THE MODEL

Ex ante models may not provide credible estimates on the economic impact of a mega-event for the reasons cited. An *ex post* model may be useful in providing a filter through which the promises made by event boosters can be strained. A mega-event's impact is likely to be small relative to the overall economy, and the primary challenge for those doing a post-event audit involves isolating the event's impact. This is not a trivial task, and those who seek insight into the question of economic impact should be cognizant of the challenges and deficiencies common to both *ex ante* and *ex post* analyses.

Several approaches are possible in constructing a model to estimate the impact an event has had on a city, and are suggested by past scholarly work. Mills and McDonald (1992) provide an overview of previous models used to explain metropolitan economic growth. They identified five theories: export base, neoclassical growth, product cycle, cumulative causation, and disequilibria dynamic adjustment. All these theories seek to explain growth through changes in key economic variables in the short-run (export base and neoclassical) or the identification of long-term developments that affect metropolitan economies in hypothetical ways (product cycle, cumulative causation, and disequilibria dynamic adjustment).

Our task is not to replicate explanations of metropolitan economic growth, but to use past work to help identify how much growth in economic activity in U.S. cities hosting the FF is attributable to the event. To this end we have selected explanatory variables from past models to help establish what economic activity would have been in the absence of the FF. Estimating the economic impact of the FF used involves a comparison of the projected level of economic activity without the event to the actual levels of economic activity that occurred in cities hosting the FF. The success of this approach depends on our ability to identify those variables that explain the majority of observed variation in growth in economic activity in host cities. To isolate the mega-event's impact, both external and internal factors need to be considered. External factors might include, for example, a relocation of people and economic activity from the "rust/frost belt" to the "sun belt," changes in the disposition of the federal government toward revenue sharing, and changes in the demographic character of urban America. Internal factors might include a change in the attitude of local politicians toward fiscal intervention, a natural disaster, or unusual demographic changes. One technique would be to carefully review the history of cities in general and particular and incorporate each potentially significant change into a model. An alternative is to represent a statistic for a city for a particular year as a deviation from the average value for that statistic for cohort cities for that year. Such a representation over time will in effect "factor out" general urban trends and developments. For example, if we identify a particular city's growth in employment as 15% over time, but cities in general are growing by 10%, then we would conclude that this city's pattern deviates from the norm by 5%. It is the 5% deviation that requires explanation and not the whole 15%, for our purposes in this study.[4]

In modeling those factors that are unique to individual cities, it is helpful to identify some conceptual deficiencies characterizing the demand side of *ex ante* and *ex post* models that exaggerated economic impact estimates. Many prospective economic impact studies, particularly those that are older, fail to make a distinction between gross and net spending changes that occur as a consequence of hosting a mega-event. *Ex post* studies' failure to factor out the city's own secular growth path could embellish an estimate of the contribution of the NCAA basketball tournament. *Ex ante* studies even in very sophisticated forms are based usually on the premise that important economic relationships remain unchanged. It is, after all, historical experiences that define the statistics upon which prospective impact estimates are based. However, if the event is significant in a statistical sense, will not the event modify historical experience? We cannot claim a significant impact, and at the same time claim that history will be unaltered. Our model, therefore, in various ways "factors out" the city's historical experience. To continue with our example from above, if history tells us that a city experiences a growth in employment that is 5% above the national average, before and after a mega-event, then it would be misguided to attribute that additional 5% to the mega-event. If after the event, the city continued to exhibit employment increases 5% above the national norm, the logical conclusion is that the mega-event simply supplanted other economic developments that contributed to the city's above-average rate of growth. It will be particularly interesting to see if rates of economic growth forecast for cities hosting the NCAA tournament approximate what an *ex post* model not adjusted for a city's secular growth path would conclude.

The alternative to the technique outlined to this point, would be to carefully review the history of cities in general and particular, and explicitly incorporate each potentially significant change into the model. This technique has practical limitations to which past studies attest. Economists who have sought to explain growth using this technique have followed traditional prescriptions, and have developed demand- or supply-centered models through which to explain growth. To assess the relationships between costs and growth, see Mills and Luansende (1995), Terkla and Doeringer (1991), and Goss and Phillips (1994). Other scholars such as Duffy (1994) and Wasylenko and McQuire (1985) have combined both demand and supply arguments. Both supply and demand models have strong theoretical underpinnings. Those who utilize a demand approach with some version of employment as the independent variable base their theory on the notion that the demand for labor is ultimately derived from the demand for goods and services. Those who favor a supply approach would argue that cost factors are the most critical in explaining employment in a metropolitan statistical area (MSA) or region.

Given the number and variety of variables found in regional growth models and the inconsistency of findings with regard to coefficient size and significance, criticisms of any single model could logically focus on the problems posed by omitted variables. Any critic, of course, can claim that a particular regression suffers from omitted-variable bias; it is far more challenging to address the problems posed by not including key variables in the analysis. In explaining regional or metropolitan growth patterns, at least some of the omitted variable problem can be addressed through a careful specification of the dependent variable. As noted above, representing relevant variables as deviations from city norms leaves the scholar a more manageable task, namely that of identifying those factors that explain city growth after accounting for the impact of those forces that generally have affected regional or MSA growth. For example, a variable is not needed to represent the implications of federal revenue sharing, if such a change affected cities in ways proportionate to changes in demographic characteristics, e.g., population, used to calibrate the size of the revenue change for any particular city. Of course, instead of representing the MSA dependent variable as a deviation from a national mean and its own secular growth path, a national mean and the MSA's growth path can be represented as independent variables. In fact, we chose to represent the MSA mean rate of employment growth and the city's growth path for employment for the previous three years as independent variables.

Following the same logic, independent variables should also be normalized, that is, represented as a deviation from an average MSA value or as a fraction of the MSA average. It is important, for example, to model the fact that relocating a business could occur as a consequence of wages increasing in the MSA under study or a slower rate of wage growth in other MSAs. What matters is not the absolute level of wages in city i, but city i's wage relative to that of its competitors. What we propose, therefore, is an equation for explaining metropolitan employment growth that incorporates those variables that the literature identifies as important, but specified in such a way that those factors common to MSAs are implicitly included.

The purpose of *ex ante* studies is to provide a measure of the net benefits a project or event is likely to yield. To our knowledge there is no prospective model that has the capacity for measuring the net benefits of a project relative to the next best alternative use of those funds. If we assume that the best use of funds has always occurred prior to a mega-event, then the growth path observed for a city can be construed as optimal. If this optimal growth path, identified by the city's secular growth trend, decreases after the mega-event occurs, then the evidence does not support the hypothesis that a publicly subsidized mega-event put those public monies to the best use. A negative or even insignificant coefficient for the NCAA basketball tournament variable is prima facie evidence that the mega-event is less than optimal. Everything discussed in this section of the paper to this point is intended to define the regression analysis that will be used to assess changes in income attributable to the FF in host cities based on historical data between 1970 and 1999 for the FFM and between 1982 and 1999 for the FFW.[5]

Equation (1) represents the model used to predict changes in income for host cities:

$$\partial Y_t^i = \beta_0 + \beta_1 \sum_{i=1}^{n} \frac{\partial Y_t^i}{n_t} + \beta_2 \partial Y_{t-1}^i + \beta_3 W_t^i + \beta_4 T_t^i + \beta_5 OB_t^i + \beta_6 TR_t^i + \varepsilon_t^i \qquad (1)$$

where for each time period t,

∂Y_t^i = % change in income (GDP) in the ith metropolitan statistical area (MSA),

n_t = number of cities in the sample,

W_t^i = nominal wages in the ith MSA as a percentage of the average for all cities in the sample,

T_t^i = state and local taxes in the ith MSA as a percentage of the average for all cities in the sample,

OB_t^i = a dummy variable for oil boom and bust cycles for selected cities and years,

TR_t^i = annual trend, and

ε_t^i = stochastic error.

For the purposes of our analysis, the functional form is linear in all the variables included in equation (1). The equation was calculated for each host metropolitan area over the period identified in the previous paragraph for the FFM and FFW. For two host sites, Dallas–Fort Worth in 1986 and East Rutherford, New Jersey, in 1996 for the FFM, the economic impact was es-

timated for Dallas and Fort Worth and Newark and New York City separately. For most cities, autocorrelation was identified as a significant problem and therefore, the Cochrane-Orcutt method was used for all regressions.
Not every variable specified in Equation (1) emerged as a statistically significant predictor in the regression model for every city. Insignificant variables were removed from the model until only predictors significant at the
5% level remained. In all cases, average income growth was a significant predictor with the other variables being significant in a smaller number of the
cities. The variables used for each city are shown in Table 2.

As mentioned previously, rather than specifying all the variables that may
explain metropolitan growth, we attempted to simplify the task by including independent variables that are common to cities in general and the ith
MSA in particular. In effect, we have devised a structure that attempts to
identify the extent to which the deviations from the growth path of cities in
general $(\Sigma \partial Y_t^i / n_t)$ and city i's secular growth path ∂Y_{t-1}^i,[6] are attributable
to deviations in certain costs of production (wages and taxes), and dummy
variables for the oil boom/bust cycle.

Relative values wages and tax burdens are all expected to help explain a
city's growth rate in employment as it deviates from the national norm and
its own secular growth path. As mentioned above, past research has not produced consistency with respect to the signs and significance of these independent variables. Some of the inconsistency can be attributable to an
inability to separate cause and effect.

For example, we would expect higher relative wages over time to reduce
the rate at which employment is growing in an MSA relative to other cities.
That would be true, all things being equal, if wages determined employment.
If, however, high rates of employment increased an MSA's wage relative to
that of other cities, it may be that the opposite sign emerges. We do not have
as a consequence a priori expectations with regard to the signs of the coefficients.

That should not be construed as an absence of theory about key economic
relationships. As noted earlier, we included those variables that previous
scholarly work found important.

RESULTS

The model identified in Table 2 for each city is used to estimate income
growth for each city for each year analyzed, 1970–1999 for the FFM and
1982–1999 for the FFW. The predicted income growth is then compared
to the actual income growth that each MSA experienced for the year in which
the city hosted the FF. The predicted city real incomes are based on data
for the individual cities covering the period 1969 through 1999. Using the
difference between actual and predicted growth for the host city's economy,

Table 2
Variables Used in Model to Predict Income Growth

Host MSA	Predictors					
Albuquerque, NM	Constant	Avg. Growth				
Atlanta, GA	Constant	Avg. Growth				
Austin, TX	Constant	Avg. Growth	Taxes (%)	Trend		
Charlotte, NC	Constant	Avg. Growth	Wages (%)	Trend		
Cincinnati, OH	Constant	Avg. Growth	Taxes (%)	Trend		
Dallas, TX	Constant	Avg. Growth	Taxes (%)	Lagged Income Growth	Trend	Oil Bust
Denver, CO	Constant	Avg. Growth	Wages (%)			
Fort Worth, TX	Constant	Avg. Growth				
Greensboro, NC	Constant	Avg. Growth				
Houston, TX	Constant	Avg. Growth	Oil Bust			
Indianapolis, IN	Constant	Avg. Growth				
Kansas City, MO	Constant	Avg. Growth				
Knoxville, TN	Constant	Avg. Growth	Wages (%)	Trend		
Lexington, KY	Constant	Avg. Growth				
Los Angeles, CA	Constant	Avg. Growth				
Minneapolis, MN	Constant	Avg. Growth	Trend			
New Orleans, LA	Constant	Avg. Growth				
New York, NY	Constant	Avg. Growth	Trend			
Newark, NJ	Constant	Avg. Growth	Wages (%)	Trend		
Norfolk, VA	Constant	Avg. Growth				
Philadelphia, PA	Constant	Avg. Growth	Wages (%)	Taxes (%)	Trend	
Richmond, VA	Constant	Avg. Growth	Trend			
Salt Lake City, UT	Constant	Avg. Growth	Taxes (%)			
San Antonio, TX	Constant	Avg. Growth				
San Diego, CA	Constant	Avg. Growth				
San Jose, CA	Constant	Avg. Growth				
Seattle, WA	Constant	Avg. Growth				
St. Louis, MO	Constant	Avg. Growth				
Tacoma, WA	Constant	Avg. Growth	Wages (%)	Trend		
Tampa, FL	Constant	Avg. Growth				
Washington, DC	Constant	Avg. Growth				

a dollar value estimate of this difference can be determined. If it is assumed that any difference between actual and predicted income can be accounted for by the presence of the FF, then a dollar estimate of the impact of the NCAA basketball tournament for cities hosting the event can be generated. Estimates for the real economic impact of the FFM and FFW based on regressions for equation (1) are recorded in Tables 3 and 4, respectively.

Table 3
Estimated Real Economic Impact on Host Cities from the FFM, 1970–1999

Yr	Final Four Location	Actual Growth	Predicted Growth	Diff	Net income gains/ losses	t-stat	Real Income ($000s)	St. Res.
70	College Park	5.186%	2.856%	2.330%	1,646,176	2.29	70,651,320	0.0102
71	Houston	5.180%	5.184%	-0.004%	-1,415	0.00	36,981,510	0.0235
72	Los Angeles	4.317%	4.362%	-0.045%	-70,679	-0.03	157,065,115	0.0138
73	St. Louis	2.730%	3.223%	-0.493%	-242,814	-0.76	49,203,393	0.0065
74	Greensboro	-1.256%	-1.359%	0.103%	16,838	0.13	16,394,609	0.0077
75	San Diego	2.428%	0.497%	1.931%	617,429	1.80	31,973,621	0.0107
76	Philadelphia	3.619%	3.630%	-0.011%	-11,117	-0.02	102,070,263	0.0072
77	Atlanta	5.844%	5.411%	0.433%	185,267	0.45	42,770,498	0.0096
78	St. Louis	3.665%	4.394%	-0.729%	-389,427	-1.12	53,418,826	0.0065
79	Salt Lake City	1.572%	1.879%	-0.307%	-49,872	-0.22	16,253,420	0.0137
80	Indianapolis	-3.732%	-2.372%	-1.360%	-369,660	-0.95	27,184,118	0.0143
81	Philadelphia	0.260%	0.164%	0.096%	100,339	0.13	104,368,055	0.0072
82	New Orleans	0.409%	0.216%	0.193%	52,899	0.16	27,372,301	0.0122
83	Albuquerque	6.118%	3.858%	2.260%	225,330	1.40	9,969,697	0.0161
84	Seattle	4.060%	5.937%	-1.877%	-837,648	-1.06	44,621,753	0.0177
85	Lexington	4.122%	4.748%	-0.625%	-48,800	-0.48	7,802,668	0.0129
86	Dallas	3.088%	3.893%	-0.805%	-558,260	-0.82	69,349,066	0.0098
86	Fort Worth	3.180%	5.516%	-2.336%	-694,457	-1.57	29,728,452	0.0149
87	New Orleans	-2.523%	-1.323%	-1.200%	-327,808	-0.98	27,326,363	0.0122
88	Kansas City	2.136%	3.606%	-1.470%	-579,044	-1.38	39,384,302	0.0107
89	Seattle	6.049%	5.006%	1.043%	605,511	0.59	58,030,571	0.0177
90	Denver	1.861%	0.682%	1.179%	530,055	0.86	44,953,686	0.0137
91	Indianapolis	0.623%	-1.344%	1.967%	686,591	1.38	34,901,643	0.0143
92	Minneapolis	4.648%	3.393%	1.255%	943,036	1.35	75,122,731	0.0093
93	New Orleans	1.328%	1.046%	0.282%	82,519	0.23	29,271,596	0.0122
94	Charlotte	5.014%	4.314%	0.700%	224,538	1.01	32,095,003	0.0069
95	Seattle	2.394%	3.719%	-1.325%	-867,355	-0.75	65,483,377	0.0177
96	Newark	2.022%	1.784%	0.238%	155,950	0.28	65,525,280	0.0086
96	New York City	3.603%	3.847%	-0.244%	-695,103	-0.16	284,878,337	0.0151
97	Indianapolis	3.355%	3.267%	0.088%	36,570	0.06	41,635,975	0.0143
98	San Antonio	7.050%	7.133%	-0.083%	-31,282	-0.08	37,464,702	0.0109
999	Tampa/ St. Petersburg	1.751%	3.364%	-1.613%	-1,029,775	-1.03	63,826,713	0.0156
	Average	2.631%	2.670%	.039%	-44,278	.02	52,448,368	0.011

Table 4

Estimated Real Economic Impact on Host Cities from the FFW, 1982–1999

Year	Final Four Location	Actual Growth	Predicted Growth	Difference	Net income gains/losses	t-stat	Real Income ($000s)	St. Res.
1982	Norfolk, VA	2.386%	1.107%	1.279%	301,173	1.14	23,548,604	0.0112
1983	Norfolk, VA	5.438%	4.334%	1.104%	274,075	0.99	24,829,141	0.0112
1984	Los Angeles	6.106%	5.549%	0.557%	1,126,315	0.40	202,210,958	0.0138
1985	Austin, TX	9.650%	8.855%	0.795%	140,125	0.44	17,615,321	0.0179
1986	Lexington, KY	4.062%	4.762%	-0.701%	-56,905	-0.54	8,119,584	0.0129
1987	Austin, TX	-1.332%	0.689%	-2.021%	-359,706	-1.13	17,801,691	0.0179
1988	Tacoma, WA	3.158%	4.881%	-1.722%	-206,003	-0.83	11,959,528	0.0208
1989	Tacoma, WA	3.964%	4.473%	-0.509%	-63,226	-0.25	12,433,616	0.0208
1990	Knoxville, TN	2.794%	1.865%	0.929%	123,285	0.84	13,266,060	0.0111
1991	New Orleans	1.389%	-0.600%	1.989%	561,798	1.63	28,252,166	0.0122
1992	Los Angeles	0.653%	0.930%	-0.277%	-656,728	-0.20	237,085,976	0.0138
1993	Atlanta	4.156%	3.426%	0.730%	632,556	0.76	86,651,567	0.0096
1994	Richmond, VA	2.610%	2.273%	0.337%	85,097	0.29	25,260,772	0.0117
1995	Minneapolis	3.139%	3.809%	-0.670%	-545,102	-0.72	81,384,321	0.0093
1996	Charlotte, NC	4.293%	4.390%	-0.097%	-34,150	-0.14	35,342,319	0.0069
1997	Cincinnati	3.648%	3.867%	-0.219%	-96,373	-0.31	43,992,399	0.0070
1998	Kansas City	6.544%	6.620%	-0.076%	-38,603	-0.07	50,555,987	0.0107
1999	San Jose	11.925%	4.775%	7.150%	5,482,913	3.38	76,684,098	0.0212
	Average	**4.145%**	**3.667%**	**0.477%**	370,586	0.32	55,388,562	0.0133
	Excluding San Jose	**3.686%**	**3.602%**	**0.084%**	69,860	0.14	54,135,883	0.0129

Table 3 records various estimates derived from the regressions for the individual cities that enable computation of the dollar differences between actual real income growth rates and the estimated increase (decrease) in real dollar income (1999 dollars) for the host city generated by the model. The most important conclusion suggested by the numbers in Table 3 is that the FFM induced a statistically significant outcome only once. That occurred in 1970 when College Park, Maryland, hosted the tournament. The size of the impact indicates the presence of other unusual and substantial economic activity in College Park in 1970, which may have been statistically attributed to the FFM, but improperly so.

Although only a single site produced a statistically significant net gain or loss in real income from the FFM, it is noteworthy that the model used generates a differential between the actual and estimated city incomes of a mere −.039 percent. Using this model, the average real economic impact (in 1999 dollars) from the FFM over the period 1970 through 1999 is estimated at −$44.28 million, or the model indicates that the average host city experienced a reduction in real income of $44.28 million as a consequence of the event. This compares to typical booster estimates predicting gains ranging from $25 million to $110 million. The median estimated economic impact equaled a loss of $6.44 million. The model estimates indicate that fifteen (seventeen) of the host cities experienced real gains (losses) from the FFM. Since but one outcome emerged as statistically significant in the sample of 32 MSAs, not too much should be read into these estimates of gains and losses. But the consistency of statistically insignificant outcomes does cast doubt on the credibility of at least the more robust booster claims for a financial windfall from hosting the FF.

Table 4 records results relating to the economic impact of the FFW for the period 1982 through 1999. The outcomes for the FFW parallel that for the FFM in several respects. First and foremost, all outcomes proved statistically insignificant except for the 1999 tournament hosted by San Jose.

The San Jose result very likely reflects frenzied economic activity in Silicon Valley relating to the Internet boom during that time period. Second, if San Jose is eliminated, the average difference between the predicted and actual growth rates in real income for the host MSAs equaled something less than one-tenth of one percent. Third, negative and positive net real income outcomes associated with the tournament were equivalent for the FFW if San Jose was included, but exhibited a greater incidence of negative outcomes if San Jose was excluded. These outcomes taken together approximated those from the FFM. One noteworthy difference between the FFW and FFM results relates to the average net change in real income induced by the tournament. Recognizing the substantial caveat relating to the interpretation of a statistically insignificant outcome, the results indicate that the FFW generated on average a net gain in income equal to approximately $70 million dollars.

One possible explanation for this observed difference between the men's and women's tournament may be the choice of host cities. The FFW has tended to be held in cities that are not otherwise normally considered prime tourist or convention destinations, such as Norfolk, Virginia; Austin, Texas; and Knoxville, Tennessee. If these cities do not normally attract significant numbers of business or recreational travelers, the tournament will not crowd out these other visitors, leading to a smaller substitution effect. The FFM has more commonly been held in "destination" venues such as New Orleans or Seattle, cities that would be more likely to attract other visitor travel even in the absence of the sporting event.

Despite the paucity of statistically significant outcomes for the FF, we can use confidence intervals to develop a range for the likely impact for the FFM and FFW. If we use a 95% confidence interval to establish an estimated range of economic impact from the FF, expressed in 1999 dollars, the range of impact for the FFM is a $103.6 million positive impact to a $117.4 million negative impact. Using a 95% confidence interval, the economic impact of the FFW (excluding San Jose) ranges from a $168.1 million positive impact to an $86.5 million negative impact.

Several explanations exist for the range of economic impacts. First, the model does not explain all the variation in estimated income, and, therefore, not all the variation can be attributable to the FF. Information in Tables 3 and 4 indicates variation in the residuals that is non-trivial from year to year for some cities. Heteroscedasticity (variance of a disturbance term is not the same across observations), therefore, does pose a problem. We have addressed this problem by standardizing the residuals, and using that statistic in estimating p-values.[7] The heteroscedasticity problem is particularly apparent in cities such as Houston (FFM), Tacoma (FFW), and San Jose (FFW). It is arguable that each of these metropolitan economies is dominated by a cyclical industry—oil in Houston, forestry in Tacoma, and computer related activity in San Jose, for example—and that explains the variation in their disturbance terms.

Second, the FF is not held on consecutive days. The "crowding-out" effect covers a weekend and a Monday evening when the championship is played. It may be that this scheduling interferes with two weeks of alternative conference activity and thus induces a more substantial crowding-out effect than the number of games might otherwise suggest.

Third, the spending of residents of the host city may be altered to the detriment of the city's economy. Residents may not frequent areas in which the event occurs or the fans stay. Fourth, if the games are televised, some fans may stay inside to view the games rather than going out as they normally might.

It is important to realize that the host cities for the FF are large, diverse economies for which even a sports mega-event will account for a small portion of that city's annual economic activity. For example, in Lexington, Kentucky, the smallest host city in our sample, even a $100 million dollar increase in economic activity would raise the city GDP by only 1.28%, a statistically insignificant amount given the standard error of the estimates for the city's regression model. While a $100 million dollar impact would not emerge as statistically significant for any single city, one would expect that on average, host cities would have higher than expected economic growth in Final Four years. An average increase of $100 million over a large sample of cities may emerge as statistically significant even if the increase is not significant in any single city. While it is not uncommon for an individual city to deviate from its expected economic growth path by even $1 billion in a given year, it

Table 5
Probabilities for Various Levels of Economic Impact Induced by the FFM

Economic Impact	Probability of such an impact or greater having occurred
$103.6 million	5.00%
$100.0 million	5.55%
$78.45 million	10.00%
$50.00 million	19.47%
$25.00 million	31.41%
$ 0.00 million	45.83%
negative	54.17%

would be quite unusual for a sample of 18 or 32 cities to exhibit lower than expected economic growth if a mega-event should, according to boosters, be contributing up to $100 million in unanticipated economic benefits. Tables 5 and 6 provide estimates on the probabilities that various levels of economic impact will be induced by the FFM and FFW respectively based on the observed economic growth rates and the calculated standard errors. Inspiration for these tables derived from the claims for economic impact noted in the paper's introduction.

Table 6
Probabilities for Various Levels of Economic Impact Induced by the FFW

Economic Impact	Probability of such an impact or greater having occurred	Probability of such an impact or greater having occurred (excluding San Jose)
$150.0 million	25.25%	7.68%
$100.0 million	49.71%	21.42%
$99.50 million	50.00%	21.64%
$75.00 million	62.70%	32.25%
$50.00 million	74.39%	45.04%
$40.75 million	78.00%	50.00%
$25.00 million	83.50%	58.42%
$ 0.00 million	90.10%	70.80%
negative	9.90%	29.20%

As the estimates recorded in Table 5 indicate, our analysis of the FFM suggests that the event has a greater chance of imparting a negative economic impact than of benefiting the host communities. Gains of the magnitude indicated by the most optimistic promoters of the Men's Final Four are highly remote. The results presented in Table 6 of our analysis of the Women's Final Four are more encouraging for the boosters, with an economic impact of about $40 million being predicted in the model that excluded the San Jose outlier. It is significant to note, however, that an economic impact of zero for the FFW cannot be rejected at a reasonable level of certainty even including San Jose in the model.

One final set of calculations can be made with this data. We have previously noted that a major shortcoming of all *ex post* economic analyses of mega-events is the fact that even the biggest spectacles, such as the FF, have relatively small economic impacts compared to the size of the cities that host the event. Because of this fact, one should expect that any economic gains from hosting these events, should any gains exist, should be more likely to surface in smaller host cities. As mentioned previously, a $100 million increase in GDP represents 1.28% of Lexington's 1985 economy, while the same $100 impact represents merely 0.035% of New York City's 1996 GDP. Any economic benefit imparted by the FF would be likely to be obscured by natural but unpredictable variations in the New York City economy, but would be more liable to show up in Lexington's much smaller economy. Therefore, if the FF really does have a significant economic impact, there should be a significant negative correlation between city size and the difference between actual and predicted economic growth. In fact, the simple correlation between these two variables is −0.024, or almost nonexistent. The Spearman Rank-correlation between the two variables, which should account for any undue influence in the simple correlation statistic caused by particularly large host cities such as Los Angeles and New York City, is 0.067. Not only is the correlation nearly zero, in this case it actually has the incorrect sign. This result gives further credence to the idea that the economic impact of these events is small.

Similarly, one should expect that the number of visitors to the event should influence the total economic impact. Over the past 30 years, the FFM has been held in venues ranging from mid-sized basketball arenas holding 15,000 to 20,000 fans to large, indoor football stadiums that are converted to basketball arenas for the event. These stadiums can hold from 40,000 to 65,000 fans. If the boosters are correct, the larger the number of attendees, the larger the expected economic impact. If the adherents to the "crowding-out" hypothesis are correct, the larger number of attendees will simply result in a larger number of other visitors being crowded out of the metropolitan area. The economic impact, therefore, will be the same regardless of the size of the venue. In fact, the simple correlation between the estimated real dollar impact of the event and the number of attendees for the FFM is −0.007. The lack of correlation between the number of attendees and the observed economic impact suggests that bigger crowds don't lead to bigger gains, but simply lead to bigger displacements of regular economic activity.

CONCLUSIONS AND POLICY IMPLICATIONS

The NCAA Final Four tournaments for men and women have achieved sports mega-event status. Cities vigorously compete to host the Final Four because a perception exists that the event provides a financial windfall in the short run through exporting a sports service, and in the long run through image enhancement. This paper has analyzed the short-run economic impact. High-profile sporting events generally require substantial expenditures on a campaign to attract the event; state-of-the-art infrastructure; and security, which taken together generally imply a significant commitment of public resources. The ability of a city to attract a Final Four often depends on convincing a sometimes skeptical public that hosting the event generates economic profit. A motive for exaggerating the impact of a mega-event clearly exists, and that explains the purpose for this assessment of the impact of the NCAA basketball tournament finals for men and women.

The evidence suggests that the economic impact estimates provided by Final Four promoters routinely exaggerate the true economic impact of the event. The fundamental flaw in booster estimates pertains to underplaying the substantial substitution effects that accompany mega-sports events. In short, the event not only stimulates spending by nonresidents, it also reduces spending by other nonresidents and residents alike. An accurate assessment of first-round changes in net new spending induced by the Final Four is critical to precise renderings of its economic impact on the host city. The evidence presented suggests that neither the Final Four for Men or for Women boost the local economy much if at all. The highest probability corresponds to the event having a zero or negative economic impact for the FFM, and just over a 5% probability exists that the event will stimulate the host economy by more than the $100 million estimated by some event promoters. For the FFW, the results suggest a nearly 30% probability that the event will have a negative economic impact, and nearly an 80% probability that the event will generate an economic impact of $100 million or less. In an analysis of the Final Four for men over a 30-year period and for women over an 18-year period, only on two occasions did either event emerge as inducing a statistically significant change in the host city's real income. The consistency of the statistically insignificant findings coupled with low probabilities for achieving the economic benefit typically ascribed to the event by its advocates argue for restraint in committing substantial public resources to the event. The evidence indicates that the economic impact of the Final Four will more likely be the equivalent of a financial "air ball" than an economic "slam dunk."

NOTES

1. Scholars refer to the early 1980s as the post-federalist period. The Reagan administration had reduced federal revenue sharing, and, this development coupled with the flight of businesses from city centers, compelled a more entrepreneurial approach on the part of cities to their economic problems. These forces as well as financial developments in professional sports explain in large measure the spate of stadium, convention center, and hotel construction that has occurred in cities throughout the United States in the last two decades.

2. It could be argued that if multiple cities bid for the event, then the winning bid is likely to exceed the event's marginal revenue product. It is in the interest of the NCAA to encourage as many cities as possible to bid for its tournament.

3. It is not altogether clear whether occupancy rates increase during mega-events. It may be that the most popular convention cities, those most likely to host the Final Four, would experience high occupancy even if they are not successful in hosting them. Evidence, however, suggests that room rates increase substantially during sports mega-events, but questions regarding the final destination of those additional earnings remain.

4. It should be remembered that our intent here is not to focus on what accounts for all growth in cities. Rather our task is to determine how much a mega-event contributes to a city's economy. It is true that trend-adjusting does not provide any economic insight about those factors responsible for metropolitan growth, but adjusting for trends enables us to focus attention on a smaller component of growth for a city, which a mega-event may help explain.

5. It should be noted that the women's field has experienced a steady expansion in terms of the number of teams participating. In particular the field grew 32 to 40 teams in 1986, 40 to 48 teams in 1989, and 48 to 64 teams in 1994. This expansion is noteworthy for the purposes of this report because there arguably should be a positive correlation between the size of the FFW field and economic impact.

6. Growth rates for employment in the previous year were used to account for estimation problems created by a single aberrant year that could occur for a variety of reasons to include a natural disaster or a change in political parties with accompanying changes in fiscal strategies. Technically speaking, the model was more robust with this specification, and the values for the cross correlation coefficients did not suggest a multicollinearity problem.

7. The residuals in the "Difference" column in Tables 3 and 4 are divided by the standard deviation of the yearly residuals for the appropriate city. The mean of these standardized residuals is divided by the square root of 32 or 18 (the sample size for FFM and FFW, respectively) in order to find a t-statistic with 31 and 17 ($= n-1$) degrees of freedom. The resulting p-values shown in Table 5 assume normality of the residuals.

APPENDIX: CITIES AND YEARS USED TO ESTIMATE MODELS IN TABLES 3 AND 4

City	1969 Population	1969 Rank	1999 Population	1999 Rank	Wage Data availability	Region
Albany, NY	797,010	50	869,474	68	1969-1999	Mideast
Atlanta, GA	1,742,220	16	3,857,097	9	1972-1999	Southeast
Austin, TX	382,835	88	1,146,050	49	1972-1999	Southwest
Baltimore, MD	2,072,804	12	2,491,254	18	1972-1999	Mideast
Bergen, NJ	1,354,671	26	1,342,116	44	1969-1999 (State data 1969-1999)	Mideast
Birmingham, AL	718,286	54	915,077	65	1970-1999 (State data 1970-1971)	Southeast
Boston, MA	5,182,413	4	5,901,589	4	1972-1999	New England
Buffalo, NY	1,344,024	27	1,142,121	50	1969-1999 (Average of cities)	Mideast
Charlotte, NC	819,691	49	1,417,217	42	1972-1999	Southeast
Chicago, IL	7,041,834	2	8,008,507	3	1972-1999	Great Lakes
Cincinnati, OH	1,431,316	21	1,627,509	33	1969-1999	Great Lakes
Cleveland, OH	2,402,527	11	2,221,181	23	1969-1999	Great Lakes
Columbus, OH	1,104,257	33	1,489,487	40	1972-1999	Great Lakes
Dallas, TX	1,576,589	18	3,280,310	10	1972-1999	Southwest
Dayton, OH	963,574	42	958,698	63	1969-1999	Great Lakes
Denver, CO	1,089,416	34	1,978,991	25	1977-1999	Rocky Mountains
Detroit, MI	4,476,558	6	4,474,614	7	1976-1999	Great Lakes
Fort Lauderdale, FL	595,651	70	1,535,468	38	1969-1999 (State data 1988-1999)	Southeast
Fort Worth, TX	766,903	51	1,629,213	32	1976-1999 (State data 1976-1983)	Southwest
Grand Rapids, MI	753,936	52	1,052,092	58	1976-1999	Great Lakes
Greensboro, NC	829,797	48	1,179,384	47	1972-1999	Southeast
Greenville, SC	605,084	67	929,565	64	1969-1999 (State data 1969)	Southeast
Hartford, CT	1,021,033	39	1,113,800	52	1969-1999	New England
Honolulu, HI	603,438	68	864,571	69	1972-1999	Far West
Houston, TX	1,872,148	15	4,010,969	8	1972-1999	Southwest
Indianapolis, IN	1,229,904	30	1,536,665	37	1989-1999	Great Lakes
Jacksonville, FL	610,471	66	1,056,332	57	1972-1999 (State data 1988-1999)	Southeast
Kansas City, MO	1,365,715	25	1,755,899	28	1972-1999	Plains
Las Vegas, NV	297,628	116	1,381,086	43	1972-1999	Far West
Los Angeles, CA	6,989,910	3	9,329,989	1	1969-1999 (State data 1982-1987)	Far West
Louisville, KY	893,311	43	1,005,849	61	1972-1999	Southeast
Memphis, TN	848,113	45	1,105,058	55	1972-1999	Southeast
Miami, FL	1,249,884	29	2,175,634	24	1969-1999 (State data 1988-1999)	Southeast
Middlesex, NJ	836,616	47	1,130,592	51	1969-1999 (State data 1969-1999)	Mideast
Milwaukee, WI	1,395,326	23	1,462,422	41	1969-1999	Great Lakes
Minneapolis, MN	1,991,610	13	2,872,109	13	1972-1999	Plains
Monmouth, NJ	650,177	62	1,108,977	53	1969-1999 (State data 1969-1999)	Mideast
Nashville, TN	689,753	57	1,171,755	48	1972-1999	Southeast
Nassau, NY	2,516,514	9	2,688,904	16	1969-1999	Mideast
New Haven, CT	1,527,930	19	1,634,542	31	1969-1999 (Average of cities)	New England
New Orleans, LA	1,134,406	31	1,305,479	45	1972-1999	Southeast

APPENDIX (*Continued*)

City	1969 Population	1969 Rank	1999 Population	1999 Rank	Wage Data availability	Region
New York, NY	9,024,022	1	8,712,600	2	1969-1999	Mideast
Newark, NJ	1,988,239	14	1,954,671	26	1969-1999 (State data 1969-1999)	Mideast
Norfolk, VA	1,076,672	36	1,562,635	36	1972-1999 (State data 1973-1996)	Southeast
Oakland, CA	1,606,461	17	2,348,723	19	1969-1999 (State data 1969-1987)	Far West
Oklahoma City, OK	691,473	56	1,046,283	60	1969-1999	Southwest
Orange County, CA	1,376,796	24	2,760,948	15	1969-1999 (State data 1982-1987)	Far West
Orlando, FL	510,189	76	1,535,004	39	1972-1999 (State data 1988-1999)	Southeast
Philadelphia, PA	4,829,078	5	4,949,867	5	1972-1999	Mideast
Phoenix, AZ	1,013,400	40	3,013,696	12	1972-1999 (State data 1972-1987)	Southwest
Pittsburgh, PA	2,683,385	8	2,331,336	21	1972-1999	Mideast
Portland, OR	1,064,099	37	1,845,840	27	1972-1999	Far West
Providence, RI	839,909	46	907,795	66	1969-1999	New England
Raleigh Durham, NC	526,723	73	1,105,535	54	1972-1999	Southeast
Richmond, VA	673,990	60	961,416	62	1972-1999	Southeast
Riverside, CA	1,122,165	32	3,200,587	11	1969-1999 (State data 1982-1987)	Far West
Rochester, NY	1,005,722	41	1,079,073	56	1969-1999	Mideast
Sacramento, CA	737,534	53	1,585,429	34	1969-1999 (State data 1982-1987)	Far West
St. Louis, MO	2,412,381	10	2,569,029	17	1972-1999	Plains
Salt Lake City, UT	677,500	58	1,275,076	46	1972-1999	Rocky Mountains
San Antonio, TX	892,602	44	1,564,949	35	1972-1999	Southwest
San Diego, CA	1,340,989	28	2,820,844	14	1969-1999 (State data 1982-1987)	Far West
San Francisco, CA	1,482,030	20	1,685,647	29	1969-1999 (State data 1982-1987)	Far West
San Jose, CA	1,033,442	38	1,647,419	30	1972-1999 (State data 1982-1987)	Far West
Seattle, WA	1,430,592	22	2,334,934	20	1972-1999 (State data 1982-1999)	Far West
Syracuse, NY	708,325	55	732,920	73	1969-1999	Mideast
Tampa, FL	1,082,821	35	2,278,169	22	1972-1999 (State data 1988-1999)	Southeast
Tulsa, OK	519,537	74	786,117	71	1969-1999	Southwest
Washington, DC	3,150,087	7	4,739,999	6	1972-1999	Southeast
W. Palm Beach, FL	336,706	105	1,049,420	59	1969-1999 (State data 1988-1999)	Southeast

Complete data on population, income, and employment was available for all cities from 1969 to 1999. This implies that data on real income growth and on real income growth lagged one year was available from 1971 to 1999. Data regarding state and local taxes as a percentage of state GDP was available for all cities from 1970 to 1999, and was obtained from the Tax Foundation in Washington, DC. Wage data from the Bureau of Labor Statistics Current Employment Statistics Survey was available for cities as described above. When city data was not available, state wage data was used in its place. When possible, the state wage data was adjusted to reflect differences between existing state wage data and existing city wage data. When an MSA included several primary cities, the wages of the cities were averaged together to create an MSA wage as noted in the Appendix.

The "Oil Bust" dummy variable was included for cities highly dependent on oil revenues including Dallas, Denver, Fort Worth, Houston, New Orleans, Oklahoma City, and Tulsa. The variable was set at a value of 1 for boom years, 1974–1976 and 1979–1981, and at –1 for the bust years, 1985–1988. While this formulation does imply that each boom and bust is of an equal magnitude, the variable does have significant explanatory value nonetheless.

Each city was placed in one of eight geographical regions as defined by the Department of Commerce. The region to which each city was assigned is shown in the Appendix. Employment, income, and population data were obtained from the Regional Economic Information System at the University of Virginia, which derives its data from the Department of Commerce statistics.

Part IV
Labor Issues in College Sports

8

College Football and Title IX

Michael A. Leeds, Yelena Suris,
and Jennifer Durkin

INTRODUCTION

For all the controversy it has generated in the sports world, Title IX of the 1972 Education Amendments to the 1964 Civil Rights Act was not designed specifically to ensure gender equity in sports. Strictly speaking, Title IX prohibits institutions that receive federal financial assistance from excluding anyone from "any educational program or activity" on the basis of sex (see Educational Development Center, 1997; Seligman and Wahlbeck, 1999; and Zimbalist, 1999a). However, the impact of Title IX—and the controversy it has engendered—has been most evident in the sports realm. All agree that it has dramatically expanded athletic opportunities for girls and young women. Some go so far as to attribute American Olympic and World Cup triumphs, even the creation of two professional women's sports leagues—the WNBA in basketball and the WUSA in soccer—to Title IX. These advances have come at a high cost. Many colleges claim that the only way they could equalize opportunities for women and for men was by reducing opportunities for men. Several colleges have eliminated highly successful men's programs—such as the swimming and gymnastics teams at UCLA—and attributed their actions to Title IX (Lynch, 2001). Some sports, such as men's gymnastics and wrestling, are in danger of disappearing from college campuses, a trend some attribute to Title IX.

Despite or perhaps because of the fact that it seldom appears in any of the specific policies designed to comply with Title IX, intercollegiate football has figured prominently in the arguments surrounding gender equity in intercollegiate sports. Some see football programs, with their bloated squads and expenses, as a major impediment to gender equity. Others see football as a cash cow, without which the steps that have been taken toward gender equity would not be possible.

This paper clarifies the role that football programs play in subsidizing women's athletics. We show that some of the net revenues generated by major football programs do find their way into women's sports, though the figure is extremely small. We also show that expenditures on football programs come at the expense of women's athletics. The net impact of pursuing major intercollegiate football is thus negative unless the net revenues from football are extremely high.

In the next section, we provide a brief background on the impact of Title IX and how observers and researchers have regarded its relationship to major intercollegiate football programs. In Section III, we develop a theoretical model that shows why schools choose to spend so much more on football than on women's sports. The model, when combined with institutional detail, also predicts what factors lead some schools to have greater disparities in spending on men's and women's sports than others have. Finally, the model shows how profitable sports, like football, can be used to subsidize less profitable sports. Since Title IX directs schools to fund opportunities for women, one would expect schools to use the profits from football to subsidize women's athletic programs, allowing them to avoid the painful choices between cutting back the number of unprofitable women's sports or the number of unprofitable men's sports.

We test these hypotheses in Section V using data on colleges with Division I women's athletics programs, which we describe in Section IV. We find that, despite Title IX, schools have continued to underfund women's athletics and that even most profitable football programs provide little revenue for women's sports. A highly profitable program may still represent a drain on women's sports if the expenditures on the sport pull more resources away from women's sports than the profits provide. We thus build upon previous findings by including both expenditures and profits of the football program in the regression equation. A conclusion follows.

THE IMPACT OF TITLE IX—AND ATTITUDES
TOWARD IT

The impact of Title IX on intercollegiate women's sports was swift and impressive. Between the 1971–72 academic year and 1986–87, the number of women participating in intercollegiate sports more than quadrupled from 30,000 to over 120,000, and participation rates rose from 1.7% to 5.2%. Since then, however, the growth of women's sports has slowed dramatically. In 1997–98, 157,000 women participated in intercollegiate sports, corresponding to a participation rate of 5.5%. Since the mid-1980s, much of the gain women have made relative to men has come from the decline in the number of men participating in intercollegiate sports from 234,000 in 1997–98 to 239,000 in 1985–86 (figures from General Accounting Office, 2000). As a result, in the late 1990s, women still accounted for less than 40% of all college athletes and athletic scholarships (see Zimbalist, 1999a).

Some claim that the slowing gains by women stem from the ambiguous legal interpretations of Title IX's objectives. The courts have ruled that schools can satisfy the dictates of Title IX in any of three ways. They can provide athletic opportunities for women that are "'substantially proportionate' to the school's mix of male and female students" (Seligman, 1999, 520). Alternatively, they can show a history of increasing opportunities for women. Failing proportionality and good faith effort, they can simply show that the needs of women have been "fully and effectively accommodated." That is, schools can argue that they do not provide equal opportunities because the women at their school do not care to have them (see Seligman and Wahlbeck, 1999; Zimbalist, 1999a).

One of the roadblocks facing Title IX may stem from the financial strain that the rapid growth of women's athletics programs has placed on many athletic departments. The Chronicle of Higher Education collected data on expenditures from reports by colleges under the Equity in Athletics Disclosure Act (the Chronicle's data underlie much of the General Accounting Office report). These data show that in 1995–96, 290 of the 303 Division I women's programs operated at a deficit (see Naughton, 1997). Colleges have frequently responded to these fiscal pressures either by continuing to underfund women's athletics or by cutting back on unprofitable men's sports. These responses have engendered two very different attitudes toward football, the most profitable and most expensive of college sports.

Some see football, especially the "big-time" Division I-A programs, as a major impediment to implementing Title IX. (For an explanation of the Division I-A program, see the Appendix.) They claim that the large sums spent on big-time football prevent schools from meeting the provisions of Title IX. Some see no point in including football in Title IX calculations, since, in the words of Frank Deford, "[b]ig-ticket football is to sports what guinea pigs are to livestock" (Deford, 2000). According to this point of view, football is less an intercollegiate competition than an entertainment event. While they did not share Deford's view of sport as entertainment, football coaches did appear at a special Congressional hearing to appeal for special treatment of their sport in meeting Title IX standards. They claimed that including football in the mix would create unreachable targets for women's sports. Moreover, they expressed concern that de-emphasizing football in order to satisfy the dictates of Title IX would alienate football's audience and jeopardize its profitability. This, in turn, would reduce the spillovers that a successful football program provides to less profitable sports.

Advocates of this view see football as a cash cow from which less profitable women's sports can benefit. As a result, they object to cutting expenditures on football and to any policy that will make football less profitable. In the words of Calli Theisen Sanders, Associate Director of Athletics at the University of Alabama at Birmingham:

> Our [women's] scholarship budgets have increased. And when we talk about expanding our women's programs now it is not "if," it is "what and when." And it wouldn't have been that way without football. (Naughton, 1997)

Fleisher et al. (1992) assert that the surpluses generated by sports like football and basketball often subsidize sports that fail to cover their expenses. Similarly, Sperber (1990) claims that "big-time athletic departments" funded almost half of their women's sports with the profits of their men's programs. Conversely, when a football program fails to run the expected surplus—as has recently happened at the University of Minnesota—other sports feel the financial strain (Craig et al., 2001).

Rishe (1999) and Agthe and Billings (2000) provided empirical support for these claims. Using the data found in Naughton (1997), Rishe showed that profits from football underwrite unprofitable men's and women's sports. Agthe and Billings used NCAA data to show that the gap between Title IX dictates and actual compliance with Title IX was inversely related to the profits of the football team. They also found that state schools complied more fully with Title IX.

Data from Naughton and the NCAA show the impact of a "big-time" football program on an athletic department's finances. Over two-thirds (67.3%) of all the athletic departments in Naughton's sample lost money, with a median loss of $1,887,000. By contrast, almost two-thirds (61%) of the athletic departments that had Division I-A football programs made money, with a median profit of $970,000. Division I-A football programs ran a median profit of $1,173,000. This success did not extend to smaller-scale football programs, since football programs as a whole ran a median loss of $241,000.

A first glance at women's programs in the sample seems to support the "cash cow" view of major football programs. The higher profits associated with Division I-A football seemed to allow women's programs to run greater deficits. The median loss for all women's programs was $1,025,000, while the median loss for women's programs at schools with Division I-A football programs was $1,619,000. The result, as seen in Table 1, is that, on average, women's programs at schools with Division I-A football programs receive about $600,000 more than women's programs at other schools.

While women's programs at Division I-A schools receive more funding, their share of total athletic expenditures is smaller. Table 1 shows that the added expenditure on women's sports is dwarfed by a $1.5 million increase in spending on men's sports. The raw data thus do not provide clear evidence on whether big-time football helps women's athletics.

THEORETICAL FRAMEWORK

Since the turn of the century, colleges and universities have viewed football as a vehicle for raising their visibility (e.g., Lawrence, 1987). They have seen it as a way to instill pride in their alumni and to attract the attention of potential applicants (e.g., McCormick and Tinsley, 1987; Baade and Sundberg, 1996). Athletic departments help universities maximize the esteem with which the public at large regards them, what other studies have termed "prestige" (e.g., James, 1986). These models typically assume that schools maximize prestige by manipulating research budgets and expenditures on graduate programs. Theoretical models have so far ignored the role played by athletics in building the reputations of universities, a role acknowledged by the president of Oklahoma University in the 1950s, when he called upon the state legislature to build a university of which the school's football team could be proud.

We assume that an athletic department's contribution to the prestige of a university is a function of the quality of three sports: a generic women's sport, w; a generic men's sport, m; and football, f. We assume that the prestige function is twice continuously differentiable and additively separable in its arguments. We also assume that it displays diminishing marginal returns to the quality of each program:

$$\pi_i = \pi_i(Q_f, Q_w, Q_m) = \pi_{fi}(Q_f) + \pi_{wi}(Q_w)\pi_{mi}(Q_m)$$

$$\frac{\partial \pi_{ji}}{\partial Q_j} > 0, \quad \frac{\partial^2 \pi_{ji}}{\partial Q_j^2} < 0, \tag{1}$$

where π_i is the prestige accruing to institution i and Q_j is the quality of sport j, as measured in quality units ($j = w, m, f$). Additive separability is equivalent to assuming that the prestige generated by a school's football team does not affect the prestige generated by its other sports. While allowing for prestige spillovers would be more general, it would not alter the basic results.

If athletic departments maximized prestige subject to a pre-specified budget with no institutionally imposed constraints, they would spend much less on the less profitable sports or on the unproductive aspects of the more profitable sports. Fleisher et al. (1992) suggest that athletic directors try to spend any profits generated by their more popular sports in order to keep the revenue within the Athletic Department. This claim is a modified version of bureaucratic "budget maximization" first proposed by Niskanen (1968). We employ this observation by assuming that athletic departments face a zero profit constraint. (One could capture unprofitable Athletic Departments without altering the basic results by adding a fixed subsidy to the model.) Specifically, we assume that athletic departments maximize prestige subject to:

$$R_j^i(Q_f) + R_w^i(Q_w) + R_m^i(Q_m) = C_f^i(Q_f) + C_w^i(Q_w) + C_m^i(Q_m), \tag{2}$$

where $R_j^i(Q_j)$ is the revenue generated by sport j at institution i and $C_j^i(Q_j)$ is the price per quality unit of sport j to institution i. Quirk and Fort (1994) show that revenue for professional teams are a function of a team's performance. We assume a similar relationship between the quality of a school's team and the revenue it generates. In addition, we assume that increasing quality has a decreasing impact on revenue (we ignore "championship effects"), so $(dR^i)/(dQ_j) > 0$ and $(d^2R^i)/(dQ_j^2) < 0$ for all i and all j. Finally, we assume that the marginal cost of quality is positive and increasing $(dC^i)/(dQ_j) > 0$ and $(d^2C^i)/(dQ_j) > 0$.

Cost functions may vary from institution to institution because of varying efficiency in generating quality. A school with a particularly good coaching staff or with a tradition of winning teams has lower marginal costs than an otherwise equivalent school that lacks either characteristic. For example, the marginal cost curve for Penn State's football team lies below Temple's.

When a school maximizes its prestige function subject to its budget constraint (for simplicity we drop the school index, i), one gets the familiar first order condition:

$$\frac{\partial\pi/\partial Q_j}{\partial\pi/\partial Q_k} = \frac{dC_j/dQ_j - dR_j/dQ_j}{dC_k/dQ_k - dR_k/dQ_k}. \tag{3}$$

Intuitively, equation (3) says that the department sets the ratio of marginal benefits from any two sports (the marginal impact of quality on the school's prestige) equal to the ratio of net marginal costs (the difference between the marginal cost of quality and the marginal revenue of quality). It follows that a school will add quality units to sport j if equation (3) is upset by a rise in the marginal impact of quality in sport j on prestige, a rise in marginal revenue for sport j, or a fall in marginal cost for sport j, all things being equal.

Figure 1 shows a simple example in which two sports at a school share a common marginal prestige function and a common marginal revenue function (for simplicity set at 0) but have different marginal cost functions. Assume that the marginal cost of quality for sport j, however, is much lower

Figure 1
Differences in Price Lead to Differences in Funding Marginal Cost/
Marginal Prestige

Marginal Cost/Marginal Prestige

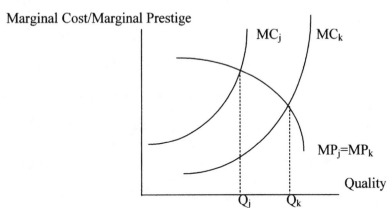

than the marginal cost of quality for sport k. In this situation, the athletic department will "purchase" more quality in sport j than in sport k. This may explain why some schools have "big-time" reputations in some sports but not in others (e.g., Georgetown University has a national profile in basketball but has a Division III football program).

Marginal prestige functions also vary among sports and schools. The pressure to maintain a high-profile football program is likely to be greatest among state schools, for whom the pressure to maintain a high profile with state legislators provides additional incentive to maintain prestige (e.g., Thelin, 1994). The added pressure helps explain why 21 of the Top 25 ranked football programs in final ESPN rankings for the 2001 season were state schools (the exceptions were Miami, Syracuse, Stanford, and Boston College).

Athletic departments have not willingly invested in women's sports because they do not believe that women's sports generate much prestige or support. In terms of our model, $(\partial \pi)/(\partial Q_f)$ is large, but $(\partial \pi)/(\partial Q_w)$ is close to zero for small values of $Q_f = Q_w$. As a result, athletic departments try to emphasize the quality of their football programs at the expense of women's sports, even when one ignores the implications for revenues (see Figure 2).

The high cost of equipment and facilities and the need for a relatively large number of players all make the marginal cost of quality much larger for football than most other sports. High marginal costs and the large amounts of quality purchased by football programs (especially in Division I-A) explain the prominence of football in athletic budgets and the disproportionate prestige that football generates.

Equation (3) shows that athletic departments apply a form of the equimarginal principle when purchasing quality for different sports. In addition,

Figure 2
Differences in Prestige Lead to Differences in Funding Marginal Prestige

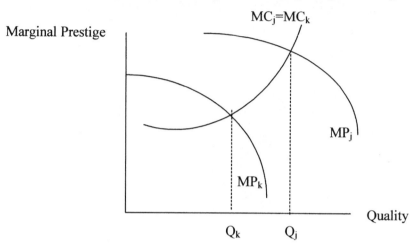

casual observation suggests that football generates much greater marginal prestige at $Q_f = Q_m = Q_w = 0$ than do either of the other sports. We shall also assume that football generates a profit over some range $0 < Q_f < Q^*$ while neither of the other sports generates a profit over any value of Q_m or Q_w. In such a setting, schools make football the foundation of their athletic program, investing in the quality of their football team until marginal prestige falls and net marginal cost rises enough for the school to want to spend an additional dollar on another sport. According to this model, the dollars invested in other sports come from the profits generated by football. The athletic department will invest in additional sports until the profits generated by football are dissipated.

Because women's sports and many men's sports generate little if any publicity and almost all of them lose money (see above as well as Fulks, 1998), schools would choose to provide little or no funding for women's sports or the lesser-known men's sports. Consider, for example, the limiting case in which the generic women's sport generates no prestige ($\partial \pi / \partial Q_w = 0$) and loses money ($dC_w / dQ_w - dR_w / dQ_w > 0$). Since devoting resources to football generates prestige and income, the athletic department will be at a corner solution, as it will never fund the women's sport (or the generic men's sport) because

$$\frac{\partial \pi / \partial Q_w}{\partial \pi / \partial Q_m} = 0 < \frac{dC_w / dQ_w - dR_w / dQ_w}{dC_m / dQ_m - dR_m / dQ_m}. \tag{4}$$

More generally, a school will willingly fund the women's sport only if football and the generic men's sport generate sufficiently low marginal prestige or sufficiently high net marginal costs at a low enough level of funding.

Title IX upsets the equilibrium in which women's sports are under-funded by effectively dictating that a portion of the profits generated by football goes towards women's sports. Since Title IX requires schools with equal numbers of male and female undergraduates to spend the same amount on men's and women's sports and since women's sports are generally unprofitable, schools that obey Title IX spend more of the profits from football on women's sports than they would if left to their own devices. If football generates more prestige and less net cost than the generic men's sport at the unconstrained optimal funding level, then the school will fund the women's sport in this model by cutting back on the generic men's sport. If the mandated expenses on the women's sport and the net marginal costs of the generic men's sport are high enough and the prestige generated by the generic men's sport is low enough, then the athletic departments will fund the women's sport by closing down the generic men's sport in order to satisfy Title IX. In terms of equation (3), this will be true if $\Omega > C(Q_m^*)$, where Ω is the mandated level of funding and Q_m^* is the optimal level of funding for the men's sport, and if

$$\frac{\partial \pi_m / \partial Q_m}{\partial \pi_f / \partial Q_f} < \frac{dC_m / dQ_m}{dC_f / dQ_f} - \frac{dR_m / dQ_m}{dR_f / dQf}. \tag{5}$$

at $Q_m = 0$.

The foregoing analysis leads to several testable hypotheses. According to the proportionality criterion, schools with a larger percentage of women in their undergraduate population should spend more on women's athletics. Similarly, schools that spend more on men's athletics should also spend more on women's athletics. The expenditure, however, may not rise equally across all sports. Athletic departments will sacrifice other men's sports in order to protect their football programs from the impact of Title IX. Finally, as noted above, many claim—and Rishe (1999) and Agthe and Billings (2000) have shown—that profits from football programs underwrite the losses from women's sports. This need not mean that football is good for women's sports. If the expenditure on football drains away more funds than the profits add, then even a profitable program may harm the opportunities available to women. We test these hypotheses with the OLS regression equation:

$$S_i = \beta' X_i + \tau \Pi_i + \rho \Upsilon_i + \mu Z_i + \psi M_i + \varepsilon_i, \tag{6}$$

where

S_i is expenditure on women's athletics at school i;
X_i is a vector of characteristics of school i;
Π_i is the profits generated by football at school i;
Υ_i is the percentage of the undergraduate student body that is female;
Z_i is expenditure on football at school i;
M_i is expenditure on other men's athletic programs at school i.

If schools obey the proportionality provision of Title IX then one would see $\rho > 0$ in equation (6). Moreover, schools will match greater expenditure on men's sports with greater expenditure on women's sports. If schools treat all men's sports alike in terms of Title IX, then equation (6) suggests that one should observe $\mu = \psi = 1$. If the school shields football from Title IX, then it will reduce other opportunities for men to fund opportunities for women $\mu \ll 1$ and $\psi > 1$. If a school uses profits from football to fund women's sports then the coefficient on the profits of the football program (τ) in equation (6) will be positive. Alternatively, if schools disregard Title IX, we should see that all these coefficients have values that are close to zero.

The vector of variables, X, represents the values that colleges hold and the pressures on them. For example, we have suggested above that state schools are more subject to pressures to spend money on highly visible men's sports. Similarly, schools that rely on educational reputation or research prowess for their reputation may feel less pressure to emphasize men's sports at the expense of women's sports. The vector also controls for scale effects, since larger schools may spend more on women's sports than smaller schools' teams even if they do not follow Title IX as closely as the smaller schools.

DATA

Data for the estimation came from several sources. The most important source came from Gender Equity in Athletics Disclosure Statements that the Chronicle of Higher Education obtained for all schools that had Division I women's athletics programs. These data were printed in a table accompanying Naughton (1997). These statements contained information on the number of male and female athletes and the operating and recruiting expenditures and sports-related aid provided to each group, excluding expenditures on football. They also reported the revenues and expenses of the school's football team.

We computed total expenditures by adding aid, operating expenses, and recruiting expenses. The profits for football are the difference between revenues and costs. As Quirk and Fort (1994) and Fleisher et al. (1992) point out, self-reported expenditures, revenues, and profits for professional and amateur sports enterprises can be easily manipulated to meet the immediate

Table 1
Relevant Means

Variable Name	All	Div I-A
% of Schools Ranked "Most Competitive"	0.04	0.03
% of Schools Ranked "Highly Competitive "	0.12	0.19
% of Schools Ranked "Moderately Competitive"	0.56	0.66
% of Schools Ranked "Somewhat Competitive"	0.06	0.03
% of Schools Ranked "Not Competitive"	0.22	0.09
% of Students Who Are Women	0.53	0.51
% of Schools That Are State-Affiliated	0.60	0.78
% of Schools That Are Church-Affiliated	0.10	0.06
% of Schools That Are Division I-A Programs	0.36	---
Net Revenues from Football ($000s)	1101	2834
Expenditures on Football ($000s)	1961	3096
Other Expenditures on Men's Athletics ($000s)	2967	4341
Expenditures on Women's Athletics ($000s)	1113	1619
Ratio: Expenditures on Women Relative to Men	0.568	0.403

ends of the franchise or athletic department. While we acknowledge the potential for error in these data, football programs that one would expect to be highly profitable (e.g., the University of Michigan or Florida) are indeed highly profitable while schools that one would expect not to be profitable (e.g., Temple) are not.

We used *Peterson's Guide to Four-Year Colleges and Universities* for information on the location, admissions criteria, affiliation, undergraduate enrollment, and research expenditures of each school. The status of the football programs came from the NCAA Web site (NCAA, 1997), which listed all colleges in each football classification (I-A, I-AA, II, and III).

Discarding schools that did not have football programs or that did not report relevant information left 201 observations. The sample size varies slightly between the regressions due to the availability of specific variables.

Table 1 shows that schools with Division I-A football programs differed from other schools. Division I-A schools were more concentrated in the mid-range "highly" and "moderately" competitive categories. Eighty-five percent of Division I-A schools fell into these categories, but only 68% of the sample as a whole did. Consistent with the predictions from Section III, Division I-A schools were much more likely to be state schools (78% vs. 60%).

The average profits for Division I-A programs were about 2.5 times greater than for the data set as a whole. Because a few highly profitable schools could drive the overall profit figures, we also looked at the broader distribution of profits. These figures provide even stronger evidence of a difference in profitability. For the data set as a whole, over 61% of the schools lost money on their football programs, with the median loss being about $241,000. In contrast, fewer than 30% of the Division I-A football programs lost money, with a median profit of about $1.18 million.

RESULTS

The coefficients shown in Table 2 paint a dim picture of Title IX compliance. We find strong evidence that universities as a whole have failed to comply with Title IX, though some types of schools have created more opportunities for women than have others. The results also show, as demonstrated in Table 3, that while women's programs have benefited from profitable football programs, football is generally a drain on women's athletics.

Table 2 shows that schools do not follow the proportionality provision of Title IX, as the estimate of ρ, the coefficient on the percentage of women in the undergraduate student body, is statistically insignificant at any reasonable level of significance. Schools do not fund their sports programs proportionately to other men's sports either, as ψ is small in absolute value. An increase of $1,000 in funding men's sports other than football results in only $282 of increased spending on women's sports.

The negative sign on μ shows that schools go even farther than simply insulating football from women's sports. It suggests that expenditures on football come at the expense of funding for women's sports. A $1,000 increase in spending on football actually reduces expenditure on women's sports by $112.

Table 2
Determinants of Expenditures on Women's Athletics

Variable Name	Coefficient	t-stat
Constant	102.190	0.38
Highly Competitive Admissions	220.194	1.30
Somewhat Competitive Admissions	61.132	1.25
State School	-154.188	2.50
% of Undergraduate Women	128.056	0.28
Number of Undergraduates	0.006	1.57
Number of Varsity Athletes	1.389	7.65
Expenditures on Football	-0.112	3.40
Expenditures on Other Men's Athletics	0.282	11.14
Net Revenue from Football	0.034	5.26
Observations	201	
Adjusted R^2	0.831	

A profitable football program does subsidize women's sports, but the subsidy is relatively small. A $1,000 increase in a football program's net revenues increases expenditures on women's sports by $34. Using the data from Table 1, a college with the average levels of expenditure on football and profits from football would reduce expenditures by over a quarter of a million dollars. In order for a school with the average level of expenditure on football to subsidize women's sports, its football program would have to show a profit of almost $10 million. As a result, only the most profitable football programs provide a net subsidy to women's sports.

We used the results in Table 2 to simulate the impact of football programs on the funding of women's sports. The results were striking. Only nine schools had football programs that actually subsidized women's sports. These schools and their estimated subsidies appear in Table 3. All of these schools have "big-time" Division I-A programs and six of them (Auburn, Florida, Penn State, Washington, Georgia, and Texas A&M) are among the 10 most profitable football programs in the sample.

Table 3 also shows the five programs with the largest estimated drain from women's sports. Again, all the schools are from Division I-A. Only one of these schools (Tulane), however, is among the least profitable in the sample. The low ranking of the other schools stems from the large expenses on

Table 3
Predicted Net Impact of Football Expenditures

Institution	Predicted Impact on Women's Athletics
Predicted Subsidies	
Auburn University	+$301,000
University of Florida	+$301,000
Penn State University	+$243,000
University of Washington	+$211,000
University of Georgia	+$177,000
Texas A&M University	+$121,000
University of South Carolina	+$37,000
Florida State University	+$12,000
Rice University	+$8,000
Five Largest Predicted Drains	
University of Kentucky	-$613,000
Tulane University	-$638,000
University of Oregon	-$656,000
University of Nebraska	-$940,000
University of California, Los Angeles	-$944,000

football relative to the profits they make. The negative impact of these football programs on women's sports is huge. Our model predicts that two of the programs (UCLA and Nebraska) take almost $1 million per year from women's sports. These profitable schools fail to support women's sports because they choose to do so, not because they cannot afford to support them.

As predicted in Section II, not all schools have the same attitude towards women's sports. All else equal, state schools spent over $150,000 less than other schools on women's athletics. This is consistent with our hypothesis that state schools face special pressures to emphasize more prestigious programs and, as a result, they, too, choose to ignore Title IX.

In Section II we theorized that schools that can easily generate prestige in other areas feel less pressure to excel in sports. The point estimate on admissions criteria in Table II support this hypothesis, as schools with the most stringent admissions criteria spend over $200,000 more on women's athletics. The coefficient, however, is not statistically significant.

In sum, we find that Division I-A football programs have an almost uniformly negative impact on offerings for women. On average, our model predicts that a football program drains almost $184,000 per year from women's sports. Ironically, our model predicts that the football program at the University of Alabama at Birmingham, which Calli Theisen Sanders cited as a positive force in implementing the goals of Title IX, drains almost $400,000 away from the school's women's athletic programs.

CONCLUSIONS

Whatever the gains experienced by women's sports over the last 25 years, we find ample evidence that schools continue to ignore Title IX guidelines regarding the funding of women's athletics. State schools are particularly recalcitrant.

We find little justification for the claim that women's athletics benefits from the profits flowing from big-time football programs and as a result should be sheltered from the reallocative aspects of Title IX. Schools with unprofitable football programs have no surplus to provide and reduce the funds available for women's sports. A profitable football program, however, is no guarantee that women's sports will receive adequate funding. Only a few of the most profitable football programs provide a positive net subsidy to women's athletics. Almost all other schools, some of them with highly profitable football programs, actually drain funding from women's athletic programs. Indeed, some of the nation's most prestigious and successful football programs have the most harmful impact drain on women's athletics. One is thus forced to conclude that many collegiate athletic departments view violating Title IX as an optimal strategy.

APPENDIX: AN EXPLANATION OF DIVISION I-A FOOTBALL

The NCAA divides most sports into Divisions I, II, and III. Division I consists of the largest, best-known programs (e.g., basketball at Duke or tennis at Stanford). Division III consists of the smallest programs that have no pretense of professionalism (e.g., basketball at Haverford or tennis at Swarthmore). Some schools may seek to emphasize some sports while relegating others to a more recreational status (i.e., Johns Hopkins is a Division I power in lacrosse but plays Division III basketball).

Football originally followed the same divisions as other NCAA sports. The growing revenues from television broadcasts led the largest and (generally) most profitable programs to try to gain greater control over the revenue they generated and to avoid having to share TV revenue with smaller programs. The result of this power grab was the subdivision of Division I schools into Division I-A and Division I-AA. A school's football program can be classified as Division I-A if it satisfies four criteria:

1. It maintains at least eight varsity intercollegiate sports, including football.
2. It schedules at least 60% of its games against Division I-A opponents.
3. It has averaged at least 17,000 in paid attendance at home games.
4. It uses a stadium for home games with at least 30,000 permanent seats.

Lawrence (1987) points out that, unlike other divisions, which at least have the pretense of promoting equality of competition, the separation of Division I-A from Division I-AA schools is typically based on criteria (3) and (4). These criteria relate strictly to the profitability of the program.

9

Measuring Marginal Revenue Product in College Athletics: Updated Estimates

Robert W. Brown and R. Todd Jewell

INTRODUCTION

Economists generally agree that National Collegiate Athletic Association (NCAA) rules have created a monopsony market in the recruitment of players for college football and men's basketball, the two "revenue-producing" sports for colleges. The NCAA limits compensation to players, restricts their mobility between schools, and controls championship competition. As a result, players' marginal revenue products exceed their effective compensation—which amounts to the value of an athletic scholarship and a small amount of outside earnings—so that colleges capture economic rents from players. Economists have offered few empirical estimates of the revenues generated by college athletes, and for good reason: The lack of reliable data on athletic revenues and the problem of measuring player skill levels make it difficult to relate college sports revenue to player productivity.[1]

Brown (1993, 1994) provides the first econometric estimates of the rents generated by college athletes. Put simply, those papers estimate the marginal revenue product (MRP) of NCAA football and basketball players by regressing a college team's 1988–89 revenues on the number of its "premium players," defined as a college player who is drafted into the National Football League (NFL) or the National Basketball Association (NBA), holding constant other factors that influence revenues. Professional draft data proxies the skill level of an individual college football or basketball player: Each year professional sports teams search for new players to draft from college teams;

thus, a drafted player is one of the most skilled college players. Brown (1993) estimates that the MRP of a premium college football player (i.e., a future NFL draftee) exceeds $500,000 in annual revenues for his college team. A premium college basketball player (i.e., a future NBA draftee) generates approximately $1,000,000 in annual revenues for his college team (Brown, 1994).

In this paper, we add to this literature by estimating a college athlete's MRP using more recent and more extensive revenue data reported by *The Kansas City Star* for college football and basketball teams during the 1995–96 seasons. Updating Brown's estimates is important for several reasons. First, the debate surrounding the economic exploitation of college athletes remains at the core of college athletic reforms. Given the paucity of empirical estimates, economists can contribute greatly to this debate to the extent that they can offer a reliable and consistent empirical literature. Second, Brown's 1988–89 data were collected shortly after the 1984 Supreme Court case that ruled NCAA restrictions on college football television appearances violated antitrust legislation.[2] This ruling effectively deregulated the market for TV appearances by college teams, stimulating an intense competition among schools to attract lucrative television contracts. Ultimately, the Court's ruling provided the catalyst for the creation, and then the demise, of the College Football Association. Later in the 1990s, the ruling may have contributed to realignment toward super-conferences, the Bowl coalition arrangement, and more lucrative television contracts, all of which have presumably put upward pressure on athletic revenues, at least for some schools.

Third, Brown's data contain information from less than one-half of NCAA Division I-A schools, each collected on an individual basis from the athletic departments or institutions themselves.[3] Private institutions are not required by the Freedom of Information Act to release revenue information, which limited the potential sample to mostly public universities. In addition, due to the sensitive nature of the data and time costs involved in gathering the information, not all public institutions made data available. In 1997, *The Kansas City Star* gathered a more exhaustive set of college athletic revenue data from the 1995–96 season, collected in an 18-month study that benefited from *The Star*'s greater availability of resources to access federal open records requests. These data contain information on nearly all Division I-A programs, both public and private universities, creating a much larger sample with which to estimate MRP for college student athletes.

The paper proceeds by summarizing the estimation approach in Brown (1993, 1994) and Brown and Jewell (1995). We follow with a description of the 1995–96 data and then compare these data to those in the earlier studies. Finally, we report the updated MRP estimates of premium college athletes in football and basketball. The results generally support Brown's estimates: Premium college football and basketball players generate revenues in excess of their effective compensation and, moreover, the estimates are similar in size. Thus, our results strengthen and quantify the argument that the NCAA extracts monopsony rents from student athletes.

METHODOLOGY AND DATA

We assume that a college team's revenues are a function of its skill level, the quality of its opponents, its market demand characteristics, and its past success. A team's total skill level is the sum of the individual skill levels of each player it recruits. The greater number of premium players that a team acquires increases its total team skill which, in turn, generates additional revenues. Expending additional recruiting effort attracts a greater number of premium players, but there are also costs incurred during recruiting. We assume that college athletic programs weigh the revenues and costs in choosing a recruiting effort level to maximize profits. For any given effort level, however, the number of premium players a team acquires is a function of its team's pool of potential recruits, its past success, and the quality of its opponents. First, teams located near larger pools of potential recruits are able to acquire more premium players, other factors constant. Second, a successful team that gains exposure from a top ranking during previous seasons can more easily attract more premium players. Third, better players are attracted to teams that play stronger opponents.

Following Brown (1993, 1994), we estimate the marginal revenue product of a premium college player by using professional draft data to represent college player skill-level and then regress team revenues on the number of players drafted. This provides a measure of the MRP of acquiring one more of the most-skilled college football or basketball players. However, the skill level of the players acquired by a college team is endogenous to its recruiting effort: Since the level of recruiting effort is a function of teams' market and recruiting characteristics, the number of players drafted from a college team would be correlated with the error term. A two-stage estimation accounts for the endogeneity in acquiring recruits. First, we estimate a draft equation using the number of players drafted from each college team as the dependent variable. This is a measure of a premium college player's skill level which, in turn, is a function of a team's recruiting effort, market and recruiting characteristics, and pool of potential recruits. Second, team revenues are estimated as a function of the fitted values of a team's number of players drafted, controlling for market characteristics and opponents' team skill levels.

Total revenue data are gathered from the *Kansas City Star* and are for the 1995 season in football and the 1995–96 season in basketball. For eighteen months, a team of reporters from the *Star* traveled across twenty-three states, conducting over one thousand interviews and collecting financial, academic, and legal documents from schools. Invoking state and federal open records requests, they were able to collect records from most Division I-A schools. Our sample uses data on all Division I-A schools for which either football or basketball revenue data were collected.

College player performance is measured using professional draft data. We include information on players who are drafted in 1996, 1997, and 1998. A 1995 roster might include players who will be drafted in the spring of 1996, as well as the following 1997 and 1998 drafts. For example, a premium sophomore player contributes to 1995 team revenues but may not be drafted until 1998. Including data from only the 1996 draft would overlook this player's contributions. Freshmen student athletes on a 1995–96 team are excluded in the draft measure, unless the student athlete left school early for the professional draft; we assume that a student athlete who leaves school early is highly productive as a freshman. The NBA-draftee variable is the number of future draftees (in NBA drafts 1996, 1997, and 1998) from a college basketball team's 1995–96 roster. The NFL-draftee variable is the number of future draftees (in NFL drafts 1996, 1997, and 1998) from a college football team's 1995 roster.

Table 1 compares sample means of the new 1995–96 data with the 1988–89 sample reported in Brown (1993, 1994). Average revenues for the basketball and football samples were higher in 1995, possibly indicating that more money is going into college sports: The 1995–96 sample shows football revenues are 5.9% higher than in the 1988–89 sample, while 1995–96 basketball revenues are 29% higher than in 1988–89 (the consumer price index rose 18.6% between 1989 and 1995). Moreover, the average number of future NFL draftees is 2.99 fewer (or 37%) than in 1988–89, and the average number of future NBA draftees is 0.54 fewer (or 34% fewer) than

Table 1
Comparison of Data Sets

	1988-89 Data	1995-96 Data
Total Football Revenues Per Team	$5,399,351 (4,004,574) $n = 39$	$5,718,326 (5,241,234) $n = 87$
Total Basketball Revenues Per Team	$1,792,458 (1,554,435) $n = 46$	$2,317,949 (1,974,468) $n = 95$
Number of Future NFL Draftees Per Team	8.03 (5.24) $n = 39$	5.04 (4.76) $n = 87$
Number of Future NBA Draftees Per Team	1.57 (1.52) $n = 46$	1.03 (1.27) $n = 95$

Table 2
Descriptive Statistics

Variable	Description	Mean	Standard Dev.
MSA	1995 population of nearest Metropolitan Statistical Area	2,177,372	3,757,942
STATEPOP	1995 State population	9,549,741	8,405,382
PAC10	Pacific 10 Conference	0.11	0.31
BIG10	Big 10 Conference	0.09	0.29
BIG8	Big 8 Conference	0.05	0.22
BIGEASTFB	Big East Conference (football)	0.03	0.18
BIGEASTBB	Big East Conference (basketball)	0.07	0.26
SEC	Southeastern Conference	0.09	0.29
ACC	Atlantic Coast Conference	0.09	0.29
SWC	Southwest Conference	0.07	0.26
BBRANK9294	Basketball Average AP Rankings 1992-94	2.48	4.36
FBRANK9294	Football Average AP Rankings 1992-94	2.92	5.37
BBRANK94	Final Basketball AP Ranking 1994	2.56	5.84
FBRANK94	Final Football AP Ranking 1994	3.12	6.63

in 1988–89; thus, the 1995–96 data may contain a greater number of less-skilled teams than the 1988–89 data do. Table 2 provides descriptions and sample statistics for the remaining variables.

RESULTS

To control for the endogeneity of a college team's future draftees, we estimate a predicted value of draft picks in a first-stage estimation. The number of draft picks is a discrete variable taking on relatively small values, or count data, so that OLS estimates will have undesirable properties. Instead, we use a Poisson regression in the first-stage estimation and compute a predicted value based on the results. The results of the first-stage estimation are reported in Table 3.[4] From the data obtained from the *Kansas City Star*, we include teams that competed in NCAA Division I-A football in the NFL-Draft regression (n = 87) and those that competed in Division I basketball in the NBA-Draft regression (n = 95).

College teams located near larger pools of potential recruits can attract better players with any given level of recruiting effort. We measure recruiting

Table 3
Draft Equation Coefficient Estimates Poisson Regression (Standard
Errors in Parentheses)

Variable	NFLDRAFTEE $n = 87$	NBADRAFTEE $n = 95$
constant	1.79994 (0.37268)	-15.0740 (1699.91)
MSA	-5.29e-08*** (2.03e-08)	-2.59e-08 (3.74e-08)
STATEPOP	2.11e-08*** (7.72e-09)	1.72e-08 (1.72e-08)
FBRANK9294	0.05537*** (0.00794)	
BBRANK9294		0.09789*** (0.01920)
pseudo R²	0.3806	0.2191

**Significant at 5%.
***Significant at 1%.

pool characteristics with the population of the state where the school is located.[5] Past team success attracts premium players through expanded exposure. We capture this effect by calculating average weekly Associated Press (AP) Top-25 rankings for the three seasons prior to the 1995–96 seasons, the period in which players made their recruiting choices. During any particular week, a number one ranking earns a team 25 points, a number two ranking earns 24 points, and so on. Cumulative point rankings were divided by total weeks, yielding an average weekly point ranking: An average ranking of 15 can be interpreted as a number 10 average ranking in weekly polls over these seasons. We measure market demand characteristics, or the ability to attract a fan base, with the population of the nearest Metropolitan Statistical Area (MSA) to the school. We also include categorical variables for each conference to control for the effect of conferences in attracting players, since better players may be attracted to teams that compete in stronger conferences.[6]

As reported in Table 3, the draft equation estimates for both college football and college basketball teams show that teams in more populous states have more premium players, although this effect is only significant for football. In addition, teams with higher rankings during the recruiting period obtained more future draftees. The latter result is as expected and is important, since the ranking variable serves as an exclusion restriction to identify the second-stage estimates from the first-stage estimates.

Marginal Revenue Product Estimates

Table 4 presents the marginal revenue products of a college football player and college basketball player from OLS regressions.[7] In each case, team revenues are regressed on the fitted values of the number of future draftees (from the first-stage regression), controlling for market potential and the quality of the team's opponents. We proxy market potential with the population

Table 4
Marginal Revenue Product Estimates (Bootstrapped Standard Errors in Parentheses)

Variable	1995 Football Revenues $n = 87$	1995-96 Basketball Revenues $n = 95$
constant	1,091,955 (785,183)	891,122*** (260,964)
MSA/1 million	49,952 (149,616)	-8,586 (56,601)
NFLDRAFTEE	406,914** (179,746)	
NBADRAFTEE		1,194,469*** (278,512)
FBRANK94	214,828* (122,336)	
BBRANK94		47,666 (50,406)
PAC10	3,921,891* (2,267,883)	-472,557 (461,557)
BIG10	4,326,320*** (1,255,231)	1,560,171* (610,051)
BIG8	1,229,364 (1,598,000)	-19,269 (493,532)
BIGEASTFB	294,213 (3,189,366)	
BIGEASTBB		-1,208,661 (978,710)
SEC	6,395,138*** (1,691,822)	794,152* (467,490)
ACC	1,509,459 (1,600,363)	578,091 (720,656)
SWC	2,133,334** (1,001,533)	-630,413** (308,513)
adjusted R^2	0.6168	0.4632

*t-statistic significant at 10%.
**t-statistic significant at 5%.
***t-statistic significant at 1%.

of the nearest MSA; dummy variables measuring major conference affiliation control for the quality of opponents and for any effects of conference on attracting fan interest or television revenues. In addition, we include a team's final AP ranking in 1994 to control for the impact of previous year performance on ticket sales, especially on season ticket sales.

The results reported in Table 4 suggest that the quality of a college basketball or football team (as measured by the number of premium-quality players) has a significantly positive effect on team revenues. In the 1995 NCAA football season, another future NFL-draftee increased revenues by over $400,000; in the 1995–96 NCAA basketball season, another future NBA draftee increased revenues by over $1 million.

Recent success does not significantly impact basketball revenue and has only a marginally positive effect on football revenue; the draft measures pick up most of the effect of team quality. Major conference affiliation appears to affect athletic revenues, although it is unclear whether this is a result of exposure or overall conference quality. However, certain "power conferences" have greater potential for generating revenues. Specifically, the Pac 10, Big 10, Southeastern, and Southwest Conference generated significantly more football revenues than did other conferences in 1995, while the Big 10 and Southeastern Conferences generated greater basketball revenues. Interestingly, the Southwest Conference generated significantly less basketball revenues than other conferences in 1995–96. Thus, the merger of the Big 8 Conference and the four largest Southwest Conference schools in 1996 (to form the Big 12 Conference) may have benefited the Big 8 schools in terms of football revenues, but it probably did not positively influence basketball revenues.

CONCLUSION

Our focus in this paper is on the MRP estimates. Brown (1993) reports MRP results for a premium college football player ranging from $538,760 to $646,150. The results reported in this paper suggest that the MRP of a premium player for the 1995 NCAA football season was $406,914, or about 24% less than the lower end of Brown's estimates. The lower MRP of college football players may simply result from the fact that Brown's 1988–89 data included somewhat more successful programs. For basketball, our results suggest that the MRP of a premium player during the 1995–96 season was $1,194,469, compared to Brown (1994) estimates ranging from $871,310 to $1,283,000. So for basketball players, our estimate falls near the upper end of Brown's previous estimates.

Our updated MRP estimates from these 1995–96 data underscore Brown's earlier estimates: Athletic departments extract sizeable monopsony rents from college football and basketball players. Given that the NCAA limits effective compensation for student athletes, our estimates suggest that a college program can extract nearly $400,000 from a premium college football player and over $1 million from a premium college basketball player per year. These rents, in turn, often amount to transfers to coaches and administrators in the form of higher salaries as well as to support non–revenue producing sports or even academic programs.

The literature on college sports concentrates on the revenue-producing sports: football and men's basketball. However, due to more stringent application of Title IX in college sports programs, women's college sports have seen a substantial growth in recent years. In addition, the late 1990s saw the start of a new professional women's basketball (WNBA) league. Thus, we may expect to see a steady growth in the amount of money flowing into NCAA women's basketball in the future; since the rules for remuneration of athletes are the same across gender, we would expect college athletic programs to reap the majority of this increase in revenues at the expense of female student athletes.

NOTES

1. For a counterargument, see McKenzie and Tullock (1994), Chapter 24, pages 352–373. In addition, some argue that student athletes are "paid" by having the opportunity to get a college education. Student athletes who graduate realize more future income in the non-sports labor market than do those who do not graduate. However, given the low graduation rates for some college programs, future income potential may not be an important issue. See Sheehan (1996), Chapter 12, pages 286–312 for a calculation of the "wages" paid to student athletes. Leeds and von Allmen (2002) and Zimbalist (1999a) discuss college athletic markets. Brown (1996) estimates the additional revenues generated by special-admission athletes, and Brown and Jewell (1994, 1995, 1996) estimate racial differences in revenue-generating potentials of college athletes and related NCAA policies. McKenzie and Tullock (1994, Chapter 24, pages 352–373) provide a counterargument for NCAA rules. In this paper, the term "basketball" refers to men's college basketball.

2. *NCAA v. The University of Oklahoma and The University of Georgia.*

3. In Brown (1993, 1994, 1996), Division I-A schools are those that compete in the highest levels of NCAA competition in both football and basketball, of which there were approximately 103 in 1988–89. The number of top-level college athletic programs has increased slightly since then.

4. We also used OLS and the negative binomial regression to form predicted values. The results are not substantially different from those reported in this paper, except that an OLS first-stage estimation leads to larger coefficients on draft picks in the second-stage estimation.

5. Brown (1993, 1994) included a recruiting-pool variable developed by Rooney (1987) from 1971–72, 1976–77, and 1980–81 college rosters to calculate the percentage of players produced in each state relative to the state's athletic programs. Updated measures are unavailable, so we substitute state population for this variable; Brown and Jewell (1995) take a similar approach to estimate racial differences in revenues generated by college basketball players.

6. For the sake of brevity, we do not report the coefficients for all the conferences in Table 3. However, as expected, better conferences do attract significantly more premium players. In addition, varying the number and type of conference included as independent variables does not change the estimation in any meaningful manner: It appears that past rankings are driving most of the estimation results.

7. The standard errors in the second-stage estimation must be corrected since we are using a predicted value as a regressor. This is accomplished using bootstrap techniques. That is, the standard errors reported in Table 4 are bootstrapped from the original estimates.

10

Participation in Collegiate Athletics and Academic Performance

John Fizel and Timothy Smaby

INTRODUCTION

The stereotype of the "dumb jock" seems to have coincided with the advent of collegiate sports. Similarly, so began the tales of the unethical means by which many varsity athletes are recruited and kept eligible. Revelations such as falsified transcripts, credit for phantom courses, surrogates for tests, phony test scores, and illiterate athletes have continually tarnished the reputation of college sports (Bergmann, 1991; Sperber, 1990; Telander, 1989). These violations appear to have been exacerbated by the financial climate of contemporary sports. Winning programs attract lucrative television money, bowl and tourney bids, alumni donations, and high attendance figures. While coaches may publicly espouse that their athletes are students first and athletes second, they and their institutions have a strong financial interest in recruiting good players and keeping them eligible by whatever means possible (Knight Foundation Commission, 1991; Lederman, 1991).

Historically, the organization responsible for policing collegiate athletic programs, the National Collegiate Athletic Association (NCAA), had focused on violations of amateurism—such as athletes receiving financial inducements to play—and neglected the investigation of charges that athletes might be receiving an inferior education. Recently, however, the NCAA has enacted reforms designed to put the "student" back into "student athlete." Propositions 48 and 42 define specific academic eligibility criteria for freshmen athletes. These criteria consist of a sliding scale that focuses on the grade point average earned in 13 core high school subjects and a score on either the SAT or the ACT. Those who fall short of the standards are not able to participate, but can earn eligibility if a 1.8 GPA (out of 4.0) is maintained over 24 credits during their freshman year of college.

The NCAA has also limited athlete practice and conditioning time so that more attention could be devoted to academics. Student athletes are limited to 20 hours of practice per week, four hours per day, and a maximum of six days of practice per week. Out-of-season conditioning activities are limited to eight hours per week.

Finally, graduation rates for athletes in all sports must be publicly available. As a result, incoming athletes can be aware of the typical educational outcomes of the institution.

What effect have these reforms had on the relationship(s) between athletics and academics? Research to date typically suggests that athletic participation complements rather than undermines academic performance. Successful athletic programs have been shown to increase student interest in a given institution. The increased interest is reflected in increased applications, which permits admission personnel to be more selective in setting entrance standards. Thus, freshman classes at universities with successful athletic programs have higher average SAT scores than do freshman classes at universities with less successful programs (Bremmer and Kesserling, 1993; McCormick and Tinsley, 1987). This effect is more pronounced for big-time football programs than for big time basketball programs (Tucker and Amato, 1993). Participation in successful athletic programs also tends to increase graduation rates (Tucker, 1992; Lederman, 1991). Again, basketball participation may be an exception (Lederman, 1991). However, faculty academic performance, when measured by research output, is reduced as football success increases (Shughart, Tollison, and Goff, 1986).

Although previous studies provide important insights into the relationships between athletics and academics, they focus on the college in aggregate. They largely ignore the individual student athlete and the time allocation decisions that these individuals must make in attempting to perform admirably on the field and in the classroom. The purpose of this study is to focus on the individual athlete. Rather than examining the effects of a successful sports program on the academic performance of an entire collegiate class, we examine the effects of athletic participation on the individual student's grade point average.

MODEL OF ACADEMIC ACHIEVEMENT

Ascertaining the effect of athletic participation on a student's grade point average requires a model of academic achievement. It must capture the characteristics of the student and his/her environment. We specify the following:

$$\text{GPA} = a_0 + a_1 \text{ Human Capital} + a_2 \text{ Environment} + a_3 \text{ Support} + a_4 \text{ Activitics} + \varepsilon$$

where GPA is cumulative grade point average for each student.

Human Capital

Human capital variables include student SAT score, age, and gender. SAT score measures a student's academic capabilities upon entering college. Age is a proxy for the maturity of the student. Both are expected to be positively related to GPA. Gender, which takes a value of 1 for males and 0 for females, attempts to capture any inherent differences, should any exist, in male and female academic achievement.

Environment

The academic environment of the student includes the university environment and the home/community environment. Student GPAs may be expected to differ depending on the student's choice of major/college. While unable to make *a priori* judgments as to how a particular college choice may affect GPA after accounting for the many other factors in our achievement model, we do acknowledge that different colleges have different average GPAs, and that students often claim that certain curricula are easier than others. Student semester standing should also affect GPA, with an increase in semester standing increasing GPA. As students continue in a university they become more comfortable with their environment, have the opportunity to improve study habits, and become more focused in their educational studies and goals.

Two variables are used to describe characteristics of a student's home/community environment.[1] An increase in the median household income (MedInc) for a student's hometown suggests more educational opportunities available to the student and/or more tax revenue available to support the student's secondary education. Each would imply a higher expected university GPA. The expectations for the percent of the hometown population that is urban (PopUrb) are less clear. Anecdotally, urban environments are often associated with larger class sizes, higher crime, and harsher learning milieus, but are also associated with faster maturation by their inhabitants.

Support

Student support is the percent of full cost (as defined by the university) covered by athletic scholarships (AthlSchol), academic scholarships (AcadSchol), loans, grants, and work study. All but work study should allow students more time to pursue their studies and enhance academic performance.

Work study represents time spent on jobs in lieu of studying and therefore may limit scholastic achievement.

Activities

Data were limited concerning student activities. Variables indicating whether a student was an initiate or a pledge are used to indicate extracurricular participation in fraternities or sororities. Other extracurricular activities include participation in club sports. Women club sports (WClub) include bowling, cycling, equestrian, racquetball, rifle, rugby, alpine skiing, and soccer, whereas men club sports (MClub) include bowling, boxing, cycling, ice hockey, rifle, racquetball, rugby, alpine skiing, and volleyball. Participation in varsity sports is the key activity identified in our model. Varsity participation is the basis for defining two variables: participation in revenue-producing sports (RevAthl) and participation in non-revenue-producing sports (NoRevAthl). The revenue-producing sports are men's football, men's basketball, and women's basketball. Varsity participation is also desegregated into 13 different female and 13 different male sports programs.[2] MultiVar is used to identify individuals who participate in multiple varsity sports.

THE DATA

Data were compiled for all spring 1995, full-time baccalaureate students at Penn State University at University Park (PSU). PSU's Offices of Administrative Systems, Financial Aid, Registrar, and Student Information Systems are the sources of these data. A total of 19,566 students, including 583 varsity athletes, were identified for our sample after deleting records with missing information.

ACADEMICS AND ATHLETICS: PRELIMINARY ANALYSIS

Key concerns of the academic community are preferential treatment in admissions (or recruitment) for athletes, and academic subsidies for athletes to enhance retention and eligibility. The data in Table 1 addresses the first of these concerns. It reports average SAT scores for all students and various varsity athlete subgroups. The average SAT score of 989 for athletes is less than the overall student average of 1,030. This difference is more pronounced for women athletes (977) than for male athletes (996), and is more pronounced for athletes in revenue-producing sports (927) than for those in non-revenue sports (989). Participants in 20 of the 26 reported sports have SAT averages below the average for all students. The two lowest SAT averages are for participants in women's basketball (877) and men's football (914), both revenue-producing sports. Therefore, athletes are at a

Table 1
SAT Averages by Group

Student Group	N	Avg. SAT	Std. Dev. SAT	Student Group	N	Avg. SAT	Std. Dev. SAT
All Students	19566	1030	172	WSoccer	18	949	132
All Athletes	583	989	146	WinTrack	41	977	127
Male Athletes	369	996	150	WCross Cntry	18	967	136
Female Athletes	214	977	138	MBaseball	26	955	138
RevAthl	119	927	143	MBaskball	18	1021	143
NoRevAthl	466	1005	143	MFence	12	1012	176
WBaskball	9	877	78	MFootball	92	914	140
WFence	11	1104	180	MGolf	14	1039	91
WFldHockey	17	924	124	MGymnast	7	1076	185
WGolf	14	979	139	MLacross	39	1042	117
WGymnast	16	994	135	MSwim	23	1027	161
WLacross	22	970	113	MTennis	11	965	115
WSwim	27	995	132	MOutTrack	58	1058	136
WTennis	9	952	173	MVllyBall	15	1057	130
WOutTrack	42	981	127	MSoccer	20	1020	164
WVllyBall	12	1021	120	MWrestle	34	988	166

Table 2
College GPA and Enrollment

College (GPA)	% Athlete	% Student
Education (3.18)	9.09	6.83
Health, Human Dev. (2.97)	23.16	13.91
Arts and Architecture (2.93)	1.37	4.76
Business Admin. (2.92)	12.69	14.33
Sciences (2.92)	4.46	9.22
Liberal Arts (2.91)	16.30	14.67
Communications (2.89)	3.60	5.30
Engineering (2.83)	10.12	16.32
Earth, Mineral Science (2.78)	1.72	2.64
Agriculture (2.72)	2.57	6.56
Undergrad Studies (2.58)	14.92	5.44

Note: GPA is estimated holding constant SAT. This is done through calculating the fitted value for GPA (at the mean SAT) by estimating the following regression equation: GPA = $b_0 + b_1$ SAT + b_3 College. Using actual GPA gave similar qualitative results.

disadvantage relative to other students in terms of expected academic achievement. As a result, retention and eligibility may be a concern.

Do athletes then major in easier curricular programs to offset their SAT disadvantage? Table 2 provides data necessary to address this question, including the average student GPA for each college, and the percentage of athletes and total students enrolled in that college. Easy curricula, or "grade-inflated" curricula, should be associated with higher average student GPAs. In the two colleges with the highest estimated GPAs, athletes enroll at a disproportionately higher rate than do other students.

Athletes do appear to take "easier" courses to enhance their level of "academic achievement." The clear exception is the 14.92% of athletes who enroll in the Division of Undergraduate Studies, which has the lowest average GPA. However, this college is only for freshmen and sophomores who have yet to declare a major, so the data suggest that a larger proportion of athletes are not making significant progress toward their degrees. For the athletes that have declared a major, many attempt to offset their SAT disadvantage with an easier curriculum.

ESTIMATING THE MODEL OF ACADEMIC ACHIEVEMENT

The data in the previous section provide evidence that the academic potential for athletes is lower than that for other students (i.e., SAT scores), and that athletes may enroll in less rigorous curricula to help retain eligibility. But, these data do not tell whether the act of participating in athletics helps or hinders a student's academic achievement. Coaches and athletic competition may help structure the student athlete's life, enhance self-esteem, and lead to improved athletic and academic performance. On the other hand, student athletes may be forced to commit so much time and effort to their sports that there is a negative impact on their grades. To address this relationship between athletic participation and academic performance, we estimate our model of academic achievement.

The results of the estimation identifying varsity participation in revenue-generating and non-revenue–generating sports are reported in Table 3, and the results of estimation identifying all individual varsity sports are reported in Table 4. The results on the variables unrelated to sports participation are similar across models. As expected, higher SAT scores and higher semester standing are associated with higher GPAs. In contrast, older students and male students have lower grades than do their counterparts. The former result suggests that the increase in the population of nontraditional students may be a harbinger of lower overall GPAs at the university.

Curricular choice is important in determining GPA. For the sake of brevity, we will not interpret each coefficient. But as a group, the college variables have significant explanatory power, and within the group there is significant variation. Students from higher-income and more urban hometowns have lower academic achievement, although the effect is marginal. Student support has mixed effects on academic performance. Counter to our expectations, grant and loan recipients have reduced performance while work study recipients perform better. Perhaps, in the face of multiple demands on their time, the work study students learn to be more organized and develop better time management skills. Membership in fraternities and sororities is associated with lower academic performance.

Finally, we see that, as a group, sports club participants and non-revenue sports participants have grades comparable to those of other students. However, revenue sports participants, as a group, have significantly lower grades than do other students. The impact in the expected GPA of participants in revenue sports is –0.148. The magnitude of this effect seems small, but with an average GPA for all students equal to 2.916 and a standard deviation of 0.53, this result implies that the average revenue sport athlete has a GPA equivalent to approximately the 39th percentile of the entire student body. Moreover, this effect occurs even after controlling for SAT disadvantages and curricular choices made by the athletes.

The impact of athletic participation on GPA, however, is not uniform across sports groups. Although participants in non-revenue sports as a group exhibited no significant differences in GPA, we find that grades are significantly different in three individual non-revenue sports. Women's field hockey and men's fencing participants face dramatic declines in GPA. On the other hand, the women's swim team participants have above-average academic

Table 3
Academic Achievement Model (RevAthl and NoRevAthl)

Variable	Coefficient	t-statistics	Variable	Coefficient	t-statistics
Constant	2.199	41.82***	Semester	0.047	24.99***
SAT	0.001	51.03***	Medinc	-0.00004	1.74*
Age	-0.026	11.33***	PopUrb	-0.0005	4.30***
Gender	-0.176	24.86***	AthlSchol	0.0006	1.04
Agriculture	-0.193	9.76***	AcadSchol	0.007	22.42***
Business Admin.	0.025	1.47	Loans	-0.002	11.70***
Communications	-0.024	1.18	Grants	-0.0006	2.73***
Undergrad. Studies	-0.237	11.36***	Work Study	0.004	2.27**
Education	0.206	10.50***	Initiate	-0.057	6.07***
Earth, Mineral Sci.	-0.132	5.23***	Pledge	-0.074	2.99***
Engineering	-0.063	3.65***	WClub	-0.094	1.303
Health, Human	0.017	1.02	MClub	0.029	0.63
Liberal Arts	-0.024	1.04	RevAthl	-0.148	2.74***
Science	-0.012	0.62	NoRevAthl	-0.007	0.24
Other Colleges	0.025	0.11	MultiVar	0.089	1.74*
Adjusted R^2 = 0.2664			F statistic = 237.84		

Notes: Using two-tailed t-tests, *** indicates statistical significance at the .01 level of significance, ** at the .05 level; and * at the .10 level. The College of Arts and Architecture is used as the benchmark in assessing the effect of college on GPA.

Table 4
Academic Achievement Model (All Varsity Sports)

Variable	Coefficient	t-statistics	Variable	Coefficient	t-statistics
Constant	2.201	41.85***	MClub	0.029	0.63
SAT	0.001	50.98***	WBaskball	-0.163	1.02
Age	-0.026	11.34***	WFence	0.042	0.30
Gender	-0.176	24.47***	WFldHockey	-0.204	1.79*
Agriculture	-0.193	9.78***	WGolf	0.182	1.47
Business Admin.	0.025	1.41	WGymnast	0.035	0.29
Communications	-0.024	1.18	WLacross	-0.033	0.33
Undergrad. Studies	-0.238	11.41***	WSwim	0.102	1.72*
Education	0.207	10.52***	WTennis	-0.012	0.81
Earth, Mineral Sci.	-0.134	5.31***	WTrack	-0.234	0.79
Engineering	-0.064	3.71***	WVllyBall	-0.100	0.72
Health, Human Dev.	0.018	1.03	WSoccer	-0.008	0.07
Liberal Arts	-0.025	1.46	MBaseball	-0.146	1.60
Science	-0.012	0.64	MBaskball	-0.033	0.30
Other Colleges	0.024	0.11	MFence	-0.252	1.91*
Semester	0.047	25.01***	MFootball	-0.151	2.45**
Medinc.	-0.00004	1.79*	MGolf	-0.06	0.49
PopUrb	-0.0006	4.36***	MGymnast	0.236	1.35
AthlSchol	0.0004	0.55	MLacross	-0.082	1.12
AcadSchol	0.006	22.40***	MSwim	0.155	1.59
Loans	-0.002	11.71***	MTennis	0.223	1.60
Grants	-0.0006	2.67***	MTrack	-0.181	0.62
Work Study	0.004	2.26**	MVllyBall	-0.021	0.17
Initiate	-0.056	6.05***	MSoccer	0.09	0.90
Pledge	-0.073	2.97***	MWrestle	-0.073	0.92
WClub	-0.094	1.29	MultiVar	0.288	1.01
Adjusted R^2 = 0.2666			F statistic = 135.21		

Notes: Using two-tailed t-tests, ***indicates statistical significance at the .01 level of significance; ** at the .05 level; and * at the .10 level. The College of Arts and Architecture is used as the benchmark in assessing the effect of college GPA.

performance. Participants in all other non-revenue sports perform equivalently to their non-athletic peers.

Regarding revenue sports, the athletes exhibit no significant differences in GPAs except for men's football. Participants in men's football perform worse than their peers with comparable backgrounds. Because men's football is the only revenue sport with a significant effect on GPA, the quantitative remarks concerning revenue sports participants made in the above paragraph should apply only to those in men's football. Interestingly, men's football is the primary source of sports revenue to the university. Also, there are more athletes competing in men's football than in other sports. The ninety-two participants in men's football is almost twice the number of athletes competing in any other sport.

It is also interesting to see that multiple varsity athletes have grades that are no worse (or better) than their peers.

CONCLUSION

We compiled the data on all full-time baccalaureate students at Penn State University for spring 1995. Using these data, we examined the effects of athletic participation on classroom achievement. In the process we uncovered a number of interesting findings.

First, athletes have average SAT scores that are below those of other students. Two of the three revenue-producing sports for the university show the lowest SAT averages. This occurs despite the SAT and high school core course requirements of Propositions 42 and 48. While the initiation of these propositions may have reduced the differences between the scholastic backgrounds of athletes and nonathletes, measurable differences continue to exist. These data are consistent with admission policies that pave the way to recruit an excellent athlete who is a marginal student, but they also create a situation in which the student athlete will continually be at a disadvantage in competing with peers in the classroom.

Post-season football playoffs would exacerbate exploitation in both the athletic and academic arenas, significantly slower in advancing toward an academic degree. If the university is willing to bring in athletes as "disadvantaged" students, then the university should consider allocating more resources to help the athletes overcome their disadvantage. Even after holding constant SAT scores and curricular choices, participants in a few sports still exhibited significantly different GPAs than their student peers. Men's football, which represents the largest number of athletes, had average GPAs consistent with only the 39th percentile of the student body. The NCAA prohibits these athletes from being paid for their athletic services, despite the fact that football is the largest source of spoils revenue to the university. Now it appears that the exploitation of these athletes, the big money spoils athlete, has been extended to the classroom.

If the student athlete begins with a competitive disadvantage in the classroom, maintaining eligibility may become a problem. Perhaps in an attempt to offset this academic disadvantage, athletes opt for less rigorous curricula, as suggested by our results. If this is the primary reason for curricula choices, athletes have had their academic opportunities compromised. Our results also imply that athletes may be significantly slower in advancing toward an academic degree. If the university is willing to bring in athletes as "disadvantaged" students, then the university should consider allocating more resources to help the athletes overcome their disadvantages.

Even after holding constant for SAT scores and curricular choices, participants in a few sports exhibited significantly different GPAs than did their student peers. Men's football, which represents the largest number of athletes, had average GPAs consistent with the 39th percentile of the student body. The NCAA prohibits these athletes from being paid for their athletic services despite the fact that football is the largest source of sports revenue to the university. Now it appears that the exploitation of these athletes, the big-money sports athletes, has been extended to the classroom. Post-season football playoffs would exacerbate exploitation in both the athletic and the academic arenas.

NOTES

1. Personal data on students could not be released for use in this study, so hometown characteristics are used as proxies. The percentage of people with baccalaureate degrees in the hometown of the student was initially used in addition to the variables described in this section. However, this variable was omitted because of high collinearity with MedInc.

2. Women's indoor track, outdoor track, and cross-country were combined into one variable, WTrack, and men's indoor track, outdoor track, and cross-country were combined into one variable, MTrack, due to the high collinearity between these sports variables.

11

Managerial Efficiency, Managerial Succession, and Organizational Performance

John Fizel and Michael P. D'Itri

INTRODUCTION

Managers perform several functions that are often deemed critical to the performance of organizations. Thus, when organizations exhibit poor performance, there is a common notion that dismissing and replacing the manager will lead to improved performance. While that has intuitive appeal, both the assertion that "performance causes succession" and the counter-assertion that "succession causes performance" are subject to theoretical and empirical debate.

Amid this controversy is the problem of measuring managerial performance. Managerial performance measures in business are often difficult to define, use distorted or proprietary data, or are determined, in part, by forces outside managerial control. We use data envelopment analysis (DEA) to introduce a "new" measure of managerial performance to this debate. DEA estimates the efficiency of a given manager relative to the efficiency of all managers in the industry. This efficiency measure also determines the difference between the actual performance of the manager and what could have been achieved under "best practice" decisions. We believe this innovative measure of managerial efficiency helps to shed new light on the old yet puzzling relationships between succession and performance.

For this reexamination of the "performance causes succession" and the "succession causes performance" hypotheses we use NCAA Division I college basketball data over the period 1984–91. There are a number of reasons why basketball is a useful and convenient point of departure for our measure of managerial efficiency. First, data on input and output are readily available, and provide easy-to-interpret proxies for the productivity relationships that exist in the industry. Second, the dimensions of basketball coaching parallel those of business managers. The coaching function includes personnel decisions (recruiting, training, scheduling), motivation of personnel (allocating playing time), and strategic planning (devising and altering offensive and defensive schemes). Finally, basketball is a sport with essentially one coach. This reduces the contaminating influences other coaches might have on organizational performance, as may occur in baseball and football where larger coaching staffs are the norm.[1]

LITERATURE REVIEW

There is no dispute that managers will be replaced for poor performance as long as they are held accountable for their actions (Brown, 1982; Crain, 1977; Salancik and Pfeffer, 1980). The principal-agent problem, however, which is at the core of any model of organizations, suggests that accountability may not always exist (Fama, 1980). Managers and stakeholders may have divergent goals, and if there is no mechanism by which managers are dissuaded from acting in their own interests, managers will be free to maximize returns to themselves rather than to fulfill the performance goals of stakeholders. Under such conditions managerial shirking and/or incompetence may ensue without managerial succession (i.e., turnover). Recent analyses indicate that powerful managers are held less accountable. When managers are either members or chairs of the board of directors, organizational performance does not affect managerial succession (Fizel et al., 1990; Fizel and Louie, 1990; Dyl, 1988; Gomez-Meija et al., 1987).

How would the performance of the organization change if the manager was replaced? One theory suggests that managerial turnover is disruptive to the organization. Gouldner (1954) observed that the appearance of new managers in a gypsum plant altered accepted and expected patterns of organizational behavior, causing deterioration in morale and productivity. Moreover, the negative succession-performance relationship may ultimately create a "vicious circle." Focusing on professional baseball managers, Grusky (1963, 1964) found that managerial dismissal was more likely in poorly performing teams and that once the new manager took over, the team's performance deteriorated further. The disruptive hypothesis receives additional support from Carroll's (1984) study of U.S. newspaper publishers and Brown's (1982) study of professional football coaches.

A second theory suggests that managerial succession has no effect on performance. With roots in Aldrich's (1979) population ecology theory, this position sees organizational success as solely the result of environmental forces. Managers may lose their jobs following poor performance, but this is regarded as a scapegoating process. Gamson and Scotch (1964) note in their study of baseball managers that fired managers typically enjoy attractive employment prospects with other teams. This implies that team owners recognize that terminations are often ritualistic demonstrations of concern to lower-level employees. Brown (1982) and Liebersen and O'Connor (1972) find a similar scapegoating effect in professional football and large corporations.

Finally, Guest (1962) hypothesizes that a new manager will improve performance. This hypothesis assumes that either there is a "novelty" effect associated with the new manager, or the new manager is more competent than the departing one. Studies have disaggregated manager competence from manager succession per se to address each component of this hypothesis. Smith et al. (1984), in a study of Methodist ministers, and Pfeffer and Davis-Blake (1986), in a study of professional basketball coaches, found a positive relationship between the ability of the new manager and organizational performance; but succession, in and of itself, had no impact on performance. In contrast, Virany et al. (1992) established that both succession per se and the characteristics of the new manager altered performance.

Thus, to date no universal relationship appears to exist between succession and performance. These conflicting results may illustrate that the succession-performance relationship is dependent on the characteristics of the organizations under study. These results, however, also raise questions about the validity of previously used performance measures as well as the decision processes used to hire and fire managers. This paper addresses the former by using a measure of efficiency that explicitly addresses the manager's ability to transform inputs into output, and in so doing implicitly addresses the calculus that college administrators use in determining which coaches should be hired and retained.

PROCEDURES

The following four subsections outline the procedures employed in this research and the sources of data. The first procedure described is DEA, which is used to measure managerial efficiency. Subsequently, we describe two regression models. The first is used to identify the performance factors that are instrumental in motivating managerial succession. The second provides a short-run forecast of future organizational outcomes based on the relative performances of the new and replaced manager. Together, these models allow us to determine whether the factors that prompt succession are consistent with the factors that lead to better future organizational performance. Finally, a description of the data is provided.

ESTIMATING MANAGERIAL EFFICIENCY

Basketball utilizes a production process where team output is measured as winning percentage, W, and is partially a function of the players' talents and skills, T. As the level of talent increases, so should a team's winning percentage. Accurate evaluation of coaching efficiency must also account for the playing power of opponents, P, in order to draw a distinction between coaches who wade through paper-thin opposition to glittering win-loss records while other, perhaps more efficient, coaches may have anguishing seasons simply because they faced too much adversity for the talent they oversee. An increase in P represents an increase in opposition power or the difficulty of schedule played by a given team. Formally we say that winning percentage, W, is a function of player talent, T, and opposition power, P,

$$W = f(T, 1/P) \tag{1}$$

where $1/P$ is used so that $\partial W/\partial T > 0$ and $\partial W/\partial(1/P) > 0$.[2]

The manager or coach is the economic agent responsible for transforming inputs into wins. In addition to identifying talent, the coach must develop the players, organize and allocate playing time through the use of appropriate player combinations, and create and select strategies that affect the outcome of games. The quality of these decisions determines the coach's performance.

Empirical estimates of efficiency, E, are made using DEA, originally developed by Farrell (1957), and Charnes et al. (1978). DEA compares the efficiency of a given manager relative to the efficiency of the most efficient managers in the sample. Efficiency is characterized by a frontier isoquant that identifies the lowest input use for a given level of output, or the maximum output for given levels of inputs.

Conceptually, DEA begins by identifying managers using the fewest inputs while producing a given level of output. The "best practice" isoquant is then formed by connecting these points with piecewise linear segments. Although DEA encompasses a variety of modeling formulations, we employ a computationally efficient approach introduced by Boles (1967) to estimate efficiency. In this method the production function $W = f(T, 1/P)$ may be expressed in intensive form as $W/W = 1 = f[T/W, (1/P)/W]$ (i.e., the frontier production function), and may be depicted by the unit isoquant, W/W, shown in Figure 1. If all managers are efficient decision makers, their performance could be depicted as points along the isoquant, as is the case for managers A, B, and C. Managers such as D who fail to maximize output for their set of inputs, or use excessive inputs to achieve a given output, will lie above the isoquant. Managerial inefficiency can then be measured by the distance each manager is from the frontier isoquant.

For example, the efficiency of manager D is calculated as the ratio of the most efficient input utilization or performance within the sample of managers, line segment OD′, to the actual performance of manager D, OD. Since the actual amount of inputs utilized exceeds those of an analogous output level on the efficient frontier, the efficiency, E, for manager D is less than

Figure 1
Graphical Exposition of Data Envelopment Analysis

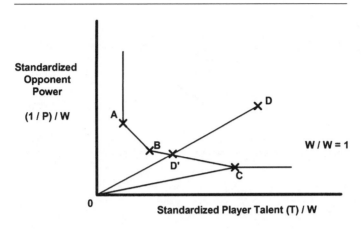

100%, indicating substandard performance. The same procedure can be used to assess the efficiency of manager C. In this case the ratio of efficient to actual performance is OC/OC, making the managerial efficiency equal to one, demonstrating that manager C is utilizing his or her resources at 100% efficiency (relative to all other managers in the sample).

In the Boles formulation, as applied here, the efficiency indices are estimated by solving a series of linear programs (LPs), one for each of the coaches. These will be indexed by k, for a total of K LPs.

In the description of the objective function and the constraint matrix, we will use the j subscript to refer to each of J coaches ($J = K$). The i index will indicate the inputs available to the coaches, where there are a total of I types of inputs. Inputs are expressed relative to the single output, the winning percentage of each coach, W_j. Thus,

$$f_{ij} = \frac{F_{ij}}{W_j} \begin{cases} i = 1, 2, ..., I \\ j = 1, 2, ..., J \end{cases} \qquad (2)$$

where:

f_{ij} = standard utilization per unit of output achieved with input i for coach j
F_{ij} = level of input type i for the jth coach
W_j = output level (winning percentage) for the jth coach

The objective of each of the K linear programs is to maximize output x_0^k by considering the impact of distributing the kth coach's resources to the most efficient coaches. In other words, the kth coach is evaluated relative to the performance of the remaining coaches in the sample. If one or more of the remaining coaches is more efficient than the kth coach, this procedure will determine the extra output the efficient coach(es) could produce using the resources available to the kth coach. The ratio of the output produced by the efficient coaches relative to the output produced by the kth coach is captured in x_0^k. If coach k is operating along the efficient frontier, there will be no advantage to reallocating his resources and x_0^k will be 1. If, however, coach k is less efficient than some of his counterparts in the sample, the value of x_0^k will exceed 1, demonstrating the potential increase in productivity. The efficiency index for each of the coaches, E_k is then $1/x_0^k$.

To recapitulate, if coach k is operating on the efficient frontier x_0^k will be 1, and $E_k(= 1/x_0^k)$ will also be 1. This indicates that coach k is 100% efficient. In contrast, suppose that coach k is inefficient and operating above the efficient frontier so that $x_0^k = 1.25$. Coach k's efficiency index would then be 0.80, indicating that coach k is only 80% as efficient as the most efficient coaches in the sample.[3]

This theoretical reallocation is achieved through the decision variables, x_j^k, the output levels that coach j could achieve with the kth coach's inputs. Constraints of the form

$$\sum_{j=1}^{J} f_{ij} X_j^k \leq f_{ik} \qquad i = 1, 2, ..., I \qquad (3)$$

establish the ability of the kth coach to transform each input into wins. The complete formulation for the kth linear program is as follows:

$$\text{Maximize:} \quad X_o^k = \sum_{j=1}^{J} X_j^x$$

$$\text{Subject to:} \quad \sum_{j=1}^{J} f_{ij} X_j^x \leq f_{ik} \qquad i = 1, 2, ..., I \qquad (4)$$

$$X_j^x \geq 0 \qquad j = 1, 2, ..., J$$

A MODEL OF PERFORMANCE CAUSES SUCCESSION

The model used to test the "performance causes succession" relationships is as follows:

$$S = \alpha_0 + \alpha_1 E + \alpha_2 T + \alpha_3 W + \alpha_4 EX + \varepsilon_1 \qquad (5)$$

where S indicates managerial succession; E, T, and W represent organizational performance benchmarks for efficiency, player recruiting and winning percentages, respectively; EX captures managerial power/reputation via the experience of the coach; α_i's are the parameters to be estimated; and ε represents the random error.

One would ordinarily assume that manager replacement is caused by poor organizational performance, and manager retention is caused by good organizational performance. But, as emphasized earlier, this relationship must address what performance benchmarks will be evaluated. In light of this uncertainty about an appropriate benchmark, three different performance measures are used. These measures are managerial efficiency, E; player recruiting or talent, T; and team winning percentage, W. The probability of succession, S, should diminish the more efficient a coach is, the more talent he has on the team (evidence of good recruiting), and the more the team wins. Hence we expect α_1, α_2, and α_3 to be negative. Since turnover of basketball coaches occurs most frequently after a season is completed, each performance variable is calculated prior to the advent of the succession. Although managerial efficiency best captures the productivity of the manager, it remains to be seen whether actual termination decisions give more weight to this measure.

Prior studies have indicated that powerful managers may not be held accountable for poor performance (Fizel et al., 1990; Fizel and Louie, 1990). Under such conditions, shirking and incompetence may ensue without managerial turnover. Because such power is more likely to be bestowed upon an experienced coach, we use the coach's experience in years, EX, as a proxy for managerial power. A negative association with turnover, $\alpha_4 < 0$, would be expected if such power does circumvent the succession-performance relationship. An experience variable may also capture successions that occurred because of voluntary retirements. This relationship would prompt $\alpha_4 > 0$. Only empirical estimation will determine which role of experience for coaching changes is included in this sample.

Succession, the dependent variable for this model, is assigned a value of 1 if a coaching change was made during the prior season or between the prior and current season. All coaching changes, however, are not the same. Some coaches depart voluntarily as they move to better or more prestigious positions. Other coaches are terminated and have difficultly reentering the profession. The link between succession and performance is apt to be stronger for the involuntary than for voluntary successions. We supplement the use of a variable for all successions, S, with two additional variables that isolate these contrasting phenomena. For the coaches who voluntarily left one position to take another job we use SV and for coaches who left one position and remain unemployed we use SU. SV equals 1 if the exiting coach took a new coaching position within two years of his departure, and 0 otherwise; SU will equal 1 if the exiting coach could not find a new position within two years of his replacement, and 0 otherwise. Alternative lags between coaching jobs were examined, but two years provided the time horizon within which most dismissed coaches found new jobs if they were to be re-employed. Probit estimation is used because S, SV, and SU are dichotomous dependent variables.

A MODEL OF POST-SUCCESSION PERFORMANCE USING CHARACTERISTICS OF THE MANAGERS

Whereas the "performance causes succession" model provides insights into why coaches are dismissed, the future performance model seeks to explain the change in performance after a new coach takes over. As stated earlier, Smith et al. (1984), Pfeffer and Davis-Blake (1986), and Virany et al. (1992) all find that post-succession performance depends on the characteristics of the new managers. This relationship becomes the foundation of our model of short-run, post-succession performance. That model can be expressed as follows:

$$W_t = \beta_{0V} + \beta_{1V}SV + \beta_{2V}EFNEWSV + \beta_{3V}EXNEWSV + \beta_{5V}W_{(t-1)} \qquad (6a)$$
$$+ \beta_{6V}T + \varepsilon_{2V}$$

$$W_t = \beta_{0U} + \beta_{1U}SU + \beta_{2U}EFNEWSU + \beta_{3U}EXNEWSU + \beta_{5U}W_{(t-1)} \qquad (6b)$$
$$+ \beta_{6U}T + \varepsilon_{2U}$$

where W_t is team performance measured by winning percentage for the current season; SV and SU are voluntary and involuntary managerial succession, respectively; $EFNEWSV$ and $EFNEWSU$ are the efficiency of the new coach relative to the departed coach multiplied by succession type; $EXNEWSV$ and $EXNEWSU$ are the experience of the new coach relative to the departed coach multiplied by succession type; $W_{(t-1)}$ is team performance in the prior season; T is player talent; β_i's are the parameters to be estimated; and ε_{2V} and ε_{2U} represent the random error terms.

The impact of succession on performance involves both the event of the succession and the characteristics of the coaches involved in the turnover. The dummy variables SV and SU are assigned a value of 1 when managerial turnover occurs, capturing succession per se. The characteristics of the replacement coach are captured by two variables. The first is the efficiency of the new coach, calculated as the ratio of the managerial efficiency of the new coach to the managerial efficiency of the dismissed coach. The DEA-estimated efficiency level for each coach is based on the performance level in the prior season and is defined as *EFNEW*. If the organization hires a more efficient coach, then winning percentage should increase. The second characteristic is the ratio of the experience of the new coach, *EXNEW*, relative to the experience of the dismissed coach. The hypothesis is that a more experienced coach will generate better performance than will a less experienced one. Thus, as *EXNEW* increases so should performance, W_t.

The managerial characteristic variables are multiplied by the succession event to create the variables *EFNEWSV* and *EFNEWSU* and the variables *EXNEWSV* and *EXNEWSU*. These variables capture the interaction between succession and managerial ability. For example, the total effect of a voluntary succession (*SV*) on organizational performance is:

$$\frac{\partial W_t}{\partial SV} = \beta_{1V} + \beta_{2V}EFNEW + \beta_{3V}EXNEW \tag{7a}$$

where β_{1V} captures the effect of succession per se on winning percentage and the remaining elements capture the efficiency and experience characteristics of the new coach relative to the former coach. The total effect of an involuntary succession (*SU*) on team winning percentage also involves the event of succession and the characteristics of the coaching replacement:

$$\frac{\partial W_t}{\partial SU} = \beta_{1U} + \beta_{2U}EFNEW + \beta_{3U}EXNEW \tag{7b}$$

The remaining independent variables, $W_{(t-1)}$ and T, are control variables for this model. Scully (1995) has shown that performance in professional sports has a cyclical component even after controlling for coaching and player inputs. Successful teams maintain their success for the short run, then become less successful, and unsuccessful teams continue with their lack of success in the short run, then become more successful.[4] Lagged performance, $W_{(t-1)}$, accounts for this phenomenon. Player talent, T, is used to acknowledge that the player composition of the team is at least partially beyond the control of a new coach. Often the process of changing coaches does not allow adequate time for effective recruiting. Even if a new coach recruited effectively in his inaugural season, the majority of the team members would be holdovers recruited by the prior coaching staff.

All models use pooled cross-sectional and time-series data, and are estimated using generalized least squares (GLS). Nerlove (1971) points out that ordinary least squares estimations of pooled data would tend to overestimate the impact of lagged performance. GLS estimates are consistent and efficient.

DATA

Winning percentages are culled from annual issues of NCAA Basketball (1983–92). Years of coaching experience are also taken from this source.

Player talent is measured using a talent index created by Clark Francis and distributed in his publication *Hoop Scoop* (1983–92). The construction of the talent index begins by assigning every player in NCAA's Division I a rating of 1–10. The assigned score depends on the consensus evaluation of a player's talent when he graduated from high school. If a player improves dramatically in college, he can be upgraded. Each player's evaluation is automatically increased as he gains experience. A player rated among the top five in the nation is worth 10 points as a freshman but 13 points as a senior. Next, all but the top 10 players on a team roster are eliminated. This adjustment is made because teams seldom play more than 10 players on a regular basis. The sum of the value of each of the 10 players provides a team's talent rating. These talent ratings have been produced for 11 years. Over this period and in a variety of issues of *Hoop Scoop*, Francis has provided evidence that the 'surprise' teams, those that win many more games in a given season than most prognosticators predict, have been associated with large shifts in their talent ratings. Our measure of player talent therefore seems reliable.

Previous descriptions of production functions for sporting teams have defined player talent in terms of ex post performance figures such as points scored, assists, rebounds, turnovers, and so on (Scully, 1992; Clement and McCormick, 1989; Zak et al., 1979). Because these variables result from both player talent and coaching decisions, a simultaneity problem exists that may bias estimates of managerial efficiency. In contrast, the *Hoop Scoop* talent rating is an a priori measure of talent, and provides a unique opportunity to overcome the simultaneity problem.

Opponent strength is derived from the end-of-year "power" rating created by Wise Research Associates (Wise et al., 1990). The initial information used in the rating system emanates from the polling of coaches and sportswriters used to compile the UPI and AP national basketball team rankings. Using a weighted, weekly composite of these rankings, Wise Research Associates develop a season-long composite of "ranked" teams. This is extended via a mathematical formula that uses relative standings in a conference—or area of the country for teams in a conference—to develop a numerical classification for each Division I competitor. They examine each team's schedule, awarding the values based on their opponents and for games played on opponents' courts. The result is the power rating. A higher power rating indicates a more difficult schedule and diminished victory opportunities for a given level of player talent. Schedule evaluation systems like the power rating are now used by the NCAA to select teams for the end-of-year NCAA national basketball tournament.

The data set consists of 1,116 observations for 147 rent teams over the period 1984–91. Because one or more variables were not available for a given team given year, all teams are not represented in each of the eight seasons. Most of the omissions are institutions with "new" or "minor" basketball programs that were not included in the talent or power ratings. A total of 147 succession events (*S*) were identified during these years, 100 of which are involuntary successions (*SU*) and 47 of which are voluntary successions (*SV*).

DEA efficiency indices and the "performance causes succession" model are estimated using the entire set of observations. Because the post-succession performance model focuses on performance subsequent to succession, only 969 observations are able for estimation.

ANALYSIS AND INTERPRETATION

The next three subsections parallel those of the Procedures section, presenting the DEA results and the two regression models. In the final subsection, we give our conclusions.

MANAGERIAL EFFICIENCY

DEA estimates of managerial efficiency provide provocative insights into managerial performance. First, managerial efficiency furnishes a much different assessment of managerial performance than does winning percentage. The Appendix lists the top 10 coaches for each year based on both managerial efficiency and winning percentage. Only about 25% of the coaches show up on both lists in any given year. Table 1 highlights the differences with a presentation of the rank correlations between managerial efficiency and winning percentage. The rank correlations range from 0.40 for 1985 to 0.55 for 1990. The correlation for the entire sample is only 0.48, indicating that decisions based on winning percentage are not synonymous with those based on managerial efficiency.

The most efficient coaches often come from mid-basketball conferences and teams. Because recruiting quality players is typically more difficult in these institutions, the coaches may have to work efficiently to win. Also, these coaches may be working to move up the professional hierarchy of coaching. For example, J. Calhoun has been promoted from Northeastern to Connecticut, N. Richardson from Tulsa to Arkansas, A. Russo from Louisiana Tech to

Table 1
Rank Correlations Between Managerial Efficiency and Winning Percentage

Year	Pearson rho (n)	Year	Pearson rho (n)
1984	0.51 (147)	1988	0.50 (129)
1985	0.40 (147)	1989	0.44 (143)
1986	0.47 (138)	1990	0.55 (143)
1987	0.50 (128)	1991	0.53 (141)
Total sample (n = 1116): Pearson rho = 0.48			

Washington, J. Harrick from Pepperdine to UCLA, P. Gillen from Xavier to Providence, T. Penders from Rhode Island to Texas, R. Majerus from Ball State to Utah, D. Versace and S. Albeck from Bradley to the NBA, and so on.

Although coaches of the basketball power institutions appear less frequently in the most efficient lists, J. Chaney of Temple is included in four different years. Also, J. Calhoun, N. Richardson, and R. Majerus have been among the most efficient coaches when they were at both mid-level and top-level basketball schools.

Second, there is wide dispersion in managerial efficiency ratings, ranging from the expected 100% to only 4%. A distribution of the efficiency estimates by deciles is presented in Table 2. Because only three coaches were 100% efficient, and could possibly be considered outliers, managerial efficiency was estimated again with these observations removed. The resulting distribution changed little, with managerial quality still extending from 100% to 13%. Third, the mean value of managerial efficiency is 38%, indicating that the typical coach is very inefficient relative to the practices used by the best coaches in the sample.

Our subsequent examinations of firing and hiring decisions will show whether administrators actually consider productivity or focus on the easily accessible win-loss records. If the latter is true, and the wide dispersion of managerial quality is ignored, organizations that change coaches could experience large fluctuations in performance. One example is a situation where a coach of average productivity is replaced by one of the few efficient coaches, and organization performance could increase substantially. By contrast, accidentally removing a relatively efficient coach and replacing him with a relatively inefficient coach could cause performance to plummet.

Finally, Scully (1992) identifies a learning curve for baseball managers in which the efficiency of the manager increases with managerial experience. No comparable relationship for college basketball coaches is available to explain the dispersion in managerial efficiency. A correlation between managerial efficiency and experience of –0.15 is insignificant. Regressions using linear, quadratic, and log specifications of the potential relationship between efficiency and experience also produced insignificant results.

Table 2
Distribution of Managerial Efficiency Estimates

Estimates	Observations	Estimates	Observations
0.901-1.00	7	0.401-0.500	208
0.801-0.900	9	0.301-0.400	327
0.701-0.800	29	0.201-0.300	281
0.601-0.700	65	0.101-0.200	82
0.501-0.600	106	0.01-0.100	2
Mean Estimate	0.38	Std. Deviation	0.15

PERFORMANCE CAUSES SUCCESSION

The estimated "performance causes succession" models using all successions (S), involuntary successions (SU), and voluntary successions (SV) are reported in Table 3. Model 1 captures the effects of what we believe to be the dominant performance variables—managerial efficiency and player talent. Player talent identifies the success of managers in recruiting good players to the basketball program. Managerial efficiency demonstrates the ability of the manager to mold and meld that talent into a winning team. Increases in player talent and managerial quality do significantly reduce the probability of managerial removal for S and SU managers. But there is no statistically significant relationship between these performance benchmarks and the probability that a coach will leave voluntarily to attain a new job, SV. The weaker relationship between performance and succession was expected for the analysis of voluntary managerial turnover since the new opportunities for these coaches probably result from good recent performance.

Coaching tenure or years of service is added to model 2. The positive coefficients for this variable in the total succession and involuntary succession samples suggest that long-tenured coaches are more likely to be dismissed. In other words, coaches with more years of service are held more accountable for organizational performance than are their shorter-tenured colleagues. Since increased tenure does not indicate power that can be translated into lower rates of succession, prior concerns about principal-agent problems in college basketball appear unfounded.

Model 3 uses all performance proxies in conjunction with years of service. The results with respect to years of service are unchanged. Also, there continues to be little association between performance and succession for coaches departing for better jobs, SV. For all successions, S, and dismissed coaches, SU, however, the effects of team winning percentage on succession overwhelm the impact of managerial efficiency. This is simply "bottom-line" personnel decision making. Managerial productivity is overlooked in favor of 'did we win?' Perhaps armchair analysts would find this conclusion obvious, but what is important to address is whether or not past winning percentages are also good predictors of future changes in winning percentages.

POST-SUCCESSION PERFORMANCE AND CHARACTERISTICS OF COACHES

What happens to team performance once a coaching change has been made? The control variables, $W_{(t-1)}$ and T, are positive, significant, and robust across all models, as presented in Table 4. As expected, more wins in the past and more available talent both generate better winning percentages. The focal point of our analysis, however, is the variables that capture the effect of succession.

The coefficients associated with SV and SU indicate that the succession event per se is disruptive, causing subsequent performance to decline. This

Table 3
The Effect of Performance on Succession (Dependent Variables = 1 if Manager Terminated)

Variables	(1) S	(1a) SU	(1b) SV	(2) S	(2a) SU	(2b) SV	(3) S	(3a) SU	(3b) SV
Constant	-0.294	-0.133	-1.316[a]	-0.361[c]	-0.066	-1.371[a]	-0.494[b]	-0.534	-1.042[c]
	(1.34)	(0.35)	(2.76)	(1.61)	(0.17)	(2.62)	(2.11)	(1.09)	(1.57)
Mang. Efficiency E	-1.055[a]	-1.450[a]	-0.133	-0.996[a]	-1.345[a]	0.153	0.191	0.568	11.214
	(2.78)	(2.94)	(0.23)	(2.75)	(2.64)	(0.24)	(0.24)	(0.58)	(1.00)
Player Talent T	-0.011[a]	-0.016[b]	-0.008	-0.012[a]	-0.006	0.005	-0.003	0.014	-0.003
	(3.32)	(2.57)	(0.98)	(3.60)	(0.93)	(0.59)	(0.46)	(1.40)	(0.24)
Coach Exp EX	—	—	—	0.010[c]	-0.056[a]	-0.075[a]	0.011[c]	-0.055[a]	-0.068[a]
				(1.62)	(5.85)	(5.04)	(1.82)	(5.09)	(4.20)
Winning Pct W	—	—	—	—	—	—	-1.262[c]	-1.980[a]	0.833
							(1.73)	(2.97)	(1.01)
Chi-Square Likelihood Ratio	14.389[a]	10.022[a]	1.230	17.028[a]	51.506[a]	36.828[a]	20.008[a]	198.368[a]	109.962[a]

Note: Figures in parentheses are absolute value of t-statistics; levels of significance of 1, 5, and 10% are indicated by a, b, and c, respectively; all are two-tailed tests.

Table 4
The Effect of Succession on Performance (Dependent Variable = Winning Percentage)

Variables	(1a - SU)	(1b-SV)	(2a-SU)	(2b-SV)	(3a-SU)	(3b-SV)
Constant	0.241^a (13.45)	0.232^a (13.53)	0.231^a (13.12)	0.225^a (13.25)	0.231^a (13.14)	0.225^a (13.26)
Prior Win Pct $W_{(t-1)}$	0.372^a (11.57)	0.383^a (12.05)	0.401^a (12.63)	0.401^a (12.66)	0.400^a (12.61)	0.400^a (12.63)
Player Talent T	0.003^a (9.99)	0.003^a (10.04)	0.003^a (9.67)	0.003^a (9.88)	0.003^a (9.70)	0.003^a (9.88)
Succession SU	-0.029^c (1.78)	—	-0.282^c (6.42)	—	-0.288^a (6.53)	—
Succession SV	—	-0.026 (1.10)	—	-0.305^a (4.61)	—	-0.307^a (4.64)
Effic. New Coach x SU	—	—	0.229^a (6.21)	—	0.224^a (6.35)	—
Effic. New Coach x SV	—	—	—	0.281^a (4.51)	—	0.273^a (4.32)
Exp. New Coach x SU	—	—	—	—	-0.012 (1.38)	—
Exp. New Coach x SV	—	—	—	—	—	0.012 (0.72)
Adjusted R^2	0.370	0.369	0.399	0.385	0.401	0.384
F-statistics	151.86^a	150.90^a	129.12^a	121.11^a	103.82^a	96.94^a

Note: Figures in parentheses are absolute value of t-statistics; levels of significance of 1, 5, and 10% are indicated by a, b, and c, respectively; all are two-tailed tests.

result is robust across all models, except (1b), and for both types of succession. The magnitude of the effect is small in model (1a), amounting to approximately one to two fewer wins per 30-game season. In models (2a), (2b), (3a), and (3c) the disruptive effect is approximately eight to nine fewer wins per season. Possibly the omission of the manager efficiency variable in equation (1a) biased the succession coefficients toward zero.

These results are consistent with the literature suggesting that the appearance of new coaches can alter expected and accepted patterns of organizational behavior. College basketball often involves close personal relationships between coaches and the players they have recruited and worked to develop. The new coaches who replace these familiar mentors have different personalities, expectations, and basketball systems. Therefore, it is not surprising to find the young players adversely affected by coaching changes.

In contrast, performance subsequent to succession improves when the managerial efficiency of the new coach exceeds that of the prior coach. Not surprisingly, this effect is found to be larger for coaches progressing in their careers, *EFNEWSV,* than for terminated coaches, *EFNEWSU,* whose careers have stalled or ended. In the former case, hiring a more efficient replacement is to hire a better coach than the already productive coach who is departing. In the latter case, the new coach is more productive but relative to the lower standard established by the departing coach.

New and better coaches can improve team performance but never by enough to offset the disruptive effects of succession per se. In other words, the total effect of *SE* and *SU* on performance, as outlined by Equations (7a) and (7b) and estimated using the mean values of *EXNEW* and *EFNEW* and the relevant parameter estimates from Table 4, is negative. Specifically, the evaluation of Equations (7a) and (7b) is as follows:

$$\frac{\partial W_t}{\partial SV} = \beta_{1V} + \beta_{2V} EFNEW + \beta_{3V} EXNEW$$

$$\text{or} \quad \frac{\partial W_t}{\partial SV} = 0.307 + 0.273(0.032) + 0.012(0.032) \tag{7a}$$

$$= -0.2943;$$

$$\frac{\partial W_t}{\partial SU} = \beta_{1U} + \beta_{2U} EFNEW + \beta_{3U} EXNEW$$

$$\text{or} \quad \frac{\partial W_t}{\partial SU} = -0.288 + 0.244(0.108) + 0(0.103) \tag{7b}$$

$$= -0.2616;$$

where β_{3U} is insignificant and represented by zero. The net effect of succession, whether *SV* or *SU*, is about seven to eight additional losses per season.

The experience of the new coaches, relative to the departed coaches, has no significant effect on performance. Personnel decisions should ignore experience as a decision criterion in favor of focusing on managerial efficiency. Experience is not related to productive management.

CONCLUSIONS

Good organizational performance decreased the probability of managerial turnover in college basketball, as one would expect. Although recruiting prowess and managerial efficiency appeared to be important determinants of managerial succession, the function of efficiency was overwhelmed by the inclusion of winning percentage. Simply put, basketball coaches retain their jobs if they win. Also, they can lose their jobs if they do not win even if they are very efficient.

When managerial succession does occur, the subsequent performance of the organization typically declines. This extent of diminished performance due to the succession event per se can be minimized but not overcome if the new coach is more efficient than the old coach. However obvious this may seem, it is important to reemphasize that our study indicates that winning percentage is a more dominant retention criterion than is efficiency. Because there are few highly efficient coaches and great differences in the ranking of coaches when using winning percentage versus managerial efficiency, administrators who select new coaches based on winning percentages are often going to select new coaches who are less efficient than the departed coach. Such a hiring process will exacerbate the performance loss associated with the succession event.

A more appropriate guide to hiring decisions is an evaluation of relative efficiency. Granted, one would not expect all administrative personnel to use DEA techniques to measure the relative efficiency of their staff, but the use of a similar calculus in the decision-making process would be preferred to using simple, bottom-line criteria. In fact, the efficiency calculus is more intuitive than the DEA model might suggest. DEA simply examines the internal and external environment within which the manager works, and then assesses how well the manager has done relative to others in a similar environment. Thus, it is possible for a manager to be efficient with a modest bottom line if he has limited resources, faces stiff competition, or is in an industry where firms typically earn modest returns. It is also possible for a manager to be inefficient with a high bottom line if he has extensive resources, has little competition, or is in an industry where firms typically earn high returns. The gist of this paper is to look at manager productivity, not firm returns, for determining whether managerial succession is appropriate.

NOTES

1. Although a head basketball coach may be most talented in recruiting and game strategy and rely on his one or two assistants for teaching the fundamentals to players, he is closer to the production process than if he had 8 to 11 assistants such as in football. Perhaps, in either football or basketball, one could argue that the hiring of assistants and delegating tasks to assistants is yet another managerial decision that coaches must make. Under that premise the number of assistants is irrelevant to the efficiency calculation.

2. Clearly, some schools may be interested in results other than winning percentage, such as conference championships, invitation to NCAA tournaments, and winning conference tournaments. Nevertheless, these outcomes are all the result of, or result in, winning. Thus, winning percentage is an excellent output proxy. Also, NCAA tournament invitations are based on a combination of win percentage and strength of schedule, which validates our use of the power input proxy.

3. DEA efficiency estimates capture only technical efficiency, the relationship of inputs to outputs. The choice of input use based on input prices and an input budget is not addressed. Following the dictates of NCAA recruiting procedures, one could, however, argue that the price of college players is similar across basketball schools. Also, analysis of coaching efficiency relative to compensation is precluded because compensation data are not available.

4. Specifically, for professional basketball Scully (1995) finds positive correlations with values lagged one year, negative correlations with values lagged two and three years, and positive correlations with values lagged four and five years. On p. 94 he states that this pattern "is similar to the patterns for [professional] baseball and football."

APPENDIX: RANKINGS OF TOP 10 MANAGERS BY YEAR AND PERFORMANCE CRITERION

Managerial Efficiency		Team Winning Percentage	
Name	Institution	Name	Institution
1984			
*1. J. Calhoun	Northeastern	J. Thompson	Georgetown
2. K. Mackey	Cleveland St.	D. Smith	North Carolina
3. C. Ellis	South Alabama	R Meyer	DePaul
*4. J. Chaney	Temple	N. Richardson	Tulsa
5. J.D. Barnett	Va. Commonwlth	G. Lewis	Houston
6. B. Donewald	Illinois St.	B. Tubbs	Oklahoma
7. A. Russo	Louisiana Tech	J. Hall	Kentucky
8. C. Williams	Santa Clara	J. Calhoun	Northeastern
*9. N. Richardson	Tulsa	J. Chaney	Temple
10. B. Oates	St. Mary's	L. Henson	Illinois
1985			
1. H. Egan	San Diego	J. Thompson	Georgetown
2. J. Calhoun	Northeastern	A. Russo	Louisiana Tech
3. B. Donewald	Illinois St.	D. Kirk	Memphis St.
4. J. Harrick	Pepperdine	L. Carneseca	St. Johns
*5. J. Chaney	Temple	J. Tarkanian	UNLV
6. B. Grant	Fresno St.	B. Frieder	Michigan
7. J. Sexson	Butler	B. Tubbs	Oklahoma
8. B. Oates	St. Mary's	G. Sullivan	Loyola-Chicago
*9. A. Russo	Louisiana Tech	J.D. Barnett	Va. Commonwlth
10. K. Mackey	Cleveland St.`	J. Chaney	Temple
1986			
*1. J. Calhoun	Northeastern	M. Kryzewski	Duke
2. J. Harrick	Pepperdine	D. Versace	Bradley
3. H. Egan	San Diego	L. Brown	Kansas
*4. P. Gillen	Xavier	E. Sutton	Kentucky
5. D. Haskins	Texas-El Paso	K. Mackey	Cleveland St.`
*6. D. Versace	Bradley	J. Tarkanian	UNLV
7. J. Brandenburg	Wyoming	L. Carneseca	St. Johns
8. S. Metcalf	Texas A&M	B. Frieder	Michigan
9. J. Chaney	Temple	J. Calhoun	Northeastern
10. K. Mackey	Cleveland St.`	P. Gillen	Xavier
1987			
1. J. Calhoun	Northeastern	M. Kryzewski	Duke
2. L. Anderson	BYU	J Meyer	DePaul
3. J. MacDonald	Kent St.	J. Chaney	Temple
4. C. Coles	Central Michigan	D. Smith	North Carolina
5. T. Eagles	Louisiana Tech	B. Knight	Indiana
6. J. Brandenburg	Wyoming	T. Davis	Iowa
7. K. Fogel	Northeastern	J. Thompson	Georgetown
*8. J. Chaney	Temple	W. Sanderson	Alabama
9. K. Mackey	Cleveland St.`	G. Keady	Purdue
10. G. Catlett	W. Virginia	J Boeheim	Syracuse
* On Both Lists in Given Year			

APPENDIX (*Continued*)

Managerial Efficiency		Team Winning Percentage	
Name	Institution	Name	Institution
1988			
1. B. Braun	E. Michigan	J. Chaney	Temple
2. T. Eagles	Louisiana Tech	L. Olson	Arizona
*3. P. Gillen	Xavier	B. Tubbs	Oklahoma
*4. S. Albeck	Bradley	G. Keady	Purdue
*5. L. Anderson	BYU	P. Gillen	Xavier
6. K. Mackey	Cleveland St.`	S. Albeck	Bradley
*7. B. Dees	Wyoming	B. Tubbs	Oklahoma
8. T. Penders	Rhode Island	E. Sutton	Kentucky
9. G. Ida	Baylor	B. Dees	Wyoming
10. N. Richardson	Arkansas	L. Anderson	BYU
1989			
*1. R. Majerus	Ball State	R. Majerus	Ball State
*2. L. Nance	St. Mary's	D. Versace	Bradley
3. J. Crews	Evansville	L. Henson	Illinois
4. J. Pimm	UC-Santa Barbara	J. Thompson	Georgetown
5. T. Eagles	Louisiana Tech	G. Catlett	W. Virginia
6. T. Arrow	South Alabama	B. Tubbs	Oklahoma
*7. S. Morris	LaSalle	L. Nance	St. Mary's
8. N. McCarthy	New Mexico St	R. Haddad	Jacksonville
*9. R. Haddad	Jacksonville	P. Carlesimo	Seton Hall
10. T. Barone	Creighton	S. Morris	LaSalle
1990			
*1. N. McCarthy	New Mexico St	S. Morris	LaSalle
2. J. MacDonald	Kent St.	J. Tarkanian	UNLV
*3. S. Morris	LaSalle	N. Richardson	Arkansas
4. R. Herrin	Southern Illinois	R. Williams	Kansas
5. J. Loyd	Louisiana Tech	P. Gillen	Xavier
6. B. Grant	Colorado St.	B. Tubbs	Oklahoma
*7. P. Gillen	Xavier	N. McCarthy	New Mexico St
8. D. Hunsacher	Ball St.	J. Calhoun	Connecticut
9. R. Reid	BYU	J. Heathcote	Michigan State
10. B. Parkhill	Penn St.	P. Westhead	Loyola Marymnt
1991			
1. B. Braun	E. Michigan	J. Tarkanian	UNLV
*2. R. Majerus	Ball State	N. Richardson	Arkansas
*3. J. Molinari	N. Illinois	R. Majerus	Ball State
4. B. Collier	Butler	R. Ayers	Ohio St.
5. H. Egan	San Diego	B. Knight	Indiana
6. K. Fogel	Northeastern	D. Smith	North Carolina
7. M. Ida	Texas Christian	M. Kryzewski	Duke
8. T. Barone	Creighton	J Boeheim	Syracuse
9. D. Hunsacher	Ball St.	J. Molinari	N. Illinois
10. N. McCarthy	New Mexico St	P. Carlesimo	Seton Hall
* On Both Lists in Given Year			
Correlation managerial efficiency and winning percentage **= 0.505**			

Part V

Competitive Balance in College Sports

12

Institutional Change in the NCAA and Competitive Balance in Intercollegiate Football

Craig A. Depken II and Dennis P. Wilson

INTRODUCTION

Since Scully (1989) introduced the empirical analysis of competitive balance in professional sports, various theoretical and empirical approaches have been developed to address the desirability of competitive balance, its impact on attendance (among other variables), and how various aspects of a sport might influence competitive balance. This paper contributes to this literature by investigating the effect of various organizational changes on competitive balance in collegiate football.

The analysis of competitive balance in sports follows the formula developed in the Structure-Conduct-Performance (SCP) literature that evolved during the first half of the 20th century. The SCP approach typically relates the structure of an industry, e.g., the number of firms, to an industry's conduct, e.g., price or innovation, and an industry's performance, e.g., profit margins or efficiency. While it is often difficult to quantify many traditional measures of conduct and performance in sports industries, several proxy measures of industry performance have been developed, some of which are used in this study. The SCP approach is used here to investigate how the NCAA regulatory process has impacted the competitive balance of college football.

Relatively few studies exist investigating competitive balance in sports other than professional baseball. One market in particular that has been ignored in the sports economic literature is intercollegiate athletics. The governing body of college athletics, the National Collegiate Athletic Association, has undergone multiple changes in its approach to college athletics, particularly in how schools interact with students before and after they arrive on campus. In this paper, we address how various rules changes have impacted the competitive balance of Division I-A football. We find that the NCAA rules changes have had different impacts on the distribution of winning in college football, as measured by the concentration of outcome-based points similar to that of professional hockey.

Our findings run counter to the stated purpose of changes in NCAA regulations, to wit improved competitive balance, a more "level playing field," and a protection of the spirit of amateur sport. Rather, our results tend to support a rent-seeking explanation of regulatory change, a phenomenon common to bureaucratic assemblies. Our findings share more with the claims of many "insiders" and popular-press authors investigating the mechanics of the NCAA regulatory process.

Because of space limitations, we restrict this investigation to only a few of the most important changes in the regulation of college football; the initial formation of the NCAA; the initial ban on scholarships; the creation of a viable enforcement mechanism; the limits placed on high-school grade point averages; the creation of multiple divisions in NCAA football; and the creation of the Bowl Championship Series (BCS) rating system. This list of rule changes does not address all possible influences of the NCAA on the competitive balance of college football, yet initiates the investigation.

The paper is structured as follows. The next section outlines our methodology and its relation to the existing literature. Section 3 presents our data and empirical models and discusses our results. The final section offers concluding remarks and suggestions for future research.

COMPETITIVE BALANCE IN SPORTS

A number of theoretical models of sports leagues have been developed in attempts to describe the incentives and methods of operation of a league and its member franchises (Demmert, 1973; Noll, 1994; El-Hordiri and Quirk, 1971; Scully 1989, 1995; Quirk and Fort, 1994; Vrooman, 1995; and Rascher, 1997). Special attention has been given to professional sports and explaining the effects of such things as baseball's antitrust exemption, the reserve clause, and revenue sharing. Competitive balance represents a general measure of how evenly playing talent is distributed among member teams. This is commonly deemed important because the more even the distribution of playing talent, the greater the uncertainty of a given contest's outcome, which in turn affects the demand for the contest. Because the uncertainty of each contest's outcome may influence both attendance and broadcast revenue, the overall competitiveness of the league can be of significance important to league members (Depken and Wilson, 2001).

The desirability of competitive balance is distinctly an empirical question. If competitive balance enhances attendance and/or revenues, then professional sports leagues would wish to promote balance. Thus, the desire to enhance balance would be supported by fans, team owners, and players (Wilson, 2001). There is little reason to suspect a different argument to hold in college athletics, although the uncertainty of outcome hypothesis may be less important to gate revenues because of the nature of college sports fans.[1] Indeed, the NCAA makes it clear that part of its mission is to provide as balanced a playing field as possible so that the spirit of amateur sports is allowed to flourish without the impediments of profit motives. However, like all cartels or organizations, there comes a point at which the desires and goals of an organization member contradict what is in the best interest of the group as a whole. Thus, the individual members' interest in performance excellence may override their interest in the group remaining competitively balanced. The result of such individual interests is of concern here.

The literature of public choice, of which Buchanan and Tullock (1965) is a seminal example, suggests that institutional factors may influence how the benefits of the individual are balanced with the benefits of the group. In their approach, Buchanan and Tullock suggest that special interest, or pressure groups, may naturally arise out of a decision-making process in which the benefits and costs of decisions are not equally shared.

This characterization seems to fit the NCAA well, as shown by DeBrock and Hendricks (1997) and Fleisher et al. (1992). While the majority of NCAA members are small schools, they share the benefits that accrue to the organization as a whole through the revenue-generating ability of large programs. However, because of the NCAA's attempts to regulate the interaction of schools with potential and matriculated student athletes, it is possible, in keeping with the Buchanan-Tullock hypothesis, that pressure groups may arise. These pressure groups may seek to alter competitive balance so to limit the rent-generating ability of other programs and/or to protect their own rent-generating capacity. Such voting behavior has been found to have significantly influenced the passing of such NCAA regulations as Proposition 42 and Proposition 48 (Fleisher et al., 1992).[2]

Anecdotal evidence suggests that NCAA regulations can often be trivial and nonsensical. For example, Rule 13.4.1 (h) makes it a violation of NCAA regulations for an athletic department to have more than one color of printing "between the covers" of its media guide. Furthermore, the student-athlete handbook can have only one color of printing, including the cover (NCAA, rule 13.4.1(l)). While there may be some pressing need to limit the number of colors printed on recruiting material, it seems more probable that smaller schools wish to limit the ability for larger programs to spend lavishly on printed materials, which might be a marginal issue for a potential recruit. The NCAA Division I-A handbook is replete with such rules and regulations that rival these for their triviality.

The empirical analysis undertaken here allows for initial insight into the impact of institutional changes on the competitive balance in college football. If the regulatory changes are motivated by pressure groups, one might expect competitive balance to be adversely affected. On the other hand, if regulatory changes were for the "public good" of NCAA members, institutional changes would be expected to enhance competitive balance. The field of industrial economics has long been concerned about market concentration. Issues such as profitability, advertising, pricing, research and development, innovation, and efficiency have been related to various measures of market concentration, developing several stylized facts. The techniques developed in this literature have, of late, been applied to professional sports in a variety of ways (see Horowitz, 1997 and 2000; Depken, 1999 and 2002; Eckard, 1998 and 2001).

Market concentration measures are numerous and varied. All have the common characteristic that the larger the number, the more concentrated the industry and the smaller the concentration measure, the less concentrated the industry. Loosely speaking, lower concentration measures correlate with more competitive industries, whereas more concentrated industries approach oligopoly and monopoly. Many concentration measures have been developed, including the Concentration Ratio, the Gini coefficient, the standard deviation, the entropy measure, and the Herfindahl-Hirschman Index (HHI; see Kamerschen and Lam, 1975 for an overview). This investigation employs the HHI index, although it is expected our results would be robust to various different measures of concentration.

The HHI is calculated as the sum of squared market shares, where market share can be defined either as a percentage of industry output, or if products are sufficiently differentiated, as a percentage of industry revenue. Some useful properties of the HHI include its restriction from below at zero, and from above at 10,000, corresponding to perfect competition and perfect monopoly, respectively. The HHI is also rather sensitive to changes in market shares over time, unlike some other linear measures. The HHI is a non-linear transformation of the standard deviation (see Depken, 1999) and can be related to other measures of industry concentration (see Kamerschen and Lam, 1975). However, when the number of firms in the industry increases, there is a natural decline in the HHI, thereby creating the potential for an identification problem. The decline in the HHI may indicate a more competitive industry compared to previous periods with fewer firms, even if no additional structural changes occurred in the industry.

The traditional use of the HHI as a measure of industry structure is to investigate its influence on various measures of conduct, e.g., pricing, innovation, or advertising. In turn, it is postulated by the Structure-Conduct-Performance (SCP) model that the conduct of the market will influence the performance of the industry, e.g., profitability, distribution, and efficiency.

Unfortunately, the data conducive to testing how the structure of the collegiate football industry influences the conduct and performance of the industry are not available over a sufficient time span. In such an approach, the structure of college football, as measured by concentration of output, would be used to explain other variables of interest.

Rather than treat the structure of college football as an exogenous variable, as in a traditional SCP approach, we consider the structure of the industry as endogenous, influenced by regime changes in the regulatory environment of the industry. Thus, we investigate how the "structure" of an industry, as measured by the ultimate distribution of output in the market, is influenced by the "structure" of the industry, as measured by the regulatory environment in which industry output is produced.

In many industries, the fundamentals that help determine the structure may be common macroeconomic issues, weakly exogenous from the industry and perhaps common to all other industries as well, e.g., mandated minimum wages, workplace safety requirements, and so on. However, in sports leagues this is not the case. Most organized leagues can be viewed as cartels, differing only in the degree of control that the cartel-governing body has over the day-to-day operations of the cartel members. Since the cartel does regulate the environment of all the cartel members, the changes to the cartel's agreement might influence the ultimate distribution of team outputs, however measured.

Therefore, in a traditional SCP study, we would investigate how the distribution of wins or player talent might influence variables such as attendance or television revenues. In professional baseball, the number of games played by each team is equal, and there is always a winner and a loser, i.e., no ties. Therefore, it is possible to consider a five hundred winning percentage for all teams as indicating perfect competitive balance. Because the average winning percentage in professional baseball is always five hundred, Scully's proposal to look at the variance in winning percentage is appropriate. However, in sports in which the number of games varies across teams, in which the number of teams in the league changes over time, or in which ties are possible, the appropriateness of using the variance of winning percentage as a measure of competitive balance is questionable.

This study uses performance points as a measure of team strength. Although NCAA football does not use performance points in team rankings, we use the measure to accommodate the possibility of ties. Performance points are a common measure of team strength when ties are possible. Performance points are determined by granting two points for every victory and one point for every tie (losses carry no weight). Therefore, unlike winning percentages, which would treat a tie and a loss with equal weight, the performance points measure grants marginal weight to a tie. Performance points are most easily recognized from the National Hockey League. Here, we identify competitive balance as an even distribution of performance points without considering exogenous factors, such as coaching, weather, and fan support, which might influence the success of a team.

To measure concentration, we calculate the HHI of performance points. However, as mentioned above, there are problems in comparing HHI's from different time periods when there are different numbers of firms included in the calculation. Therefore, we also calculate the difference between the actual concentration and the ideal concentration, which occurs when each team has an egalitarian market share of performance points. The ideal HHI is defined as 10,000/N, where N is the number of firms (teams) included in the calculation. As the number of teams in Division I-A college football has changed over time, it is appropriate to normalize the actual HHI by the ideal. The deviation from an ideal egalitarian distribution is measured as dHHI = HHI − 10,000/N, where N is the number of teams included in the market. While it is unlikely that perfect competitive balance would be exhibited in any given year, we investigate whether regulatory changes instituted by the NCAA have a statistical impact on competitive balance over time. If the stated purpose of the NCAA regulations is to promote competitive balance, then these regulatory changes should cause a decline in the concentration of performance points allowed in college football.

However, as pointed out in the public choice literature, regulatory changes may also be a form of rent seeking on the part of a voting bloc. If voting bloc theory holds for the NCAA, it is also possible that the NCAA regulatory changes are motivated by rent-seeking agendas on the part of one or more member schools. In this case, we would expect regulatory changes to cause an increase in the disparity among teams, which is a movement away from the ideal distribution of performance points. Anecdotal evidence suggests that many of the regulatory changes in the NCAA have been motivated by rent-seeking or rent-protection.

AN EMPIRICAL INVESTIGATION OF COMPETITIVE BALANCE IN COLLEGIATE FOOTBALL

Our data describe all Division I-A football teams from 1888 through 2001, and were obtained from James Howell.[3] For each year, the performance points for each team in NCAA Division I football and the market share of each team are calculated. To connect to the existing literature, we also calculate the variance of performance points for each year. Using market shares, we calculate the HHI and dHHI for performance points for each year. The HHI series is depicted in Figure 1. Figure 1 indicates that the competitive balance in NCAA football has steadily improved over time. While this is clearly a desirable outcome of the NCAA regulatory environment, we seek to identify whether specific regime changes in the NCAA regulatory environment have had an enhancing or deleterious impact on competitive balance.

Figure 1
Performance Points HHI (1888–2001)

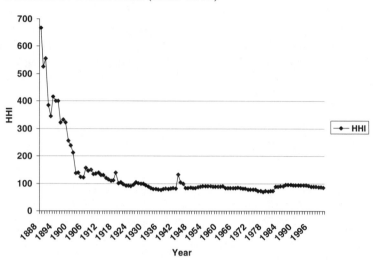

To facilitate a statistical test, we estimate the following stochastic relationship for each concentration measure:

$$DEP_t = \beta_0 + \beta_1 NCAA_t + \beta_2 SANITY_t + \beta_3 ENFORCE_t + \beta_4 GPA16_t$$
$$+ \beta_5 DIVIAA_t + \beta_6 BCS_t + \beta_7 TIME_t + \beta_8 TEAMS_t + \beta_9 DEP_{t-1} + \varepsilon_t,$$

where DEP_t is a measure of the concentration of performance points in NCAA football, and ε_t, is a mean-zero error structure. Three different measures of the concentration of performance points in NCAA football are employed. Following Scully (1989), we first use the variance of performance point within the NCAA to measure the level of competitiveness. Next, two alternative measures of competitiveness are used: the HHI and the dHHI.

The independent variables delineate major regime changes that the NCAA has implemented in the regulation of collegiate football and control for further influences of the measures of competitiveness. Each regime change is modeled as a dummy variable equal to zero for years before the regulation was implemented and one thereafter. The variable NCAA marks the creation of the NCAA as the recognized body charged with reforming and regulating collegiate football starting in 1906.[4] The NCAA was formed, in part, to resolve the problem of excessive violence and to standardize the rules of college football.[5] It is expected that the implementation of the NCAA would improve the competitive balance of collegiate football, as only a restricted number of schools were originally included in the association. These schools were commonly among the most prominent football programs of the time.

The variable SANITY marks the implementation of the so-called "sanity code" in 1949 that imposed regulations on the recruitment and retention of student athletes. In particular the "sanity code" restricted scholarships for athletic activities and implemented rules that regulated when and how schools could contact prospective students. The NCAA deems this regulation more significant than other attempts at regulation, because it created an enforcement mechanism to handle violations. A Compliance Committee became the arbiter of suspected violations investigated by the Fact-Finding Committee. If the sanity code aided competitive balance, one would expect a negative coefficient on this variable.

The Compliance Committee was effectively stripped of its enforcement powers in 1951 when the Council of the NCAA repealed the definition of what financial aid entailed and who was responsible for its administration (Fleisher et al., 1992). In 1953, the NCAA created a viable enforcement mechanism given permission to sanction schools for violating regulations, including the limitation of scholarships, television appearances, and post-season play, reflected in the variable ENFORCE. This legislation provided the NCAA with greater credibility with respect to potential violators because penalties could be issued without membership approval and between conventions. If the enforcement of regulations successfully improved competitive balance, we would expect a negative coefficient on this variable.

The NCAA implemented a minimum high-school grade point average for incoming student athletes in 1965. The minimum, set at 1.6 out of a possible 4.0, would be expected to reduce competitive balance in the short to medium run as many universities, notably Southern schools, voiced opposition to this particular regulation. Schools with high academic standards stood to gain from this regulatory change, whereas those with lower academic standards would be expected to take longer to adjust to the new limitations. The effect of this restriction is captured by the variable GPA16.

In 1981, the NCAA realigned collegiate football by introducing multiple divisions. Many schools were relegated to Division I-AA or lower status based upon their level of competition, their average attendance, and school size. At the time of the change, 50 schools lost their Division I-A status. One impact of this regime change would be to improve competitive balance, as reflected in the concentration measures used here, by removing many of those schools that consistently performed relatively poorly. However, the overall impact of this regime change, as captured by the variable DIV1AA, is ambiguous. This is because the reduction in the number of teams in Division I-A football, coupled with the subsequent changes in scheduling, alters the distribution of talent and the relative status of the remaining teams in Division I-A football. This is true because a team in the middle of the performance distribution before the multiple division frameworks might find itself at the bottom of the distribution afterwards.

The last regime change included in this model is the implementation of the Bowl Championship Series (BCS) rankings for postseason play in 1996. There are four bowls that compose the BCS; the Fiesta Bowl, the Orange Bowl, the Rose Bowl, and the Sugar Bowl. The eight participants to the BCS are made up of the conference champions of the Atlantic Coast, Big East, Big 10, Big 12, Pac 10, and Southeastern Conferences plus the next two highest ranked teams.[6] The BCS was intended to make the ranking of Division I-A teams more objective, so to avoid as much controversy as possible in determining the National Champion. While the BCS has its detractors, it arguably changed the way collegiate football schedules are created. In particular, it limited the number of Division I-AA (and lower) opponents a team could play in a given year, removed or reduced the impact of point differentials in wins and losses, and made strength of schedule an important factor in determining the rankings of teams. Thus, the implementation of the BCS would have an ambiguous impact on competitive balance. The BCS would enhance competitive balance if more teams were able to reach higher rankings through wins and strength of schedule. On the other hand, the BCS might perpetuate the dominance of a small number of teams, thereby reducing competitive balance.

To proxy for other time-dependent influences on competitive balance, we include a linear time trend that starts from the beginning of our sample (TIME). To control for the effect the number of teams in the NCAA has on the variance in performance points and the concentration of performance as measured by the HHI, the variable TEAMS is included. To accommodate first-order serial correlation, we include a once-lagged dependent variable on the right-hand side (DEP_{t-1}). The summary statistics of these variables are reported in Table 1 and the results are reported in Table 2.

Table 1
Variable Definitions and Descriptive Statistics of the Data

Variable	Description	Mean	SD	Min	Max
VARP	Variance in Points Scored	28.483	11.89	15.410	76.52
PHHI	HHI of Points Scored	168.89	159.67	84.552	1045.73
dPHHI	PHHI from Ideal	38.184	54.85	12.143	379.06
NCAA	Post NCAA Formation (1906)	0.842	0.366	0	1
SANITY	Post Sanity Code (1948)	0.465	0.501	0	1
ENFORC	Post Enforcement (1953)	0.430	0.497	0	1
GPA16	Post 1.6 GPA Requirement (1965)	0.316	0.467	0	1
DIVIAA	Post Division I-AA Breakup (1981)	0.175	0.382	0	1
BCS	Post BCS Creation (1995)	0.053	0.224	0	1
TIME	Linear Time Trend	57.50	33.05	1	114
TEAMS	Number of Division I-A Teams	98.81	31.60	15	145
N	Number of Observations	114			

Table 2
Regression Results

Independent Variable	Dependent Variable VARP	Dependent Variable PHHI	Dependent Variable dPHHI
Constant	51.001***	171.695***	40.755**
	9.31	3.36	2.22
NCAA	-19.939***	-8.519	19.937
	6.53	0.42	1.48
SANITY	0.343	-6.428	6.092*
	0.18	0.79	1.92
ENFORCE	-2.187	-14.292**	3.054*
	1.24	2.57	1.79
GPA16	5.183***	5.933	3.902*
	3.95	1.38	1.90
DIVIAA	-4.358*	-46.339***	6.398**
	1.71	3.05	2.57
BCS	0.879	-5.568	2.555
	0.57	1.41	1.40
TIME	0.231***	1.153**	-0.307**
	3.04	2.48	2.18
TEAMS	-0.212***	-1.652***	
	3.48	4.05	
LAGGED DEP	2.10e-4	0.650***	0.582***
	1.10	6.71	4.05
N	113	113	113
Adj. R2	0.8247	0.9590	0.8634

*Indicates significance at 10% level.
**Indicates significance at 5% level.

Column 1 of Table 2 reports the regression results using the variance of performance points. While the variance in performance points in the NCAA has been declining over time, the various regime changes instituted by the NCAA have had a significantly different impact on the variance of performance. The creation of the NCAA and the splitting of NCAA football into Division I and Division I-AA are found to improve the competitiveness of NCAA football. However, the implementation of minimum GPA of 1.6 is found to increase the concentration of playing talent at the expense of competitiveness. The effect of the variables SANITY, ENFORCE, and BCS is not found to be statistically different from zero. These results indicate that NCAA decisions have little impact on the competitiveness of NCAA football.

An alternative measure of competitive concentration is the HHI, results of which are presented in column 2 of Table 2. These results indicate that the implementation of a credible enforcement policy, ENFORCE, and the splitting of the NCAA into multiple divisions, DIV1AA, significantly decreased the HHI of performance points. This indicates that these regime changes altered the operating environment in a manner that improved competitiveness. However, the formation of the NCAA, the Sanity Code, the minimum GPA, and the implementation of the BCS did not significantly alter the competitiveness of college football when measured by the HHI.

In both measures of competitive balance, the variance and the HHI of performance points, the number of teams competing in the NCAA is found to improve the competitive balance of the NCAA. However, as shown in Depken (1999), the HHI is a nonlinear transformation of the variance. The intertemporal comparison of HHI indices does not account for differences in the number of teams included in the calculation. An increase (decrease) in the number of teams included in Division I-A football will naturally decrease (increase) the HHI. As can be seen from Table 1, the average number of teams classified as Division I-A has changed rather dramatically over time. While the average number of teams included in the concentration measures is approximately 98, the minimum number of teams was 15 and the maximum number of teams was 145. The relatively large variance of teams with Division I-A status has the potential of distorting the intertemporal comparisons of the HHI. This is the purpose for calculating the dHHI, effectively normalizing the actual HHI so that intertemporal comparisons are more consistent. The dHHI measures how the actual HHI differs from an ideal distribution of points scored and points allowed, i.e., every team has an equal market share. While the expected parameter signs do not change, these final regressions indicate whether the NCAA regulatory changes shift the distribution of performance points allowed closer to or further from an ideal distribution.

From column 3 of Table 2, it is apparent that the various regulatory changes included on the right-hand side of the regression have had an impact on the distribution of performance points within the NCAA. However, unlike the common justifications that such regime changes are in the best interest of competitiveness, the Sanity Code, credible enforcement policy, the minimum GPA, and the dividing of the NCAA into multiple divisions are found to have a significant negative influence on the competitiveness of NCAA football. The implementation of the BCS is also found to be detrimental to competitiveness, but is only significant when using a one-tailed test. This consistent implementation of regimes that harm competitive balance lends credence to the public choice hypothesis of special interest voting behavior for determining the direction of the NCAA. Only the implementation of the NCAA is found to have improved the competitiveness of college football, and it is significant only in a one-tailed test.

The linear time trend indicates that the concentrations of performance points have been declining over time. This could be caused by any number of possible reasons. One might be a reduction in the cost of information acquisition on the part of schools. As schools become more aware of the potential football talent throughout the entire country, the recruitment of football players may become less costly. Alternatively, a supply-side influence could also cause this general decrease. As transportation costs have declined over time, the costs of attending schools further away from home have likewise declined. Therefore, student athletes may be willing to attend schools in different regions of the country than where they attend high school. Which influence dominates, the supply-side or the demand-side, is an avenue for future research.

CONCLUSIONS

To summarize, this paper has investigated whether institutional changes in the NCAA have had beneficial or deleterious effects on competitive balance in Division I-A football. As in any organization that uses voting as a decision-making process, the potential for special interest-pressure groups arises (Buchanan and Tullock, 1965). Pressure groups would be expected to seek out or to protect private rents, thereby altering the "playing field," in college athletics.

Using data from all Division I-A football teams from 1888 through 2001, we generate three different measures of competitive balance, using performance points as a measure of team strength. Following Scully (1989), we calculate the variance in performance points for each year of the sample. Scully predicted that perfect competitive balance would imply a zero variance in winning percentage. We extend his intuition to the performance points measure. We also calculate the HHI for performance points, understanding that perfect monopoly and perfect competition are not possible. Over time, an increase (decrease) in the HHI indicates a decrease (increase) in competitive balance. Finally, we accommodate the changing number of teams with Division I-A status over time by calculating the difference between the HHI of performance points and the ideal (egalitarian) distribution.

We limit our investigation to only a few of the hundreds of institutional changes that the NCAA has experienced over the past 80 years. Among those under investigation here are the initial formation of the NCAA, the Sanity Code, the creation of a credible enforcement mechanism, minimum high-school GPA requirements, relegation of many schools to Division I-AA status, and the creation of the Bowl Championship Series system. These institutional changes might be expected to enhance (reduce) competitive balance, in which case the various measures of competitive balance would decline (increase) after enactment.

We find that over time, Division I-A football has become less balanced, although for the variance and HHI of performance points, it seems that the institutional changes have had some benefit, particularly the creation of the NCAA, creation of a credible enforcement mechanism, and the relegation of many schools to Division I-AA status. However, neither the variance nor the HHI is easily comparable intertemporally if the number of teams included in the calculation is changing dramatically over time. This is the case in Division I-A football.

Therefore, it is concluded that the difference from the ideal level of concentration is the more appropriate measure on which to focus. Using this measure, almost all of the institutional changes modeled here have had a negative impact on competitive balance, supporting the special interest-pressure group hypothesis. This hypothesis claims that if all members of the group do not share equally in the costs and benefits of decision-making, which is clearly the case in the NCAA, pressure groups will naturally arise and seek to exploit the differences in costs and benefits.

Our findings suggest that pressure groups may motivate many of the institutional changes in the NCAA, to the detriment of one of the NCAA's stated goals, competitive balance. These findings run counter to the "public good" argument that many spokespeople suggest as the motivations for NCAA rules changes, yet support the claims of some NCAA insiders that many institutional changes are motivated by "sour grapes" on the part of one or more member institutions.

NOTES

1. However, the uncertainty of outcome may be of significant importance in determining the value of television broadcast.

2. Proposition 48 tied a student athlete's eligibility to their performance on the SAT/ACT and a minimum high school GPA for a defined core curriculum. A student athlete who did not meet all Proposition 48 criteria but achieved a cumulative 2.0 high school GPA was categorized as a "partial qualifier," eligible for financial assistance but not to participate in athlete endeavors their first year. Proposition 42 later eliminated the category of "partial qualifiers."

3. The data are available at www.jhowell.net. At his website, Mr. Howell describes in detail how he gathered and confirmed the data used in this study.

4. The NCAA was originally known as the Intercollegiate Athletic Association of the United States, and changed its name to the National Collegiate Athletic Association in 1910.

5. President Theodore Roosevelt thought it necessary to convene a meeting with several schools in 1905, a year in which 18 deaths and 159 serious injuries occurred in collegiate football games (Lewis, 1969).

6. Through the 2001–2002 season, none of the at-large participants in the BCS had come from outside these six conferences.

13

Is There a Short Supply of Tall People in the College Game?

David J. Berri

INTRODUCTION

The purpose of this paper is to investigate competitive balance across three team sports played under the auspices of the National Collegiate Athletic Association. On the surface, such a topic appears quite straightforward. The reader should be warned, though, that the discussion of this straightforward topic will take a long and winding road till it reaches its final destinations. The road will begin, not in college, but with a review of the level of competitive balance achieved by a variety of professional team sports. From professional sports we will move on to a brief discussion of two apparently unrelated topics, macroeconomics and evolutionary biology. Only after such side trips will we return to the topic of interest, competitive balance in college sports.

THE SHORT SUPPLY OF TALL PEOPLE
IN THE PRO GAME

Competitive balance in team sports is typically examined for an individual sport, with the primary topic being the impact various institutions and policies have upon the dispersion of wins.[1] Inter-sport comparisons, in contrast, are not frequently offered. An exception to this general trend is the seminal work of Quirk and Fort (1994).[2] who did offer measures of competitive balance[3] for the four major North American professional team sports leagues:

Major League Baseball (MLB), the National Football League (NFL), the National Basketball Association (NBA), and the National Hockey League (NHL). Their analysis revealed that of this group, the NFL was the most competitive while the NBA had the greatest disparity in the distribution of wins.

If one extends this analysis to a larger sample of professional sports leagues, a pattern emerges that may alter how industry insiders and academic observers perceive the issue of competitive balance.[4] Table 1 reports the level of competitive balance in five different sports: baseball, basketball, American football, hockey, and soccer, for the following leagues: the American and National League in baseball, the National Basketball Association (NBA) and American Basketball Association (ABA), the National Hockey League (NHL) and World Hockey Association (WHA), the National Football League (NFL) and the American Football League (AFL), and the Bundesliga, North American Soccer League (NASL), and Major League Soccer (MLS). In order to facilitate comparison, only years in which leagues simultaneously existed in the sport are examined.

With the exception of hockey, the sport with the smallest sample of simultaneously existing leagues, the level of competitive balance within each sport is quite similar.[5] Furthermore, levels of competitive balance between sports are quite different, with soccer being the most competitive and the sport of basketball reporting the greatest dispersion in the distribution of wins. In essence, these results suggest a somewhat startling interpretation. Where much of the literature on the subject has focused on institutions and policy, the results reported in Table 1 suggest that competitive balance in a league is primarily determined by the sport the league chooses to play.

Following such a contention, why would basketball be less competitive than football (either American or international)? One explanation for the lack of competitive balance in professional basketball, to be further expanded below, is that this sport suffers from a short supply of its most important resource, tall people. The purpose of this work is to see if a similar pattern of competitive balance can be observed in college sports. In other words, is there a short supply of tall people in the college game?

MACROECONOMICS AND EVOLUTIONARY BIOLOGY

From professional sports we next move on to the next logical step in a paper on college athletics, the subject of macroeconomics. The 20th century saw a split in the field of macroeconomics. With the Keynesian revolution, economists in this tradition argued that government policy could alter a nation's economy. The neoclassical tradition, which existed prior to Keynes and was re-invigorated by the work of Milton Friedman and Robert Lucas, argued that government policy was either ineffective or potentially harmful.

Potentially a similar split exists in the literature on competitive balance.

Table 1
Competitive Balance Across Various Professional Team Sports

Sport	League	Years	Average Level of Competitive Balance
Basketball	National Basketball Association (NBA)	1967-1968 to 1975-1976	2.59
	American Basketball Association (ABA)	1967-1968 to 1975-1976	2.60
Baseball	American League (AL)	1901-2000	2.12
	National League (NL)	1901-2000	2.08
Hockey	National Hockey League (NHL)	1972-73 to 1978-79	2.59
	World Hockey Association (WHA)	1972-73 to 1978-79	1.89
Football	National Football League (NFL)	1960-2000	1.51
	Canadian Football League (CFL)	1960-2000	1.48
	National Football League (NFL)	1960-1969	1.57
	Canadian Football League (CFL)	1960-1969	1.58
	American Football League (AFL)	1960-1969	1.58
	National Football League (NFL)	1987-2000	1.46
	Canadian Football League (CFL)	1987-2000	1.59
	Arena Football League	1987-2000	1.57
Soccer	Bundesliga	1964-1995	1.32
	North American Soccer League (NASL) and Major League Soccer (MLS)	1967-1984, 1996-2000	1.34

As noted, most researchers focus their attention on one specific league. The purpose of such research is to investigate how changes in league institutions and policies impact the level of competitive balance. In other words, much of this work presumes the competitive balance is a factor within the control of league policies.

In contrast, the work of Simon Rottenberg (1956) and Stephen Jay Gould (1986, 1996) suggests that league policy is not the primary force behind the levels of competitive balance that we observe. Rottenberg's invariance principle argues that the distribution of playing talent does not depend on the distribution of property rights. Whether the league employs a reserve clause, granting ownership of talent to the owners of the teams, or free agency, which allows the players to sell their services in a competitive market, talent will migrate to where it generates the highest revenue. In other words, the institutions of the reserve clause, amateur draft, and free agency do not impact the distribution of team wins.[6] The work of Stephen Jay Gould also suggests that league policy may not be the primary determinant of competitive balance.[7]

Gould, though, is not an economist, but rather made his name as a biologist, where he was best known for offering accessible expositions on the nature of biological evolution. One such effort concerned the decline of the .400 hitter in professional baseball. Although many have argued that the inability of modern players to achieve this level of efficiency reflected a decline in the abilities of the modern hitter, Gould argued that the disappearance of this feat represented the evolution in the skills of the average player.

To understand Gould's argument, you must first understand the physical nature of athletic talent. As Gould argues, the human body has certain biomechanical limits that training and talent cannot surpass. For example, although the best athletes can now run a mile in under four minutes, the nature of the human body does not allow this time to be reduced below two minutes. Over time, though, athletes tend to converge toward the biomechanical limit of the body. Initially, though, the population of athletes in any sport will include only a small number of persons close to the limit of human capability. The remaining population will consist of athletes much further away. Such a distribution will result in a relatively large variation in performance.

Such an argument allows us to understand why the .400 hitter has disappeared. In baseball the average hitter has generally hit for a .260 average.[8] If the population of athletes is diverse, then the player close to the limits of human capability will be able to exceed the .400 barrier. As the skill level of all major league talent improves, though, the ability to perform significantly beyond the mean declines. Hence, as Gould argues, the .400 hitter disappears.

Such an argument is echoed in the work of Zimbalist (1992). Zimbalist was interested in why MLB has become more competitively balanced in the latter decades of the 20th century. After noting the inability of owners to accurately assess the value of free agents and the potential impact of the amateur draft, Zimbalist concluded "that a more objective and powerful leveling force is at work, and that is the compression of baseball talent. . . . The difference between today's best, average and worst players is much smaller than it was twenty or forty years ago. This results in greater difficulty in selecting dominating players and in greater competitive balance among the teams" (Zimbalist, 1992). One should note that the contention that competitive balance in MLB did improve in the latter 20th century was supported by the work of Chatterjee and Yilmaz (1991), Schmidt and Berri (2001), and Eckard (2001).

The argument offered by Gould should extend beyond the sport of baseball. Returning to the evidence reported in Table 1, we see that competitive balance is greatest in the sport of soccer. Given that more people in the world participate in this sport, such a result should not surprise. The sport that is the least competitive, though, is basketball, a sport that is perhaps second most popular around the world. Shouldn't basketball have the second highest level of competitive balance?

The answer to this question lies in the nature of the athlete playing professional basketball. The average height of a young adult male in the United States is between 5'9" and 5'10".[9] The vast majority of athletes in the NBA, though, exceed this average. Furthermore, more than 15% of the players in the league are 6'11" or taller. Such a height is extremely rare in the population of both the United States and the world. In the other sports considered in Table 1, training can allow a player to improve. Such training can make a player faster and more agile, and even make him acquire needed weight. As often noted in basketball, though, one cannot teach height. The NBA's persistent discrimination of the vertically challenged dramatically reduces the population of athletes it can employ. Following Gould's and Zimbalist's analysis, if population is restricted, the variability in performance is increased and competitive balance will be worsened.

IS THERE A SHORT SUPPLY OF TALL PEOPLE IN THE COLLEGE GAME?

The evidence presented with respect to professional sports suggested that competitive balance in a professional team sport was primarily determined by the sport being played. The explanation for this contention wandered from macroeconomic theory to evolutionary biology. We now turn to the subject of this inquiry, competitive balance in college sports. Do we observe the same pattern reported for professional leagues in the college ranks?

At the onset we should note substantial differences between the nature of college and of professional sports. The most obvious difference lies in the disconnect between marginal revenue product and the athlete's wage.

Although one can argue that college athletes are compensated for their performance, it is against NCAA policy to offer compensation to any player beyond an athletic scholarship. Consequently, if the rules are followed, players do not choose a college based upon the level of compensation received, although certainly the ability of a college to provide training necessary to compete in the professional ranks is an attraction.

Additionally, institutions such as free agency or player sales do not exist. Hence, one does not expect the Rottenberg Invariance principle to apply. Players will not necessarily migrate to where they will generate the highest revenue for a college, because there is not necessarily an incentive for colleges that produce less revenue to allow their players to leave. Furthermore, the lack of explicit payment to players reduces their incentives to migrate to where they may generate the highest return.

Although other differences exist,[10] the final difference we will note is perhaps the most important to the issue at hand. For the player with professional aspirations, colleges do not represent a final destination. Rather, like minor league baseball, college sports are merely a stop upon the way toward a professional career. Consequently, the population that college teams can draw upon can be diminished by the needs of the professional ranks. Again, as populations change, we can expect the level of competitive balance to follow.

To examine the validity of this expectation, data from three college sports will be employed: football, men's basketball, and baseball. Unlike professional sports, where the number of leagues is relatively small, the NCAA has a number of conferences playing each of these sports. The specific conferences examined are the only ones to play Division I baseball, basketball, and football, and include the following[11]: Atlantic Coast, Big 10, Big 12, Big East, Big West, Conference USA, Mid-American, Mountain West, Pac 10, Southeastern, and Western Athletic Conference.[12] Unlike for an investigation into professional sports, one does need many years of data to acquire sufficient observations to arrive at rudimentary conclusions. Hence the data utilized for this inquiry will focus on seven seasons, beginning with the 1995 season and concluding with the 2001 campaign.[13] One should note that only conference standings were considered. Games involving teams from different conferences were excluded from this study.

Table 2 summarizes the level of competitive balance found in each of the three sports over the time period examined. The results with respect to football bear a strong resemblance to those observed in the professional ranks. The average level of competitive balance in college football, across the 11 conferences and seven seasons examined, was 1.55. Such a number is quite similar to the average reported for each of the football leagues listed in Table 1. Despite the employment of different institutions both across these different professional leagues and in moving from the college to the professional ranks, the level of competitive balance in American football is virtually the

Table 2
NCAA Competitive Balance Sample Statistics

SPORT	Mean	Median	Standard Deviation	Coefficient of Variation	Maximum	Minimum
Football	1.55	1.61	0.21	0.14	1.86	0.94
Baseball	1.83	1.80	0.37	0.20	3.01	0.77
Basketball	1.80	1.83	0.28	0.15	2.31	1.03

same. Such a result lends credence to the supposition that the primary driving force behind competitive balance is the underlying population of athletes, not league policy.

Given this supposition, one might expect competitive balance in both baseball and basketball to differ from the average level observed in college football. The results in Table 2 do show football to be more competitive than both baseball and basketball.[14] The results in college baseball and basketball, though, are not as obviously consistent with the work of Gould.

From Table 2 it can be seen that the average level of balance observed in college baseball is slightly better than that observed in MLB over time. One should note, though, the level of average level observed in college baseball is actually worse than the most recent history of both the American and National Leagues. One can also note that relative to basketball and football, the variability in competitive balance across both conferences and time is greatest in college baseball. Both the coefficient of variation and the range in observed values are greater in baseball.

Tables 3 through 5 offer further evidence suggesting greater variability in competitive balance in college baseball. In these tables the average level of competitive balance both for each conference and for each year are reported for each of the sports examined. What one observes is relative consistency in both football and basketball. With respect to baseball, though, the average level of competitive balance in these select conferences ranges from a high of 2.02 in 1999 to lows of 1.62 and 1.68 in 1995 and 2002, respectively.

Why would the dispersion of wins be so variable in college baseball? Again we return to the population of athletes employed. A baseball prospect in high school has two clear choices in his development as a player. He can pursue a college education, or quite often, he can immediately begin his professional career in the minor leagues. A perusal of the 2002 MLB amateur draft[15] reveals how often high school players are accepted immediately in the professional ranks. In the first round, 16 of the 30 players chosen were high school players. Clearly, the very top high school talent has a real choice. A difference between baseball and the other sports, though, is not simply the

Table 3A
Average Level of Competitive Balance in Select NCAA Football Conferences
1995–2001

Conference	Average Level of Competitive Balance
Atlantic Coast Conference	1.69
Big 10 Conference	1.61
Big 8 Conference	1.69
Big East Conference	1.55
Big West Conference	1.26
Conference USA	1.42
Mid-American Conference	1.54
Mountain West Conference	1.51
Pac 10 Conference	1.57
Southeastern Conference	1.59
Western Athletic Conference	1.50
RANGE (MAX-MIN)	**0.43**

choice facing the top talent. The 50th and last round of baseball's amateur draft also drew at least half of its talent from the high school ranks. Although some of these players will not sign with a Major League club, the choice to begin a professional career for players not currently considered the best is clearly a viable option in baseball.

College baseball teams face not only professional competition for the top high school talent, but also competition for players who are not likely ever to play in the Major Leagues. Consequently, the level of talent on any col-

Table 3B
Average Level of Competitive Balance in NCAA Football

Season	Average Level of Competitive Balance
2001	1.53
2000	1.50
1999	1.47
1998	1.60
1997	1.58
1996	1.57
1995	1.59
RANGE (MAX-MIN)	**0.13**

Table 4A
Average Level of Competitive Balance in Select NCAA Baseball Conferences 1995–2000, 2002

Conference	Average Level of Competitive Balance
Atlantic Coast Conference	1.91
Big 10 Conference	1.43
Big 8 Conference	1.80
Big East Conference	1.84
Big West Conference	2.05
Conference USA	2.02
Mid American Conference	1.92
Mountain West Conference	1.54
Pac 10 Conference	1.85
Southeastern Conference	1.67
Western Athletic Conference	1.96
RANGE (MAX-MIN)	**0.62**

lege team may consist of players destined to play in the Majors, players who may someday play Minor League baseball, or players who will never play professionally. If the members of a conference all employ players at one of these levels, competitive balance should be quite high. If some teams, though, can briefly employ the top level of talent while other teams are forced to employ players who will never play professionally, the dispersion of wins should be much greater.[16]

Table 4B
Average Level of Competitive Balance in NCAA Baseball

Season	Average Level of Competitive Balance
2002	1.68
2000	1.91
1999	2.03
1998	1.85
1997	1.90
1996	1.76
1995	1.62
RANGE (MAX-MIN)	**0.42**

Table 5A
Average Level of Competitive Balance in Select NCAA Men's Basketball Conferences 1995–1996 to 2001–2002

Conference	Average Level of Competitive Balance
Atlantic Coast Conference	1.85
Big 10 Conference	1.86
Big 12 Conference	1.86
Big East Conference	1.61
Big West Conference	1.75
Conference USA	1.70
Mid American Conference	1.87
Mountain West Conference	1.72
Pacific 10 Conference	2.07
Southeastern Conference	1.62
Western Athletic Conference	1.91
RANGE (MAX-MIN)	**0.46**

Although the results with respect to football and baseball are of interest, the question posed at the onset of this paper clearly focuses on basketball. Do the results reported in Tables 3 and 5B support the conclusion that a short supply of tall people plagues the college ranks? The answer, at least superficially, is negative. Competitive balance in college basketball is lower than that in college football, but still quite similar to that found in college baseball, and clearly better than that in professional basketball.

Table 5B
Average Level of Competitive Balance

Season	Average Level of Competitive Balance
2001-02	1.78
2000-01	1.77
1999-00	1.89
1998-99	1.75
1997-98	1.92
1996-97	1.77
1995-96	1.74
RANGE (MAX-MIN)	**0.18**

The explanation for the difference may again lie in the nature of the amateur draft. Unlike the MLB draft, which lasts for 50 rounds and is used to stock both parent club and its Minor League affiliates, the NBA has only two rounds. In the NBA, a player drafted in the first round is guaranteed a three-year contract. In essence, they are guaranteed a spot in the NBA. Although second-round talent is frequently sent to Europe, many of these players are also given an opportunity to begin their professional careers in the NBA.

Hence, unlike professional baseball, the NBA generally extracts only the very best talent from the college ranks. Virtually all of the top players in the NBA today did not play four years of college basketball. Increasingly, players are skipping college and moving directly to the NBA. By taking the very best talent, the ability of teams to consistently dominate college basketball is diminished. Consequently, competitive balance in college basketball would tend to be compressed relative to the NBA.

One may argue, though, that a similar problem exists in college football. Players often leave college before they have completed four seasons. Football players, though, do not skip college and furthermore, relative to the NBA, do not often leave after only one or two seasons of college. Additionally, despite the efforts of the NFL, American football is not an international sport. Unlike basketball or baseball, players are not employed in the NFL who received their training outside the United States. Consequently, college football is able to employ virtually all of the best talent graduating from American high schools. Such a privilege does not exist in either of the other two sports examined.

In sum, the argument offered in this exposition is that the relationship between the college sports and the professional ranks is a primary determinant of the level of competitive balance observed. In baseball, where the population of players has the greatest choice, the level of competitive balance shows the greatest variation. In basketball, where the very best talent is quickly extracted, competitive balance tends to be compressed. Finally, in football, where the population of players bears the greatest similarity to that employed in the professional ranks, competitive balance is quite similar.

CONCLUSIONS

At the heart of this paper is a rather bold contention. Competitive balance, a factor believed to be of great importance to the health of a sports league, is not primarily controlled by the institutions and policies adopted by the league. Rather, the underlying population of players the sport can employ primarily determines competitive balance.

One should note the use of the word *primary*. If one wishes to understand differences in the level of competitive balance between sports, one likely need examine the nature of the population employed. Changes in competitive balance within a sport may indeed be impacted by league policy. Certainly much of the research into college football is consistent with this contention. The impact of these institutions, though, likely occurs only with the range of possibilities dictated by the underlying population.

NOTES

1. For example, Grier and Tollison (1994), Horowitz (1997), and La Croix and Kawaura (1999) have examined the amateur draft. The institution of free agency was the focus of the work of Balfour and Porter (1991), Butler (1995), Horowitz (1997), and Eckard (2001). Furthermore, much of the work on college football [see Depken and Wilson (2004), Eckard (1998), and Bennett and Fizel (1995)] has focused on how institutions impact competitive balance in the sport.

2. The work of Vrooman (1995) also examined more than one sport.

3. Quirk and Fort offered a variety of measures of competitive balance. The measure, though, most applicable to a comparison across sports was derived from the writings of both Noll (1988) and Scully (1989). Such a measure is calculated as follows:

Competitive Balance =

1. $\dfrac{\text{Actual Standard Deviation of Winning Percentage}}{\text{Idealized Standard Deviation of Winning Percentage}}$

2. Idealized Standard Deviation = $[\text{AWP}/N^{0.5}]$

    AWP = Average Winning Percentage

Such a measure will be utilized throughout this present study. One should note that a variety of alternative competitive balance measures have been offered in the literature. These include the dispersion and season-to-season correlation of team winning percentages (Butler, 1995; Quirk and Fort, 1994; Balfour and Porter, 1991), the relative entropy approach (Horowitz, 1997), the Gini coefficient, (Schmidt, 2001; Schmidt and Berri, 2001), and the Herfindahl-Hirschman index (Depken, 1999). Although many of these may represent a higher level of math than the work of Noll and Scully, such measures are not designed for the examination of multiple leagues each playing schedules of different lengths.

4. The reported data and resulting pattern with respect to professional sports first appeared in Berri and Vicente Mayoral (mimeo). The work is also referenced in Schmidt and Berri (mimeo).

5. Berri and Vicente-Mayoral (mimeo) tested whether or not the above reported means are statistically equivalent via the standard student t-tests employed. The t-stat was calculated by these authors for the following league pairs: The NBA and ABA from 1967–68 to 1975–76; the NHL and WHA from 1972–73 to 1978–79; the Bundesliga and NASL from 1967 to 1984; the NFL and CFL from 1960 to 2000; the NFL and AFL from 1960 to 1969, the NFL and Arena Football League from 1987 to 2000; and the NL and AL from 1900 to 2000. Except for the NHL and WHA, Berri and Vicente-Mayoral report that every league pair was found to have a statistically equivalent average level of competitive balance. As reported by Berri and Vicente-Mayoral (mimeo), the level of competitive balance achieved in the

brief history of the WHA was quite similar to the level achieved in the history of the NHL.

6. In addition to the findings reported in Table 1, empirical support for Rottenberg's position can be found in the work of Schmidt and Berri (mimeo) and well as the work of Lee and Fort (mimeo). Each of these works examined the level of competitive balance in Major League Baseball across time. The work of Schmidt and Berri found no significant impact in the level of competitive balance from the institutions of an amateur draft or free agency, once the model controlled for the integration of baseball and the inflow of foreign talent. The work of Lee and Fort reported no significant breaks in the competitive balance time series after 1954. In other words, the amateur draft, instituted in 1965 and free agency, instituted after the 1976 season, did not significantly impact the level of competitive balance in the sport.

7. Chatterjee and Yilmez (1991) also had this interpretation of Gould's work.

8. With the exception of the 1920s and 1930s, Gould demonstrates that the mean batting average has generally remained between .250 and .270 throughout the 20th century.

9. Statistical Abstract of the United States (1999): Table 243. Young adult male is defined as being between the ages of 20 and 29.

10. For a complete description of the nature of college sports, one is referred to Fizel and Bennett (2001).

11. The data for football and basketball came from the following web site: http://www.infoplease.com/colsport.html. Standings data for college baseball was derived from two sources. Craig Gowens provided standings data up till the year 2000 at the following web site: http://ccwf.cc.utexas.edu/~ckgowens/ncba/archive/confstndg.html.

For the year 2002, the web site of Rick Rollins was consulted: http://www.pronetisp.net/~rrollins/02stndgs.htm.

The Collegiate Baseball Newsletter listed the two college baseball sites: http://www.baseballnews.com/. Although a number of colleges play hockey, the teams are not organized in the aforementioned conferences.

12. Following the 1995 season, the Big 8 added four teams and became the Big 12. Also, in 1999 the Mountain West conference began playing. The teams from this conference came from the Western Athletic Conference, which had expanded to 16 teams in 1996.

13. Specifically, college football was examined for seven seasons, beginning in 1995 and ending in 2001. The years examined for college basketball began with the 1995–96 campaign and concluded with the 2001–02 season. College baseball was examined for the years 1995–2000 and also the 2002 season.

14. A standard t-test does indicate that the average level of competitive balance in football is statistically different than the average achieved in baseball or basketball.

15. Details on the 2002 MLB amateur draft were found at the web site of ESPN: http://espn.go.com/mlb/2002mlbdraft.html.

16. The author wishes to acknowledge the helpful comments of Martin Schmidt in constructing the discussion of competitive balance in college baseball.

14

The Impact of Cartel Enforcement in NCAA Division I-A Football

Craig A. Depken II and Dennis P. Wilson

INTRODUCTION

The task undertaken in this paper is to determine what impact NCAA sanctions and investigations have on the competitive balance of Division I-A football conferences. The departure point for our analysis is the empirical evidence, presented by Fleisher et al. (1992) that football programs come under NCAA scrutiny after a rapid increase in winning percentage, a success rate that tends to decline when NCAA sanctions are imposed. This paper investigates two conflicting hypotheses about the role of NCAA rules enforcement. One claim is that the NCAA acts in the best interest of the amateur spirit of collegiate sports, thereby ensuring a "level playing field," and encouraging competitive balance. An alternative claim is that the NCAA enforces rules to protect the relative dominance of "big-time" programs, a claim that would be supported if NCAA rules enforcement promotes greater concentration of football success in the hands of fewer schools.

We estimate the impact of NCAA football probations and investigations on various measures of competitive balance in Division I-A football conferences. We relate competitive balance to historical competitive balance, a time trend, whether the NCAA had a credible enforcement mechanism, the number of teams, the number of in-conference probations binding in the current year, and the percentage of conference teams on probation.

Using data describing ten major Division I-A football conferences from 1888 through 2001, in a pooled model, in which marginal impacts are restricted to be the same across conferences, we find that NCAA sanctions tend to reduce competitive balance, on average. However, a greater percentage of schools in a conference on probation enhances competitive balance, arguably because of a reduction in overall cheating. Unfortunately, not all conferences reflect these findings in conference-by-conference estimations. We address some possible reasons for these contradictory results and anticipate that future efforts will resolve this impasse.

The remainder of this paper is structured as follows. The next section outlines a brief history of the NCAA regulation and the theoretical impacts of rules enforcement on competitive balance. Then we describe our data and empirical methodology and present our results. The final section offers concluding remarks and avenues for future research.

AN OVERVIEW OF NCAA ENFORCEMENT

The history of the NCAA has been well documented by other authors, e.g., Fleisher et al. (1992) and Eckard (1998). Specific to our study, it is useful to outline the history of the NCAA enforcement process as it has evolved since the so-called Sanity Code in 1948. Prior to 1946, the NCAA was a loosely tied, voluntary organization that assisted in scheduling and providing uniform on-field rules. The growing popularity of college athletics and potential revenues provided institutions with the incentive to develop a method of centralized decision-making and collusive agreements for both the input and the output market. In 1946, the "Principles of Conduct of Intercollegiate Athletics" was drafted. This document was incorporated into the NCAA constitution in 1948 and became known as the "sanity code." The sanity code imposed regulations on the recruitment and retention of student athletes. In particular, the sanity code restricted scholarships for athletic activities to only tuition and fees and limited the financial contact of alumni with prospective students. The NCAA deemed this regulation more significant than other attempts at regulation because it created an enforcement mechanism to handle violations. A Compliance Committee became the arbiter of suspected violations investigated by the Fact-Finding Committee. The only form of punishment available to the Compliance Committee was the termination of the individual school's NCAA membership, to be determined by a vote of all NCAA schools. Member institutions deemed this punishment too severe and stripped the Compliance Committee of its punitive role in 1951.

In 1953, member institutions agreed to provide the Committee of Infractions (formally the Compliance Committee) with a multitude of powers to penalize rules violators in a manner less severe than termination; some of these penalties included the limitation of scholarships, television appearances, and postseason play. Further credibility was provided to the Committee of

Infractions because punishments could be leveled without general membership approval. A centralized enforcement mechanism made it possible for the NCAA to centrally organize operational procedures in the input and output markets.

As is well known, the number of lucrative bowl games has increased over the past 40 years, contemporaneous with increased media and stadium revenues available to football programs.[1] Therefore, the potential gain to cheating has increased, if cheating is expected to improve on-field performance in the near-term. According to the Becker (1968) approach, if the gains to illegal behavior increase, either the odds of detection and punishment or the penalties imposed must increase to deter illegal behavior.

The NCAA penalty schedule is similar to punishments applied in general society. More egregious cheating carries increased severity of penalties (on paper). While the NCAA does have the so-called death penalty at its avail, this punishment has been applied only to Southern Methodist University in 1987 (although the death penalty was not permanent). More often, sanctions (in football) include limitations on available scholarships, television appearances, and post-season play (see Figure 1).

The intuition underlying these forms of punishments seems twofold: (1) reduce the revenue of the sanctioned program or school and (2) reduce the ability of the program/school to recruit new student athletes, thereby reducing competitive status as a further penalty. While it is debatable whether sanctions are a good mechanism to limit illegal behavior, especially if those who bear the punishment did not commit the cheating, it is clear that NCAA sanctions have this dual potential impact on the targeted program/school.

Over the past 40 years, the average number of football-based investigations has increased steadily; likewise for the number of overall investigations

Figure 1
Sanction Types (1953–2001)

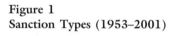

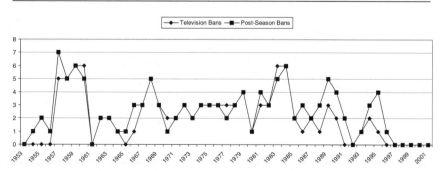

Figure 2
Football Probations (1953–2001)

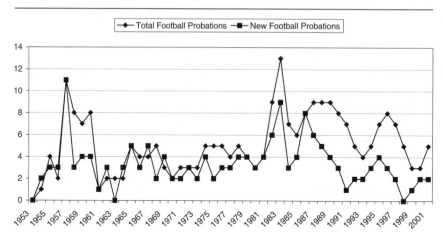

(see Figures 2 and 3, respectively). Over the same time period, the number of Division I-A football teams has varied from a minimum of 104 teams (in 1987) to a maximum of 147 teams (in 1977). However, in 2002 the NCAA employed only 15 field investigators. While investigators may be quite adept at detecting actual or potential cheaters, whistle-blowers, both named and anonymous, may also play an important role in rules enforcement.

Given the limited number of investigators, whistle-blowers would seem to be the most likely source of increased accusations, investigations, and

Figure 3
Total Non-Football Probations (1953–2001)

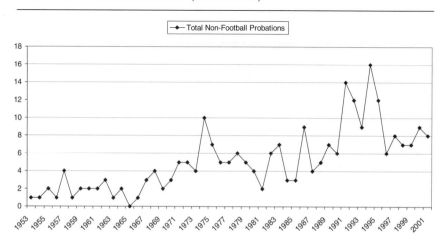

imposed penalties. This would follow from classical cartel theory; the more schools, sports, coaches, players, parents, fans, teachers, and administrators involved with NCAA athletics (however tangentially), the less likely cheating will remain secret.[2] Furthermore, much as firms often find reason to "compete" in the political and legal arena through regulations and antitrust litigation, schools may find it advantageous to strategically accuse their competitors of violations.[3] These increased dimensions of competition, while potentially inefficient uses of scarce resources, may prove useful to maintaining the solidarity of the NCAA cartel.

Three studies in the sports literature have a strong connection to the current study. Fleisher et al. (1992) investigates the probability a school will be investigated by the NCAA. They find that a dramatic increase in the winning percentage of a school's football program has a strong correlation with the chances of being investigated by the NCAA for possible rules violations. They also find that schools that are placed on probation tend to suffer significant reductions in on-field success after the NCAA enforces its regulations.

Eckard (1998) investigates competitive balance in seven major Division I-A football conferences before and after NCAA enforcement began in 1953. Eckard utilizes the variance of relative team positions over time to measure competitive balance, and tests for structural shifts in time series before and after NCAA enforcement began in 1953. He finds that competitive balance, as measured, improved in five of the seven conferences. Eckard therefore concludes that the NCAA acts as a traditional cartel by protecting the stability of relative team rankings in the conferences under its control.

Depken and Wilson (2004) investigate how competitive balance across all Division I-A football teams has been affected by various structural changes in the NCAA. Division I-A football has become less balanced over time, but a few institutional changes have had a beneficial impact on competitive balance, specifically the creation of the NCAA, the creation of a credible enforcement mechanism, and the relegation of many schools to Division I-AA status. However, many of the other major institutional changes, such as academic standards and the creation of the Bowl Championship Series, have reduced competitive balance. The findings suggest that pressure groups may motivate many of the institutional changes in the NCAA.

We extend this literature by investigating how the competitive balance of specific Division I-A football conferences changes when conference competitors are investigated or placed on probation. Our analysis initially focuses on whether NCAA enforcement actions reduce or enhance conference-level competitive balance in general.[4] We then present representative results of the impact of sanctions on competitive balance at the conference level. These latter results indicate that different conferences behave differently after NCAA enforcement.

Notwithstanding the claims by the NCAA that enforcement is specifically aimed at maintaining the spirit of amateur sport, others have argued that

NCAA enforcement is actually a way to ensure the continued dominance of historical "football powers." The NCAA's claim may have the positive by-product of improving competitive balance, whereas the latter hypothesis would predict either a decline or no change in competitive balance. Therefore, we have two plausible but competing hypotheses conducive to empirical examination.

There are plausible reasons why NCAA enforcement might naturally improve competitive balance, especially if cheating distorts balance. If an in-conference competitor comes under investigation and sanctions, it is reasonable to assume the sanctioned school ceases cheating. According to NCAA regulations, a school found guilty of a major infraction while on probation for another major infraction, or while under investigation for a major infraction, faces the so-called "death penalty." If a sanctioned school is effectively immune from new investigations, the remaining (conference) schools may have an incentive to reduce illegal behavior to avoid investigation. The intuition is similar to the common case of speeding. If all other drivers obey the speed limit, it is very risky to speed, as the potential of being caught increases dramatically. However, if a substantial number of other drivers are speeding, the individual's risk to speeding is lowered, thereby encouraging the illegal behavior.

While it is expected that a reduction in cheating may improve competitive balance, direct empirical evidence in support of this claim is lacking. Why might it be reasonable to assume an overall reduction in cheating to improve competitive balance? Most conferences are composed of schools in the same region, of roughly similar size, academic quality, (local) television exposure, and other traditional recruiting positives. Although particular schools in a conference may be renowned for their football prowess (e.g., Nebraska) and others for their basketball prowess (e.g., Duke), a reduction in overall cheating (in a particular sport) may be expected to correlate with a more "natural" distribution of player talent across the schools in a conference.

The removal of cheating may place greater pressure on coaches and schools in recruiting. Without cheating, a particular school may be less able to attract a particular player than it could if all schools are cheating. This would be consistent with the historical treatment of non-price competition wherein it is difficult *ex ante* to determine what determines consumption. However, if price competition prevails, of which cheating may be an example, schools with greater resources (to dedicate to cheating) may enjoy an advantage. Therefore, non-price competition may be more conducive to competitive balance.

However, it is important to discuss the alternative hypotheses about NCAA enforcement; namely, that it may reduce competitive balance. If all schools are caught in a prisoner's dilemma, such that all schools find cheating a dominant strategy, enforcement may reduce competitive balance if the signaling mechanism that triggers investigations of cheating is a dramatic increase in winning percentage. This would allow some schools to continue cheating, and gain a marginal advantage, if they do not trigger the investigation process.

If Fleisher et al. are correct that dramatic increases in winning percentage serve as a signal to trigger NCAA investigations, this would naturally place less dominant teams at a disadvantage. This would follow because the primary schools investigated would be those with historically less success in football compared with their short-run improvements in winning percentage; those schools with greater success in football would remain relatively immune to investigation. Whether dominant schools continue to cheat or not, competitive balance might be reduced or unaltered by enforcement if the status and success of the dominant programs remains ensured. If the NCAA investigation process is initiated only after dramatic improvements in on-field performance, this might prove observationally equivalent to a "gentleman's agreement" to enforce sanctions only on "small-time" programs.

AN EMPIRICAL TEST OF NCAA ENFORCEMENT ON COMPETITIVE BALANCE

Our empirical analysis is anchored by two reasonable yet contradictory hypotheses: one postulates that NCAA rules enforcement aims to improve competitive balance. The alternative claims that rules enforcement aims to protect the status of the schools that have consistent success in football, thereby reducing competitive balance or maintaining the status quo. The latter hypothesis centers on the empirical finding of Fleisher et al. (1992) that schools are more likely to be investigated after a significant improvement in football winning percentage. Naturally, such significant increases can occur only after a relatively low level of success. It is argued schools with historically less success in football, but that experience dramatic short-run improvements, are more often investigated and (possibly) punished for violating NCAA regulations, thereby relegating the school's football program to less success.

To measure on-field performance, we utilize a measure of performance points, as used in the National Hockey League, where a team is credited with two points for each conference win, one point for each conference tie, and zero points for a conference loss. In many years, teams do not necessarily play every possible conference opponent; schedules rotate over a set number of years. However, it is standard practice that each team plays the same number of conference opponents. Therefore, in a given year, the measure of competitive balance may be a bit misleading because one team may have a relatively strong schedule while another team enjoys a relatively weak schedule. However, it is anticipated that over time competitive balance is accurately measured. We calculate various measures of competitive balance based upon team shares of total conference performance-points: the HHI, the normalized HHI, and the variance.

We calculate the performance points for each team's conference win-loss-tie record and total performance points across each conference for each year. "Market shares" (MS) are then calculated as each team's performance points as a percentage of conference performance points, on a scale of one to one hundred. The competitive balance measures are then calculated as follows:

1. The Performance Points HHI is calculated as

$$\text{HHI} = \sum_{i=1}^{N} (\text{MS}_i)^2,$$

where N is the number of teams in the conference.
2. The Normalized HHI compares the actual HHI to the ideal, which would occur with egalitarian distribution of market shares across all teams in a conference, and it is calculated as $\text{DHHI} = \text{HHI} - 10{,}000/N$, where the latter term represents ideal (see Depken, 1999; Depken and Wilson, 2004).
3. The Variance in Performance Points represents the distribution around the mean and is calculated in the standard fashion as

$$\text{VAR} = \frac{1}{N-1} \sum_{i=1}^{N} (\text{MS}_i - \overline{\text{MS}})^2,$$

where N is the number of teams in the conference.

Some argue against the use of the total concentration measure because it does not accurately account for changes in relative standing of particular teams (Humphreys, 2002). Eckard measures the variance of relative team position as a measure of competitive balance, wherein greater variance correlates with greater competitive balance. While it is possible to measure competitive balance in this manner, it seems to lack a strong connection to the historical Structure-Conduct-Performance literature.

Indeed, the general IO literature seems agnostic about firms' relative standings when investigating competitive balance, especially in the context of extended time periods. Moreover, it is unclear whether the competitive balance of, say, ready-to-eat cereal, is fundamentally different from that of sports leagues, thereby warranting a different measure of competitive balance. In this preliminary report, we utilize traditional measures of market concentration to investigate the impact of NCAA enforcement on conference-level competitive balance.

While the level of the HHI index does not reveal much about the relative standings of any particular team (firm), it is possible to use changes in the HHI as indicators of improved competitive balance. If NCAA sanctions tend to reduce the winning percentage of the target school, the (normalized)

HHI will increase if the lost wins are distributed to teams that are above average, i.e., more dominant teams. On the other hand, the (normalized) HHI decreases, corresponding to an improvement in competitive balance, only if a sanctioned team's lost wins are distributed to those teams below average.

Our empirical analysis focuses on the impacts of these various investigative and enforcement activities on the competitive balance of Division I-A football conferences. We initially estimate each time series separately, controlling for autocorrelation inherent in the data. We estimate the following equation

$$CB_{it} = \gamma_i'CONF + \beta_1 CB_{i,t-1} + \beta_2 NCAA_{i,tt} + \beta_3 TIME_{i,t} + \beta_4 TEAMS_{i,t}$$
$$+ \beta_5 FBPROBS_{i,t} + \beta_5 PERPROB_{i,t} + \varepsilon,$$

where the β's are parameters to be estimated and ε is a zero mean error structure.

The dependent variable is the current year's competitive balance measure (either the HHI index, the normalized HHI, or the variance of performance points). The independent variables include a vector of conference dummy variables (CONF), the once lagged dependent variable ($CB_{i,t-1}$) to control for autocorrelation inherent in the data, a dummy variable that took a value of one after NCAA enforcement became credible in 1952, a time trend, the number of teams in the conference, the total number of in-conference football programs on probation that year, and the percentage of programs on probation that year.

Time is measured from the inception of the NCAA in 1905. For conferences that started at a later date, the time trends take a larger initial value to control for institutionalized behavior and customs created by the history of the NCAA. For years before the formation of the NCAA, the time trends take a negative value. Therefore, time trends should be interpreted as relative to the creation of the NCAA.

It is not clear whether competitive balance should be improving over time. While Depken and Wilson (2001) indicate that competitive balance across all Division I-A football programs has not improved over time, there seems no compelling reason to assume this result would hold on a conference-by-conference basis.

The dummy variable NCAA is included to capture any systematic impacts that the credible threat of enforcement has on competitive balance. If the formation of the NCAA enforcement mechanism aimed at curbing cheating and was successful, one would expect the variable to have a beneficial impact on competitive balance. It should be noted that this particular variable tests a similar hypothesis as undertaken by Eckard (1998).

We include the total number of football programs on probation in each conference to measure the direct impact of probations on competitive

balance. If Fleisher et al. (1992) are correct, increased probations will reduce competitive balance, i.e., have a positive marginal impact on the dependent variables, if the sanctioned team(s) sacrifice wins to above-average
teams. On the other hand, the dependent variables are expected to decline
if the sanctioned team(s) sacrifice wins to below-average teams.[5]

However, as mentioned above, the greater the percentage of conference
teams on probation (PERPROB), the greater chance any remaining school
has of being caught cheating. An increase in the odds of detection should decrease the amount of illegal behavior, all things being equal (Becker, 1968).
While we have no direct measure of the amount of clandestine cheating in any
given year, we proxy for the deterrence effect with the percentage of conference teams on probation. If an increase in the percentage of schools on probation reduces cheating, one would expect a negative marginal impact of this
proxy on the competitive balance measures employed, i.e., an improvement
in competitive balance.

Our data describe ten college football conferences: the Big 8, Big 10,
Eastern Independents, Ivy League, Mid American, Pac 10, Southeastern,
Southwest, and Western Athletic Conferences. We note that the Ivy League
was relegated to Division I-AA status in the 1982 reorganization of Division 1-A football. Historical team records are available from David Wilson
from 1888 through 2001. This data has been gathered from the schools
themselves, newspapers, media guides, and the NCAA, when possible.

For the 10 conferences, we calculate the yearly HHI, in which market
shares are calculated using the performance points measure. As NCAA

Table 1
**Descriptive Statistics of the Data Employed (Pooled Sample: ACC, Big 8,
Big 10, Eastern Independent, Ivy, Mid-American, Pac 10, Southeastern,
Southwestern and Western Athletic Conferences)**

Variable	Mean	SD	Minimum	Maximum
Performance Points HHI	1524.182	478.459	531.819	5555.555
Normalized HHI	437.526	258.509	81.360	2638.888
Variance of Performance Pts	14.208	6.418	1.066	48.622
Number of Teams	9.964	3.156	3.00	31.00
Time Trend	50.429	28.590	-17.00	96.00
NCAA Enforcement	0.575	0.464	0.00	1.00
Football Programs on Probation	0.256	0.628	0.00	4.00
% of Programs on Probation	2.738	6.759	0.00	44.44

enforcement is our focus, we total the number of schools on probation in a given year using the NCAA's Major Infractions Database. While the NCAA also maintains a Secondary Infractions Database, we do not utilize the data in this study due to the nature of the infractions. The descriptive statistics of our entire sample are reported in Table 1; conference-specific descriptive statistics are reported in Table 2.

Table 2
Descriptive Statistics of the Data Employed (Separate Samples)

Variable (*Conference*)	Mean	SD	Minimum	Maximum
Atlantic Coast				
Performance Points HHI	1663.180	214.802	1331.36	2063.49
Normalized HHI	397.793	138.090	81.360	740.740
Var. of Performance Points	15.276	5.849	3.142	27.00
Number of Teams	7.959	0.675	7.00	9.00
Time Trend	72.00	14.288	48.00	96.00
Total Football Probations	0.285	0.500	0.00	2.00
Percentage Football Probations	3.486	6.133	0.00	25.00
Big 8				
Performance Points HHI	1882.562	274.444	1485.969	2444.444
Normalized HHI	476.201	128.505	226.757	777.777
Var. of Performance Points	15.348	5.082	5.200	24.000
Number of Teams	7.223	0.884	6.00	8.00
Time Trend	56.000	19.485	23.000	89.000
Total Football Probations	0.477	0.704	0.000	2.000
Percentage Football Probations	6.076	8.972	0.000	28.571
Big 10				
Performance Points HHI	1328.561	321.010	531.819	2638.888
Normalized HHI	350.633	179.058	115.916	1210.317
Var. of Performance Points	13.938	6.092	4.285	35.111
Number of Teams	11.009	4.191	7.00	31.00
Time Trend	43.500	30.743	-9.00	96.00
Total Football Probations	0.264	0.521	0.000	2.000
Percentage Football Probations	2.598	5.161	0.000	20.000

(*continued*)

Table 2 (*Continued*)

Variable (*Conference*)	Mean	SD	Minimum	Maximum
Eastern Independent				
Performance Points HHI	1295.264	368.242	672.249	2562.326
Normalized HHI	524.192	244.826	165.477	1395.833
Var. of Performance Points	9.880	5.284	2.285	27.285
Number of Teams	13.495	2.630	7.00	21.00
Time Trend	34.00	29.877	-17.000	85.000
Total Football Probations	0.048	0.215	0.000	1.000
Percentage Football Probations	0.337	1.511	0.000	7.692
Ivy				
Performance Points HHI	1574.563	600.645	709.566	5000.000
Normalized HHI	541.460	378.258	139.860	2500.000
Var. of Performance Points	13.107	8.263	1.071	48.622
Number of Teams	10.563	3.244	4.000	20.000
Time Trend	29.500	27.279	-17.000	76.000
Total Football Probations	0.000	0.000	0.000	0.000
Percentage Football Probations	0.000	0.000	0.000	0.000
Mid-American				
Performance Points HHI	1627.480	462.029	985.041	2600.000
Normalized HHI	468.290	222.950	131.492	986.488
Var. of Performance Points	17.739	6.669	5.366	31.122
Number of Teams	9.100	2.073	6.000	13.000
Time Trend	76.500	11.690	57.000	69.000
Total Football Probations	0.025	0.158	0.000	1.000
Percentage Football Probations	0.357	2.258	0.000	14.285
Pac 10				
Performance Points HHI	1608.861	744.089	1117.685	5555.555
Normalized HHI	426.682	387.204	117.685	2638.888
Var. of Performance Points	14.798	5.321	1.066	24.177
Number of Teams	8.961	1.625	3.000	10.000
Time Trend	52.974	26.341	11.000	96.000
Total Football Probations	0.389	0.934	0.000	4.000
Percentage Football Probations	4.094	9.776	0.000	44.444

(*continued*)

Table 2 (*Continued*)

Variable (*Conference*)	Mean	SD	Minimum	Maximum
Southeastern				
Performance Points HHI	1236.086	354.599	969.529	3888.888
Normalized HHI	319.006	157.239	144.557	1388.888
Var. of Performance Points	15.479	4.937	6.666	30.878
Number of Teams	11.188	1.396	4.000	13.000
Time Trend	62.000	20.062	28.000	96.000
Total Football Probations	0.550	0.849	0.000	3.000
Percentage Football Probations	4.986	7.565	0.000	30.000
Southwestern				
Performance Points HHI	1764.187	262.525	1342.592	2839.506
Normalized HHI	451.969	222.202	88.888	1589.506
Var. of Performance Points	14.307	6.111	1.600	28.750
Number of Teams	7.703	0.813	6.000	9.000
Time Trend	49.000	23.526	9.000	89.000
Total Football Probations	0.370	0.843	0.000	4.000
Percentage Football Probations	4.291	9.687	0.000	44.444
Western Athletic				
Performance Points HHI	1555.567	392.211	755.029	2561.983
Normalized HHI	371.242	165.356	110.192	895.316
Var. of Performance Points	16.576	5.858	1.066	30.000
Number of Teams	9.00	2.631	6.000	16.000
Time Trend	76.500	11.690	57.000	96.000
Total Football Probations	0.200	0.516	0.000	2.000
Percentage Football Probations	1.958	5.306	0.000	22.222

While several of these conferences have existed for many years, several conferences including a majority of the same teams existed previously, e.g., the Big 6, which became the Big 7, which became the Big 8.[6] When it is possible to trace the genealogy of a particular conference, we include the historical lineage in a single time series. Data was also gathered on new investigations and qualified the type of probations imposed on football programs: loss of scholarship, loss of post-season play, and loss of television appearances. The correlation between new football investigations and new

Table 3

Pooled Sample Regression Results (Residuals Robust to Autocorrelation)

Variable	HHI of Performance Points		Normalized HHI of Performance Points		Variance of Performance Points	
	Parameter Estimate	Std. Error	Parameter Estimate	Std. Error	Parameter Estimate	Std. Error
ACC	1369.81*	289.345	571.997*	87.085	2.097*	1.054
BIG8	1443.89*	289.306	584.387*	81.167	3.296*	0.831
BIG10	1296.20*	277.196	535.287*	85.658	1.771**	0.932
EINDY	1391.33*	301.386	693.039*	105.572	-0.714	1.163
IVY	1401.18*	277.823	642.228*	90.231	2.103*	0.922
MIDAMER	1383.08*	305.019	640.573*	100.690	2.686*	1.240
PAC10	1314.12*	302.302	537.793*	94.933	2.438*	0.928
SEC	1264.00*	290.315	540.421*	94.056	1.297	1.043
SWC	1386.44*	280.028	556.226*	82.336	2.831*	0.834
WAC	1352.54*	296.707	583.511*	92.668	2.446*	1.137
LAGDEP	0.4508*	0.094	0.2716*	0.081	0.488*	0.043
NCAA	-69.0835	47.613	-46.673	27.308	1.451*	0.635
TIME	0.1557	1.128	-1.207**	0.652	0.027**	0.015
TEAMS	-49.7967*	13.206	-19.324*	5.174	0.299*	0.075
PROB	188.990*	97.559	114.390*	56.286	3.652**	1.988
PERPROB	-18.268*	8.675	-9.672**	5.107	-0.282	0.181
R^2	0.552		0.304		0.468	
F-stat	56.188		20.261		41.350	
N	722		722		722	

*(**)Indicates significance at the 5% (10%) level.

football probations was 1.00, whereas the correlation between new investigations and total binding probations was 0.75. We therefore include only the total number of football probations, without qualifying the type of penalty imposed.[7]

Our preliminary results for a pooled model are reported in Table 3. As the model does restrict the parameter estimates of slope parameters to be the same across the conferences, the estimated parameters reflect the average impact of NCAA enforcement on competitive balance.

The second column of Table 3 reports the results using the performance points HHI as the measure of competitive balance. Each conference intercept is statistically significant, with the Big 8 having the highest average concentration. Lagged HHI has a positive and statistically significant impact on current year concentration; 45% of the previous year's concentration is carried over into the current year. The time trend and the NCAA enforcement dummy variables are both statistically insignificant, although the signs of the parameters agree with Depken and Wilson (2004) and Eckard (1998), respectively. The more teams in the conference, the more evenly distributed are performance points.

The two variables of interest are PROB and PERPROB. The absolute number of probations tends to reduce competitive balance, perhaps supporting the intuition offered by Fleisher et al. (1992) and Eckard (1998). This support is indicated in the positive and statistically significant parameter estimate on PROB. However, as the percentage of a conference's teams on probation increases, competitive balance improves. This supports the intuition that schools tend to cheat less as the odds of being caught (and punished) increase, and indirectly supports the NCAA's contention that their enforcement activity aims only to "even the playing field."

Depending on the size of the conference and the number of teams on probation, the net impact of probations on competitive balance is actually ambiguous. Consider an original situation in which there are 10 schools in a conference and no schools on probation. A single school placed on probation would have a deleterious effect on competitive balance, increasing the HHI by 188.9 points. However, this single probation would also indicate that 10% of the schools in the conference are on probation, which would enhance competitive balance by reducing the HHI by 182.68 points. The net impact in this case would be a small increase in the HHI, indicating a slight reduction in the competitive balance of the conference.

The results for the normalized HHI, reported in column 4 of Table 3, are basically the same as those for the non-normalized HHI. The normalized HHI measures how the actual dispersion of performance points differs from the ideal, or egalitarian, distribution. The only major difference in this specification is that the time trend is negative and statistically significant at the 10% level.

The sixth column of Table 3 reports the specification using the variance of performance points as the measure of competitive balance. It is interesting that the Eastern Independents and the Southeastern Conference have intercepts that are statistically insignificant. In contrast with Eckard (1998), we find that the variance of performance points has actually increased after the NCAA enforcement mechanism was created. However, we note that we use the aggregate variance of performance points, whereas Eckard uses the decomposed variance of relative rankings of teams. Unlike the other two measures of competitive balance, only the absolute number of probations is statistically significant (at the 10% level), although the parameter estimate on the percentage of conference teams on probation does have the expected sign.

The results in Table 3 are for the pooled sample. We estimated the same specifications as in Table 3 for each conference and obtained various results. Table 4 presents the conference-specific regression results for 2 of our 10 conferences: the Southeastern and the Pacific 10. Both of these courses have rather storied histories in football, yet reveal rather different impacts of NCAA enforcement.

In the SEC, the lagged value of competitive balance, regardless of which measure is employed, has no statistical impact on the current year's value. After NCAA enforcement became credible, both the HHI and the normalized HHI reflect an improvement in competitive balance, although the

Table 4
Representative Sub-Sample Regression Results (Residuals Robust to Auto-correlation)

Variable	Parameter Estimate	Std. Error	Parameter Estimate	Std. Error	Parameter Estimate	Std. Error
Southeastern Conference						
INTERCEPT	4726.80*	1135.00	1662.28*	465.880	-4.589	4.282
LAGDEP	-0.099	0.161	-0.342	0.087	-0.034	0.106
NCAA	-239.290*	118.894	-119.699*	59.174	-1.100	1.380
TIME	-2.146	1.685	-1.302	0.934	0.166*	0.041
TEAMS	-274.677*	80.440	-104.598*	34.795	0.997*	0.353
PROB	894.261*	451.001	431.944*	219.317	16.163*	5.814
PERPROB	-96.941*	48.933	-46.824*	24.054	-1.790*	0.657
R^2	0.849		0.653		0.457	
F-stat	57.56*		19.145*		8.581*	
N	68		68		68	
Pac 10 Conference						
INTERCEPT	6129.86*	1308.67	2228.75*	556.129	-0.835	3.496
LAGDEP	-0.287	0.186	-0.349*	0.162	0.304*	0.102
NCAA	-620.537*	260.158	-320.362*	129.462	-3.890**	2.267
TIME	7.947**	4.623	2.331	2.392	0.101*	0.043
TEAMS	-466.952*	119.719	-181.939*	5.690	0.846**	0.846
PROB	442.301	489.690	151.436	352.400	-18.844*	8.413
PERPROB	-39.326	47.509	-13.371	34.180	1.837*	0.804
R^2	0.862		0.397		0.359	
F-stat	72.189*		26.489*		6.458*	
N	76		76		76	

*(**)Indicates significance at the 5% (10%) level.

parameter estimate in the variance specification does have the expected sign. The absolute number of probations tends to dramatically increase the SEC's concentration of performance points. However, the higher the percentage of SEC teams on probation the more the concentration of performance points declines, indicating an improvement in competitive balance.

These results contrast with those of the Pac 10 conference, in which the probations and percentage of teams on probation are only statistically significant in the variance specification, and then with the opposite signs. While it is perhaps natural to suspect that different conferences behave differently when the NCAA places one or more conference members on probation, we seem to lack a reasonable explanation for these qualitatively different results. Indeed, perhaps the SEC would be one conference that would not follow our intuition. The explanation of these various results is clearly an avenue of future research.

How does one explain the differences between the pooled and separate samples? An immediate possible culprit is the increased degrees of freedom available in the pooled sample, thereby reducing the potential for Type II errors.

Another possible avenue of inquiry is to investigate different bases on which to measure competitive balance. As we measure "market shares" on the basis of team performance points, there are alternatives available. One already presented in the literature is that proposed by Eckard. Others include the points scored and points allowed by each team, perhaps a more direct measure of on-field performance (see Depken, 2002, for a similar approach applied to professional baseball). These measures may prove more sensitive to the imposition of NCAA sanctions because the NCAA often limits access to scholarship athletes, not necessarily wins and losses (except for case of the death penalty). Therefore, sanctions may prove to have a greater impact on the distribution of relative offensive and defensive talent than on the overall distribution of wins and losses.

CONCLUSIONS

This paper has presented preliminary estimates of the impact of NCAA enforcement activity on the competitive balance of a sample of major Division I college football conferences. We extend the analysis of Fleisher et al. (1992), Eckard (1998), and Depken and Wilson (2004). Fleisher et al. suggest that NCAA enforcement aims to help the dominant teams in football, a sentiment that Eckard seems to support.

Whereas Eckard tests for statistical differences in the variance of relative team rankings, we employ more traditional measures of competitive balance and relate them to time trends and the absolute number of conference members on probation and the percentage of teams on probation. The former may reduce competitive balance if probation reduces the performance of a team and these extra losses are distributed to above-average teams. In a pooled model, we find that this is the case.

However, if probation also correlates with a reduction in cheating by the sanctioned team, the remaining schools face increased odds of being caught if they decide to cheat. The Becker (1968) approach to modeling illegal behavior predicts that increased odds of being caught (and punished) will dissuade illegal behavior, all things being equal. Including the percentage of teams on probation as a proxy for this deterrence effect, we find that competitive balance is improved when a greater percentage of teams are on probation.

Our pooled results do support the claim that NCAA enforcement may have the unintended consequence of reducing competitive balance, although we do find evidence that might support the NCAA's stated goal of enforcement, namely to improve competitive balance. These results indicate that different conferences react to NCAA enforcement in different ways.

NOTES

1. 2000 College Bowl Game Payouts

BOWL	Place	Payout
FIESTA	Tempe, AZ	$13.5M
ROSE	Pasadena, CA	$13.5M
SUGAR	New Orleans, LA	$13.5M
ORANGE	Miami, FL	$11–$13M
FLORIDA CITRUS	Orlando, FL	$4M
COTTON	Dallas, TX	$2.5M
OUTBACK	Tampa, FL	$2.5M
HOLIDAY	San Diego, CA	$1.9M
PEACH	Atlanta, GA	$1.8M
GATOR	Jacksonville, FL	$1.4M
LIBERTY	Memphis, TN	$1.25M
ALAMO	San Antonio, TX	$1.2M
SILICON VALLEY CLASSIC	San Jose, CA	$1.2M
INDEPENDENCE	Shreveport, LA	$1.1M
SUN	El Paso, TX	$1M
LAS VEGAS	Las Vegas, NV	$800,000
ALOHA	Honolulu, HI	$750,000
GALLERYFURNITURE.COM	Houston, TX	$750,000
HUMANITARIAN	Boise, ID	$750,000
INSIGHT.COM	Phoenix, AZ	$750,000
MICRONPC.COM	Miami, FL	$750,000
MOBILE ALABAMA	Mobile, AL	$750,000
MOTOR CITY	Pontiac, MI	$750,000
MUSIC CITY	Nashville, TN	$750,000
OAHU	Honolulu, HI	$750,000

2. Indeed, the number of high-profile whistle-blowers has increased over the past 20 years. Jan Kemp at UGA, coaches at the University of Kentucky, teachers at the University of Tennessee, criminal gamblers at the University of Minnesota, and others indicate the willingness for people to report significant violations of NCAA regulations, especially when they lack passionate interest in the success of a particular team or sport.

3. Sun, Netscape, and America Online (the latter two have now merged) eagerly support the long-running antitrust case against Microsoft. It is not difficult to find other examples in which strategic allegations of antitrust violations are sufficient to reduce the degrees of freedom of the accused in favor of the accuser.

4. This study looks only at how competitive balance is impacted by in-conference NCAA enforcement activity, although future research will also investigate how enforcement activity directed towards geographically proximate schools impacts competitive balance.

5. Additional control factors such as the number of non-football probations, lagged non-football probations, a four-year count of probations, and lagged proba-

tions were also tested. However, none were found to have a statistically significant influence on current competitive balance, regardless of how competitiveness was measured.

6. The Big 6 existed from 1928 through 1947 and included Iowa State, Kansas, Kansas State, Missouri, Nebraska, and Oklahoma. The Big 7 existed from 1948 through 1959 and included the same teams as the Big 6 with the addition of Colorado. The Big 8, which began in 1960 and lasted through 1994, included the same teams as the Big 7 with the addition of Oklahoma State. These eight teams then joined four teams from the defunct Southwest Conference to form the Big 12 in 1995.

7. We ultimately wish to test the impact of sanctions on the competitive balance of individual conferences. In this presentation, however, we focus on a pooled model that restricts the slope parameters of sanctions on competitive balance to be the same across conferences. We do, however, allow the intercepts to vary across conferences.

Bibliography

Agthe, D. and R. B. Billings. 2000. "The Role of Football Profits in Meeting Title IX Gender Equity Regulations and Policy." *Journal of Sport Management*, 14: 28–40.

Aldrich, H. 1979. *Organizations and Environments*. Englewood Cliffs, NJ: Prentice-Hall.

American Council on Education. 1997. *American Universities and Colleges*. Washington, DC: American Council on Education.

Anderson, T. 2001. "St. Louis Ready to Raise NCAA Flag If Atlanta Can't." *St. Louis Business Journal*, January 19.

Arthur Andersen, Hospitality and Leisure Services. "The Sydney Olympic Performance Survey: The Sydney Olympic Games on the Australian Hotel Industry." Mimeograph, 1–7.

Associated Press. 1998. "City sports Boosters Celebrate Final Four Success."

Atkins, L. 1996. "Next Gambling Scandal to Come as No Surprise." *The NCAA News*, http://www.ncaa.org/news/1996/961014/comment.html.

Atkinson, S., L. R. Stanley, and J. Tschirhart. Spring 1988. "Revenue Sharing as an Incentive in an Agency Problem: An Example from the National Football League." *Rand Journal of Economics*, 27–43.

Baade, R. A. 1996. "Professional Sports as a Catalyst for Metropolitan Economic Development." *Journal of Urban Affairs*, 18(1): 1–17.

Baade, R. A. and V. A. Matheson. 2000. "An Assessment of the Economic Impact of the American Football Championship, the Super Bowl, on Host Communities." *Reflets et Perspectives*, 39: 2–3, 35–46.

Baade, R. and J. Sundberg. 1996. "Fourth Down and Gold to Go? Assessing the Link between Athletics and Alumni Giving." *Social Science Quarterly*, 77(4): 789–803.

Balfour, A. and P. K. Porter. 1991. "The Reserve Clause and Professional Sports: Legality and Effect on Competitive Balance." *Labor Law Journal*, 42(1): 8–18.

Becker, G. S. 1968. "Crime and Punishment: An Economic Approach." *Journal of Political Economy*, 169–217.

Becker, G. 1985. "College Athletes Should Get Paid What They Are Worth." *Business Week*, September 30: 18.

Bennett, R. W. and J. L. Fizel. 1995. "Telecast Deregulation and Competitive Balance: Regarding NCAA Division I Football." *American Journal of Economics and Sociology* 54(2): 183–200.

Bergman, B. 1991. "Do Sports Really Make Money for Universities?" *Academe*, January/February, 77: 28–30.

Berri, D. J. and R. Vicente-Mayoral. "The Short Supply of Tall People. Explaining Competitive Imbalance in the National Basketball Association." Mimeo.

Beyer, J. M. and D. R. Hannah. (In press.) "The Cultural Significance of Sports in U.S. Higher Education." *Journal of Sport Management*.

Boles, J. 1967. "Efficiency Squared—Efficient Computation of Efficiency Indexes." *Western Economic Association Proceedings*, 24–46.

Borland, M. V., B. L. Goff, and R.W. Pulsinelli. 1992. "College Athletics: Financial Burden or Boon?" In *Advances in the Economics of Sport*, ed. G. Scully, 215–235. Greenwich, CT: JAI Press.

Bremmer, D. S. and R. G. Kesserling. 1993. "Advertising Effects of University Athletic Success." *Quarterly Review of Economics and Business*, 33: 409–421.

Brooker, G. and T. D. Klastrom. 1981. "To the Victors Belong the Spoils? College Athletics and Alumni Giving." *Social Science Quarterly*, 62, 744–750.

Brown, M. 1982. "Administrative Succession and Organizational Performance: The Succession Effect." *Administrative Science Quarterly*, 27(1): 1–16.

Brown, R. W. 1993. "An Estimate of the Rent Generated by a Premium Division I-A College Football Player." *Economic Inquiry*, 31(4): 671–684.

Brown, R. W. 1994. "Measuring Cartel Rents in the College Basketball Player Recruitment Market." *Applied Economics*, 26: 27–34.

Brown, R. W. 1996. "The Revenues Associated with Relaxing Admission Standards at Division I-A Colleges." *Applied Economics*, 28: 807–814.

Brown, R. W. and R. T. Jewell. 1994. "Is There Customer Discrimination in College Basketball? The Premium Fans Pay for White Players." *Social Science Quarterly*, 75(2): 401–413.

Brown, R. W. and R. T. Jewell. 1995. "Race, Revenues, and College Basketball." *The Review of Black Political Economy*, 23(3): 75–90.

Brown, R. W. and R. T. Jewell. 1996. "Rent Seeking in Higher Education: Voting on Academic Requirements." *Public Choice*, 88: 103–113.

Buchanan, J. and G. Tullock. 1962. *The Calculus of Consent*. Ann Arbor, MI: University of Michigan Press.

Buchanan, J. M. and G. Tullock. 1965. *The Calculus of Consent: Logical Foundations of Constitutional Democracy*. Ann Arbor, MI: University of Michigan Press.

Butler, M. R. 1995. "Competitive Balance in Major League Baseball." *American Economist*, 39(2): 46–52.

Byers, W. and C. Hammer. 1995. *Unsportsmanlike Conduct: Exploiting College Athletes*. Ann Arbor, MI: University of Michigan Press.

Carroll, R. 1984. "Dynamics of Publisher Succession in Newspaper Organizations." *Administrative Science Quarterly*, 29(1): 93–113.

Charnes, A., W. W. Cooper, and E. Rhodes. 1978. "Measuring the Efficiency of Decision Making Units." *European Journal of Operational Research*, 2(4): 429–444.

Chatterjee, S. and M. R. Yilmaz. 1991. "Parity in Baseball: Stability of Evolving Systems?" *Chance*, 4: 37–42.

Clark, B. and M. Trow. 1966. "The Organizational Context." In *College Peer Groups: Problems and Prospects for Research*, ed. T. M. Newcomb and E. K. Wilson, 17–70. Chicago: Aldine Publishing Company.

Clement, R. C. and R. E. McCormick. 1989. "Coaching Team Production." *Economic Inquiry*, 27(1): 287–304.

CNN Money. 1999. "CBS renews NCAA Basketball."

Coase, R. 1937. "The Nature of the Firm." *Economica*, 4: 386.

Coase, R. 1960. "The Problem of Social Cost." *Journal of Law and Economics*, 3: 1–44.

College Board. 2000. *The College Handbook*. New York: The College Board.

Craig, M., P. Schmid, and R. Furst. 2001. "U May Merge Men's, Women's Sports." *Minneapolis Star Tribune*, December 13, at http://www.startribune.com/stories/503/894864.html.

Crain, M. W. 1977. "On the Survival of Corporate Executives." *Southern Economic Journal*, January, 43(1): 1372–1375.

Davidson, L. 1999. "Choice of a Proper Methodology to Measure Quantitative and Qualitative Effects of the Impact of Sport." In *The Economic Impact of Sports Events*, ed. C. Jeanrenaud, 9–28. Neuchatel, Switzerland: Centre International d'Etude du Sport.

DeBrock, L. and W. Hendricks. 1996. "Roll Call Voting in the NCAA." *The Journal of Law Economics and Organization*, 12(2): 495–515.

DeBrock, L. and W. Hendricks. 1997. "Setting Rules in the NCAA Cartel." In *Advances in the Economics of Sport*, ed. W. Hendricks, 179–201. Volume 2. Greenwich, CT: JAI Press.

Deford, F. 2000. "Football is the Real Villain." *Sports Illustrated*, March, http://sportsillustrated.cnn.com/inside_game/deford/news/2000/02/22/deford_football.

Demmert, H. G. 1973. *The Economics of Professional Team Sports*. Lexington, MA: Lexington Books.

Demsetz, H. 1967. "Toward a Theory of Property Rights." *American Economic Review*, 57(2): 347–359.

Depken, C. A. II. 1999. "Free Agency and the Competitiveness of Major League Baseball." *Review of Industrial Organization*, May, 14(3): 205–217.

Depken, C. A. II. Forthcoming. "Free Agency and the Concentration of Player Talent in Major League Baseball." *Journal of Sports Economics*.

Depken, C. A. II and D. P. Wilson. 2001. "Welfare Enhancing Decisions of Cartels: The Effect of a Second Referee in the NHL." Mimeo, University of Texas-Arlington.

Depken, C. A. II and D. P. Wilson. 2004. "Institutional Change in the NCAA and Competitive Balance in Intercollegiate Football." In *Economics of Collegiate Sports*, ed. John Fizel and Rodney Fort. Westport, CT: Praeger Publishers.

Duderstadt, J. J. 2000. *Intercollegiate Athletics and the American University: A University President's Perspective.* Ann Arbor, MI: University of Michigan Press.

Duffy, N. 1994. "The Determinants of State Manufacturing Growth Rates: A Two-Digit-Level Analysis." *Journal of Regional Science,* 34: 137–162.

Dyl, E. A. 1988. "Corporate Control and Management Compensation." *Managerial and Decision Economics,* 9(1): 21–26.

Eckard, W. E. 1998. "The NCAA Cartel and Competitive Balance in College Football." *Review of Industrial Organization,* 13(3): 347–367.

Eckard, W. E. 2001. "Free Agency, Competitive Balance, and Diminishing Return to Pennant Contention." *Economic Inquiry,* 39(3): 430–443.

Educational Development Center. 1997. "Equity Online: Facts on Title IX," at http://www.edc.org/WomensEquity/title9/riley.html.

El-Hordiri, M. and J. Quirk. 1971. "The Economic Theory of a Professional Sports League." *Journal of Political Economy,* 79(1): 1302–1319.

Fama, E. 1980. "Agency Problems and the Theory of the Firm." *Journal of Political Economy,* 88(1): 288–306.

Farrell, M. J. 1957. "The Measurement of Productive Efficiency." *Journal of the Royal Statistical Association,* Series A, 120(3): 253–281.

Fizel, J. L. and R. W. Bennett. 2001. "College Sports." In *The Structure of American Industry,* ed. W. Adams and J. Brock, 323–350. Upper Saddle River, NJ: Prentice-Hall.

Fizel, J. L. and K.K.T. Louie. 1990. "CEO Retention, Firm Performance and Corporate Governance." *Managerial and Decision Economics,* 11(3): 167–176.

Fizel, J. L., K.K.T. Louie, and M. S. Mentzer. 1990. "An Economic Organizational, and Behavioral Model for the Determinants of CEO Tenure." *Journal of Economic Behavior and Organization,* 14(3): 363–379.

Fleischer, A., B. Goff, and R. Tollison. 1992. *The National Collegiate Athletic Association: A Study in Cartel Behavior.* Chicago: University of Chicago Press.

Fort, R. 2003. *Sports Economics,* 410–462. Upper Saddle River, NJ: Prentice-Hall.

Fort, R. and J. Quirk. 1999. "The College Football Industry." *Sports Economics: Current Research,* ed. J. Fizel, E. Gustafson, and L. Hadley, 11–25. Westport, CT: Praeger.

Francis, C. 1983–92. *Hoop Scoop.* Louisville, KY: Hoop Scoop Inc.

Frank, R. 1999. *Luxury Fever: Why Money Fails to Satisfy in an Age of Excess.* New York: Free Press.

Fulks, D. 1998. *Revenues and Expenses of Divisions I and II Intercollegiate Athletic Programs: Financial Trends and Relationships—1997.* Overland Park, KS: NCAA.

Gamson, W. A. and N. A. Scotch. 1964. "Scapegoating in Baseball." *American Journal of Sociology,* 70(1): 69–72.

Gaschnitz, K. M. 1997. *Professional Sports Statistics: A North American Team-by-Team, and Major Non-Team Events, Year-by-Year Reference, 1876 through 1996.* Jefferson, North Carolina: McFarland & Company.

General Accounting Office. 2000. "Gender Equity: Men's and Women's Participation in Higher Education, Report 01-128." December. Washington, DC: Author.

Goldfisher, A. 1999. "Final Four Tourney Assists Area Economy with $20M." *Silicon Valley/San Jose Business Journal.* May 14.

Gomez-Mejia, L. R., H. Tosi, and T. Hinkin. 1987. "Managerial Control, Performance and Executive Compensation." *Academy of Management Journal*, 30: 51–70.

Goss, E. and J. Phillips. 1994. "State Employment Growth: the Impact of Taxes and Economic Development Agency Spending." *Growth and Change*, 25: 287–300.

Gould, S. J. 1986. "Entropic Homogeneity Isn't Why No One Hits .400 Any More." *Discover*, August, 60–66.

Gould, S. J. 1996. *Full House: The Spread of Excellence from Plato to Darwin*. New York: Three Rivers Press.

Gouldner, A. W. 1954. *Patterns of Industrial Bureaucracy*. New York: Free Press.

Grier, K. B. and R. D. Tollison. 1994. "The Rookie Draft and Competitive Balance. The Case of Professional Football." *Journal of Economic Behavior and Organization*, 25: 293–298.

Grimes, P. W. and G. A. Chressanthis. 1994. "Alumni Contributions to Academics: The Role of Intercollegiate Sports and NCAA Sanctions." *American Journal of Economics and Sociology* 53(1): 27–40.

Grusky, O. 1963. "Managerial Succession and Organization Effectiveness." *American Journal of Sociology*, 69(1): 21–31.

Grusky, O. 1964. "Reply to Scapegoating in Baseball." *American Journal of Sociology*, 70(1): 72–76.

Guest, R. H. 1962. "Managerial Succession in Complex Organizations." *American Journal of Sociology*, 68(1): 47–54.

Hall, R. E., D. M. Lilien, G. Syeyoshi, R. Engle, J. Johnston, and S. Ellsworth. 1995. *Eviews User's Guide*. Irvine, CA: Quantitative Micro Software.

Horowitz, I. 1997. "The Increasing Competitive Balance in Major League Baseball." *Review of Industrial Organization*, 373–387.

Horowitz, I. 2000. "The Impact of Competition on Performance Disparities in Organizational Systems: Baseball as a Case Study." *Journal of Sports Economics*, 151–176.

Houck, J. 2000. "High-Stakes Courtship: Cities Build New Arenas to Bring in Major Sports Events, Hoping to Make Big Money." FoxSportsBiz.com, January 21. http://money.cnn.com/1999/11/18/news/ncaa/, posted 3/8/1999; http://www.canoe.ca/1998MarchMadness/mar31_cit.html, posted 3/1/1998; http://www.cnn.com/2001/BUSINESS/03/14/ncaa.cbs/posted 3/14/2001.

Humphreys, B. R. 2002. "Alternative Measures of Competitive Balance in Sports Leagues." *Journal of Sports Economics*, 133–148.

Humphreys, J. 1994. "The Economic Impact of Hosting Super Bowl XXVIII on Georgia." *Georgia Business and Economic Conditions*, May–June: 18–21.

Indianapolis Convention and Visitors Association. 2001. "A Sports Publication Names Indy 'Best Final Four Host,'" http://www.indygov.org/mayor/press/2001/January/01-01-12.htm.

Isidore, C. 2001. "CBS Has Pick of Winners." *CNN Money*.

James, E. 1986. "Cross-Subsidization in Higher Education: Does It Pervert Private Choice and Public Policy?" In *Private Education: Studies in Choice and Public Policy*, ed. Daniel Levy. New York: Oxford University Press.

Jung, C., K. Krutilla, W. K. Viscusi, and R. Boyd. 1995. "The Coase Theorem in a Rent Seeking Society." *International Review of Law and Economics*, 13: 259–268.

Kamerschen, D. R. and N. Lam. 1975. "A Survey of Measures of Market Power." *Rivista Internazionale di Scienze Economiche e Commerciali.* 1131–1156.

Kerr, J. L. and L. Kern. 1992. "Effect of Relative Decision Monitoring on Chief Executive Compensation." *Academy of Management Journal*, 35(2): 370–397.

Knight Commission on Intercollegiate Athletics, 1999, available at http://www.ncaa.org/databases/knight_commission/2001_report/.

Knight Ridder News Service. 1999. "Final Four's Financial Impact Hard to Gauge," Enquirer.com, http://enquirer.com/editions/1999/03/25/spt_final_fours.html.

Kotlyarenko, D. and R. G. Ehrenberg. 2000. "Ivy League Athletic Performance: Do Brains Win?" *Journal of Sports Economics*, 1(2): 139–150.

Krautmann, A. C. 1999. "What's Wrong with Scully-Estimates of a Player's Marginal Revenue Product." *Economic Inquiry*, 37(2): 369–381.

La Croix, S. and A. Kawaura. 1999. "Rule Changes and Competitive Balance in Japanese Professional Baseball." *Economic Inquiry*, 37(2): 353–368.

Lawrence, P. R. 1987. *Unsportsmanlike Conduct.* New York: Praeger.

Lederman, D. 1991. "College Athletes Graduate at Higher Rates than other Students, but Men's Basketball Players Far Behind." *The Chronical of Higher Education*, March 27, A1: A39–A44.

Lee, Y. H. and R. Fort. "Time Series Analysis of Structural Change: Competitive Balance in Major League Baseball." Mimeo.

Leeds, M. and P. von Allmen, P. 2002. *The Economics of Sport.* Boston: Addison Wesley.

Lewis, G. M. 1969. "Theodore Roosevelt's Role in the 1905 Football Controversy." *Research Quarterly.* 717–724.

Liebersen, S. and J. F. O'Connor. 1972. "Leadership and Organizational Performance: A Study of Large Corporations." *American Sociological Review*, 37(2): 117–130.

Long, I. E. and S. B. Caudill, 1991. "The impact of participation in intercollegiate athletics on income and graduation." *Review of Economics and Statistics*, 73: 525–531.

Lynch, M. 2001. "Title IX's Pyrrhic Victory." *Reason.* April.

MacDonald, D. N. and M. O. Reynolds. 1994. "Are Baseball Players Paid Their Marginal Products?" *Managerial and Decision Economics*, 15: 443–457.

Maloney, M. T. and R. E. McCormick. 1993. "An Examination of the Role That Intercollegiate Athletics Plays in Academic Achievement." *Journal of Human Resources*, 28: 555–570.

Marburger, D. R. 1997. "Gate Revenue Sharing and Luxury Taxes in Professional Sports." *Contemporary Economic Policy*, 15(2): 114–123.

McCormick, R. E. and M. Tinsley. 1987. "Athletics vs. Academics? Evidence from SAT Scores." *Journal of Political Economy* 95(5): 1103–1116.

McCormick, R. E. and M. Tinsley. 1990. "Athletics and Academics: A Model of University Contributions." In *Sportometrics*, ed. B. L. Goff and R. D. Tollison. College Station, TX: Texas A & M University Press: 193–206.

McKenzie, R. B. and G. Tullock. 1994. *The New World of Economics*, 5th ed. New York: McGraw-Hill.

Mills, E. and L. Luansende. 1995. "Projecting Growth of Metropolitan Areas." *Journal of Urban Economics*, 37: 344–360.

Mills, E. and J. McDonald. 1992. *Sources of Metropolitan Growth.* New Brunswick: Center for Urban Policy Research.

Mixon, F. G. 1995. "Athletics v. Academics: Rejoining Evidence from SAT Scores." *Education Economics,* 3, 277–283.

Mixon, F. G. and Y. Hsing. 1994. "The Determinants of Out-of-State Enrollments in Higher Education: A Tobit Analysis." *Economics of Education Review,* 13: 329–335.

Mott, R. 1996. "Associations Structure a Work in Progress." *The NCAA News,* January, 8(1): 10–12.

Murphy, R. G. and G. A. Trandel. 1994. "The Relation between a University's Football Record and the Size of its Applicant Pool." *Economics of Education Review* 13(3): 265–270.

National Collegiate Athletic Association. 1983–92. *NCAA Basketball.* Mission, KS: NCAA.

National Collegiate Athletic Association. 1997. "Colleges and Universities with Division I-A Football Programs" at http://www.ncaa.org.

National Collegiate Athletic Association. 2000. *The NCAA Online.* Indianapolis: NCAA.

National Collegiate Athletic Association. 2001. *2001–2002 NCAA Division I Manual.* Indianapolis, IN: NCAA.

National Collegiate Athletic Association. Various years and issues. *The NCAA News.* Indianapolis and Mission, KS: NCAA.

National Football League. 1999. "Super Bowl XXXII Generates $396 Million for South Florida." *NFL Times,* 58: 7.

Naughton, J. 1997. "Women in Division I Sports Programs: 'The Glass Is Half-Empty and Half-Full.'" *The Chronicle of Higher Education,* April 11, A39–A40.

Neale, W. 1964. "The Peculiar Economics of Professional Sports." *The Quarterly Journal of Economics,* 78(1): 1–14.

Nerlove, M. 1971. "Further Evidence on the Estimations of Dynamic Economic Relations from a Time Series of Cross Sections." *Econometrica,* 39(1): 359–382.

Niskanen, W. 1968. "The Peculiar Economics of Bureaucracy." *AEA Papers and Proceedings,* May, 293–305.

Noll, R. 1988. "Professional Basketball." *Stanford University Studies in Industrial Economics,* 144.

Noll, R. 1994. "Attendance and Price Setting." In *Government and Sports Business,* ed. R. G. Noll. Washington, DC: The Brookings Institution.

Noll, R. 1999. "The Business of College Sports and the High Cost of Winning." *The Milken Institute Review.* Third Quarter, 24–37.

Pfeffer, J. and A. Davis-Blake. 1986. "Administrative Succession and Organizational Performance: How Administrator Experience Mediates the Succession Effect." *Academy of Management Journal,* 29(1): 72–83.

Porter, P. 1999. "Mega-Sports Events as Municipal Investments: A Critique of Impact Analysis." In *Sports Economics,* ed. J. L. Fizel, E. Gustafson, and L. Hadley. New York: Praeger Press.

Quirk, J. and R. Fort. 1994. *Paydirt.* Princeton: Princeton University Press.

Rascher, D. 1997. "A Model of a Professional Sports League." In *Advances in the Economics of Sport,* ed. W. Hendricks, Volume 2. Greenwich, CT: JAI Press.

Rishe, P. 1999. "Gender Gaps and the Presence and Profitability of College Football." *Social Science Quarterly*, 80(4): 702–717.

Roberts, G. 1994. "Consider Everything Before Restructuring." *The NCAA News*, September 19, 4.

Rooney, J. F., Jr. 1987. *The Recruiting Game*. Lincoln, NE: University of Nebraska Press.

Rosentraub, M., R. Sandy, and P. J. Sloane. 2003. *The Economics of Sports*, New York: Palgrave.

Rottenberg, S. 1956. "The Baseball Player's Labor Market." *Journal of Political Economy*, June, 242–258.

Salancik, G. R. and J. Pfeffer. 1980. "Effects of Ownership and Performance on Executive Tenure in U.S. Corporations." *Academy of Management Journal*, 23(4): 653–664.

Schmidt, Martin B. 2001. "Competition in Major League Baseball: The Impact of Expansion." *Applied Economics Letters* 8(1): 21–26.

Schmidt, M. B. and D. J. Berri. "On the Evolution of Competitive Balance: The Impact of an Increasing Global Search." Mimeo.

Schmidt, M. B. and D. J. Berri. 2001. "Competition and Attendance: The Case of Major League Baseball." *Journal of Sports Economics* 2(2): 147–167.

Scully, G. W. 1989. *The Business of Major League Baseball*. Chicago: University of Chicago Press.

Scully, G. W. 1992. "Is Managerial Termination Rational?" In *Advances in the Economics of Sport*, ed. G. W. Scully, 1, 67–87. Greenwich, CT: JAI Press.

Scully, G. W. 1995. "Of Winners and Losers: Momentum in Sports." In *The Market Structure of Sports*, 83–99. Chicago: University of Chicago Press.

Seiford, L. 1990. "A Bibliography of Data Envelopment Analysis (1978–1989)." Working Paper, Department of Industrial Engineering and Operations Research, University of Massachusetts–Amherst.

Seigfried, J. and A. Zimbalist. 2000. "The Economics of Sports Facilities and Their Communities." *Journal of Economic Perspectives*, Summer, 95–114.

Seligman, L. and P. Wahlbeck. 1999. "Gender Proportionality in Intercollegiate Athletics: The Mathematics of Title IX Compliance." *Social Science Quarterly*, 80(3): 518–538.

Shanley, M. and C. Langfred. 1997. Reputation Building and Rose Bowls: Managing Investments in Generalized Reputation. Paper presented to the Business Policy and Strategy and Organization and Management Theory Divisions, Annual Meeting of the Academy of Management, August, Boston, MA.

Sheehan, R. G. 1996. *Keeping Score*. South Bend, IN: Diamond Communications.

Shughart, W. F., R. D. Tollison, and B. L. Goff. 1986. "Pigskins and Publications." *Atlantic Economic Journal*, 14, 46–50.

Shulman, J. L. and W. G. Bowen. 2001. *The Game of Life: College Sports and Educational Values*. Princeton, NJ: Princeton University Press.

Sigelman, L. and R. Carter. 1979. "Win One for the Giver? Alumni Giving and Big-Time College Sports." *Social Science Quarterly*, 60, 284–294.

Skousen, C. R. and F. A. Condie. 1988. "Evaluating a Sports Program: Goalposts v. Test Tubes." *Managerial Accounting*, 60, 43–49.

Sloane, P. J. 1971. "The Economics of Professional Football: The Football Club as a Utility Maximiser." *Scottish Journal of Political Economy*, 18(2): 121–146.

Smith, J. E., K. P. Carson, and R. A. Alexander. 1984. "Leadership: It Can Make a Difference." *Academy of Management Journal*, 27(4): 765–776.

Southeastern Conference (SEC). 1999. "History of the Bowl Championship Series." Birmingham, AL: SEC, Total Sports and Host Communications. http://www.secsports.com/fbo/fbc/history_bcs.html.

Sperber, M. 1990. *College Sports Inc.* New York: Henry Holt and Company.

Sperber, M. 2000. *Beer and Circus: How Big-Time College Sports Is Crippling Undergraduate Education*. New York: Henry Holt and Company.

Telander, R. 1989. *The Hundred Yard Lie: The Corruption of College Football and What We Can Do to Stop It*. New York: Simon & Schuster.

Terenzini, Patrick T. and E. T. Pascarella. 1991. *How College Affects Students: Findings and Insights from Twenty Years of Research*. San Francisco: Jossey-Bass.

Terkla, D. and P. Doeringer. 1991. "Explaining Variations in Employment Growth: Structural and Cyclical Change among States and Local Areas." *Journal of Urban Economics*, 29: 329–340.

Thelin, J. R. 1994. *Games Colleges Play*. Baltimore: Johns Hopkins University Press.

Tucker, I. B. 1992. "The Impact of Big-Time Athletics on Graduation Rates." *Atlantic Economic Journal*, 20: 65–72.

Tucker, I. B. and L. Amato. 1993. "Does Big-Time Success in Football or Basketball Affect SAT Scores?" *Economics of Education Review*, 12: 177–181.

United States Census Bureau. 1999. *Statistical Abstract of the United States*. 119th ed. Washington, DC: U.S. Government Printing Office.

Virany, B., M. L. Tushman, and E. Romanelli. 1992. "Executive Succession and Organization Outcomes in Turbulent Environments: An Organizational Learning Approach." *Organization Science*, 3(1): 72–91.

Vrooman, J. 1995. "A General Theory of Professional Sports Leagues." *Southern Economic Journal*, 61(4): 971–990.

Wasylenko, M. and T. McQuire. 1985. "Jobs and Taxes: the Effect of Business Climate on States? Employment Growth Rates." *National Tax Journal*, 38: 955–974.

Weiler, P. and G. Roberts. 1998. *Sports Law: Text, Cases and Problems*, 2nd ed. St. Paul, MN: West Group.

Williamson, O. 1975. *Markets and Hierarchies: Analysis and Antitrust Implications*. New York: The Free Press.

Wilson, Dennis P. 2001. "Cartel Behavior: The Effect of Operational Procedures in Professional Sports Leagues." Mimeo, University of Texas–Arlington.

Wise, G. L., K. L. Wise, and K. D. Wise. 1990. "Schedule Ratings: Villanova, Louisville Had Toughest Trails." *Basketball Times*, 30: 22–24.

Yoder, Marsha. 2002. "Sports Geography." Geographic Education and Technology Program, http://fga.freac.fsu.edu/academy/nasports.htm.

Zak, T. C., J. Huang, and J. L. Siegfried. 1979. "Production Efficiency: The Case of Professional Basketball." In *Sportometrics*, ed. B. L. Goff and R. D. Tollison, 103–117. College Station, TX: Texas A&M University Press.

Zimbalist, A. 1992. *Baseball and Billions*. New York: Basic Books.

Zimbalist, A. 1999a. *Unpaid Professionals*. Princeton, NJ: Princeton University Press.

Zimbalist, A. 1999b. "There's No Accounting for College Sports." *University Business*, June, 39–45.

WEB SITES UTILIZED

Arena Football.com: http://www.arenafootball.com

The Baseball Archive: http://www.baseball1.com

Collegiate Baseball Newsletter: http://www.baseballnews.com/

Craig Gowens college baseball standings: http://ccwf.cc.utexas.edu/~ckgowens/
    ncba/archive/confstndg.html

ESPN.com: http://espn.go.com/mlb/2002mlbdraft.html

Infoplease: http://www.infoplease.com/colsport.html

The International Hockey Date Base: http://www.hockeydb.com

NBA.com: http://www.nba.com

NFL.com: http://www.nfl.com

The Official Site of Major League Baseball: http://www.majorleaguebaseball.com

The Official Site of Major League Soccer: http://www.mlsnet.com

Rick Rollins college baseball standings: http://www.pronetisp.net/~rrollins/
    02stndgs.htm

Slam! Sports Official Site of the Canadian Football League: http://www.cfl.ca

Sports1: http://www.sport1.de

Index

About the Editors and Contributors

ROBERT A. BAADE has been the James D. Vail Professor of Economics at Lake Forest College since 1986. Baade has published extensively in the areas of international economics and the economics of professional and intercollegiate athletics. In the realm of sports, Baade's writing has focused in particular on the economic impact professional and amateur sports exert on their host communities. In addition to his work as a scholar, Baade served for more than 15 years as the assistant men's varsity basketball coach at Lake Forest College.

DAVID J. BERRI is assistant professor of economics at California State University–Bakersfield. His research focuses on both international trade and applied microeconomics, specifically, the economics of sports. Within this latter topic he has published papers examining the impact of labor strikes upon consumer demand, the measurement of worker productivity, the rationality of decision makers, and competitive balance.

ROBERT W. BROWN is associate professor of economics at California State University, San Marcos. He has published articles on a wide variety of topics such as college athletics, infant health, demand for abortion services, and the impact of alcohol restriction laws on drunk driving, among other topics. His current research projects focus on the economics of women's college athletics, environmental recreation in southern California national forests, and valuing environmental resources associated with watershed management.

CRAIG A. DEPKEN II is associate professor of economics at the University of Texas at Arlington. His research focuses on the economics of sports, applied price theory, and applied microeconomics.

MICHAEL P. D'ITRI has earned three degrees from Michigan State University: a B.S. degree in Chemical Engineering, an M.B.A. in Management Science, and a Ph.D. in Operations Management. He has published papers in the *International Journal of Physical Distribution and Logistics Management* and the *International Journal of Purchasing and Materials Management*. He is currently an assistant professor of Industrial Operations Management and chairman of the Business Administration Division at Dalton State College.

JENNIFER DURKIN is a Microsoft security analyst with Unisys Corporation. She will receive her B.B.A. in economics from Temple University in Philadelphia in 2003.

JOHN FIZEL is director of Penn State University's online MBA program, the iMBA. He co-edited (with Elizabeth Gustafson and Lawrence Hadley) *Baseball Economics* and *Sports Economics* and contributed a chapter on competitive balance in *Stee-rike Four! What's Wrong with the Business of Baseball?* and a chapter (with Randall Bennett) on *College Sports* in *The Structure of American Industry*. He has also published papers on a variety of sports economics topics.

RODNEY FORT is professor of economics at Washington State University, is the author of dozens of articles and monographs on sports economics, and serves on the editorial board of the *Journal of Sports Economics*. He is a regular speaker and panel participant on sports issues both in the United States and Europe. His recently published textbook, *Sports Economics* (Prentice-Hall), follows two well-known books with James Quirk, *Pay Dirt* and *Hard Ball* (both Princeton University Press). Professor Fort also has testified before the U.S. Senate on competitive balance issues and often renders expert opinion in legal cases in the United States.

BRIAN GOFF is professor of economics at Western Kentucky University. Professor Goff specializes in public sector economics, applied microeconomics, macroeconomic policy, and statistical methods. His current research focuses primarily on regulatory policy and sports economics. Dr. Goff has published several articles on sports issues, co-authored the books *The National Collegiate Athletic Association: A Study in Cartel Behavior* and *Sportometrics*, and has been a consultant with the National Basketball Association.

R. TODD JEWELL received a Ph.D. in economics from the University of California at Santa Barbara in 1992. He is currently an associate professor and economics undergraduate advisor at the University of North Texas. Dr. Jewell's research is published in economic journals such as *Southern Economic Journal, Applied Economics, Health Economics, Journal of Health*

Economics, Public Choice, and *International Journal of Industrial Organization*. In addition to the economics of college sports, his research areas include professional sports, immigration, abortion demand, and infant health.

MICHAEL A. LEEDS is associate professor of economics at Temple University in Philadelphia, PA. He is co-author (with Peter von Allmen) of *The Economics of Sports* and (with Sandra Kowalewski) of a chapter in *Sports Economics: Current Research*. His research interests include labor economics and applied microeconomics as well as the economics of sports.

VICTOR A. MATHESON is assistant professor in the Department of Economics at Williams College. He earned his Ph.D. in economics from the University of Minnesota. In addition to the field of professional sports, in which he has published several articles, his research interests include state lotteries and state and local taxation. He also works as an NCAA Division I soccer referee for the Big 10, Horizon League, and Mid-Continent conferences.

JOEL G. MAXCY joined the Department of Sport Management & Media at Ithaca College as an associate professor in 2003. He previously served as an associate professor of economics at Cortland State College. Maxcy received his Ph.D. in Economics from Washington State University in 1996. Much of his research focuses on the economics of sports and he has published several papers on this topic. His research interests also include labor relations and law and economics.

EVAN OSBORNE is associate professor of economics at Wright State University in Dayton, Ohio. He received his Ph.D. from UCLA in 1993. His sports-economics interests include college athletics and sports-gambling markets. He also conducts research on economic growth, globalization, corruption, employment discrimination, and law and economics.

ROBERT SANDY is associate professor of economics at IUPUI. In addition to the economics of sports, his publications are on occupational safety and health. He has published in the *Journal of Risk and Uncertainty, Economica, Applied Economics*, and the *Southern Economics Journal*. He is the other of one textbook on statistics and a co-author of a textbook on the economics of sports.

PETER SLOANE is professor and director of the Welsh Economy Labour Market Evaluation and Research Centre [WELMERC], University of Wales Swansea. He is also professor emeritus of the University of Aberdeen, where he was previously Jaffrey Professor of Political Economy, dean of Social Sciences and Law, and vice principal. He has published widely both in labor economics and the economics of sport. He is a Fellow of the Royal Society of Edinburgh, Fellow of the Institute for Labor Studies [IZA], Bonn, and vice president of the International Association of Sports Economists.

TIMOTHY SMABY is vice president of Curriculum Development at Schweser Study Program. Prior to joining Schweser, Tim served as an associate professor of finance and finance program chair at Penn State, Erie. As the finance program chair he developed a new finance major based on the AIMR® Body of Knowledge designed to encourage undergraduate students to enter the CFA® program. He has 10 years of teaching experience at the undergraduate and graduate levels and numerous publications in the areas of investments, corporate finance, and international finance.

PAUL D. STAUDOHAR is professor of business administration at California State University, Hayward. He is the author or editor of 19 books, including *The Business of Professional Sports* (1991), *Playing for Dollars: Labor Relations and the Sports Business* (1996), and *Diamond Mines: Baseball and Labor* (2000). Staudohar is a member of the National Academy of Arbitrators, co-founder of the *Journal of Sports Economics*, and past president of the International Association of Sports Economists.

YELENA SURIS is a financial analyst with General Electric. She received her B.B.A. in finance and accounting from Temple University in Philadelphia, PA.

DENNIS P. WILSON is visiting assistant professor of economics at the University of Texas–Arlington and was previously a faculty member at the University of Massachusetts. His research focuses on applied microeconomic topics, including market structure, competition, pricing, and discrimination.

BARRY ZEPEL spent more than 20 years as a sportswriter and sports information director for five colleges and universities, including Loyola Marymount University in Los Angeles, where he served for 11 years, also as an assistant athletic director. His writing has been published nationally and has appeared in numerous publications, including *The Los Angeles Times*. Currently he is a senior writer in public affairs for California State University, Hayward and occasionally covers Bay Area sporting events for the Associated Press.